# Unlocking the Book of
# REVELATION

Rav Sha'ul

# *Unlocking the Book of Revelation*

## by

## Rav Sha'ul

www.ravshaul.com

Special thanks to my family for all your love and support. Connie Sell thank you for your labors to edit this book to His Glory and I dedicate this book to my King who makes all thing possible. And to the Nazarenes who make this ministry possible. Special thanks to Bruce Piatt for dedicating his time to teaching this book series to hundreds of Nazarenes daily.

I dedicate this book to my wife Stephanie Fox Sides and children Stephanie Yates, Ashley Black, and Dayne Sides, and all those who have contributed to this cause below; may you all walk the path of righteousness and be granted a place in the Kingdom.

| | | | |
|---|---|---|---|
| Sherry Shaw | Andrew Genova | Lelia Dela Cruz | Bruce Piatt Sr. |
| Christinah Curtis | Deborah Bat Yah | Robin Beard-Fogg | Marie-Louise Muehlemann |
| Patrick & Gerdien Mosch | Lorry Stepp | Beth Batista | Ed Hall |
| Palmira Casanova | Ron Parker | Malakyah Malachi Malcolm | Gold Mountain Shepherds |
| Wang JANE | Joseph Franson | Joshua & Marvah Pilkerton | Alona Pakome |
| Andrew King | In Him Ministries | Ernestine James | Laura Ausmus |
| Robert Braun | Frances Frankie Oja | Scott Thompson | Roland Atencio |
| René and Carmen Spatz | Imad Laham | Ernest Hasler | Patrick Squire |
| Grace Whittaker | Sandra McGruder | Gareld McNeil | Matt Vader |
| Willie Koh | Nadybah Bat Yahuah | Nicholas Maalouf | Natzaryahu Ban Yahuah |
| Max Ard | Craig Mikic | Ariel Devar | Diversified Hawaii Consulting |
| Julie Ann Fureigh | Joseph Putol | Pato Zazzini | Jennifer Stewart |
| Raquel Bermyol | Judy Gaudet | Neville & June Shaw | Robin Beard-Fogg |
| Robert Arney | Frankellys Pena | KellyRae Breining | Jared London |
| Greg Bates | Tiffani Austin | William Netherly | Maria Acres Holst |
| Ma Durnford | Debra Docis | Gregrey Mitchell | Peggy Berger |
| Jerri Talbot | Judy Williams | Stacy Leazer Ray | John Fausett |

# TABLE OF CONTENTS

UNLOCKING THE BOOK OF REVELATION ........................................................................2

INTRODUCTION ..............................................................................................................12

WHAT IS THE BOOK OF REVELATION? ..............................................................................13

THE REVELATION OF THE HEAVENLY SCROLL ....................................................................15

THE "GLORY" OF YAHUAH ..............................................................................................17

BLESSINGS AND CURSES .................................................................................................19

You are living in DARKNESS! .......................................................................................20

THE SOURCE OF THE BOOK OF REVELATION .....................................................................25

WHEN DO THE EVENTS IN REVELATION TRANSPIRE? ..........................................................29

The Last Days....................................................................................................................30

THE WORD OF HIS TESTIMONY .......................................................................................35

A firm foundation in The Word of His Testimony.............................................................36

Our testimony is 'The Word of His Testimony'................................................................40

AND IDIOM FOR THE WORD OF HIS TESTIMONY ...............................................................45

THE SON OF MAN IS VICTORIOUS ....................................................................................47

The Heavenly Scroll .........................................................................................................47

WHO IS THE ALEPH AND TAV? ........................................................................................50

The Aleph and Tav in Scripture ......................................................................................53

Conclusion .......................................................................................................................59

I am the ALEPH and the TAV............................................................................................61

I am UINITY and PERFECTION (Perfect Unity)! ............................................................61

Was Yahusha the essence of Unity and Perfection? .......................................................61

Yahusha "came in the flesh" which is the Hebrew word 'sarki'......................................62

Yahusha was born disobedient and imperfect, he was perfected through discipline in a life on Earth.............62

THE DRAGON WHERE DID SATAN COME FROM? ...............................................................64

Rome = Babylon................................................................................................................65

FLOW OF THE BOOK OF REVELATION...............................................................................67

CHAPTER 1 ...................................................................................................................70

INTRODUCTION .............................................................................................................71

REVELATION 1 RESTORED ..............................................................................................73

Yahusha's word to the Seven   Congregations of Nazarenes ...........................................74

John's vision of   The Heavenly Scroll .............................................................................75

The Keys to The Kingdom Revealed ................................................................................76

**CHAPTER 2** .................................................................................................................................. **77**

INTRODUCTION ................................................................................................................................ 78

*Call his name Immanuel*................................................................................................................. 79

REVELATION 2 RESTORED ................................................................................................................. 82

    To the Nazarene Assembly in Ephesus,   don't compromise your first love ................................... 82

    To the Nazarene Assembly in Smyrna,   Endure Persecution and Slander ................................. 83

    To the Nazarene Assembly in Pergamum  'Overcome the Dragon' ......................................... 83

    To the Nazarene Assembly in Thyatira "Overcome the Dragon" .......................................... 85

**CHAPTER 3** .................................................................................................................................. **88**

INTRODUCTION ................................................................................................................................ 89

*The Center of the Enoch Zodiac – The Throne in Heaven* .................................................................. 89

REVELATION 3 RESTORED ................................................................................................................. 90

    To the Nazarene Assembly in Sardis   "Faith without Works is Dead Works" ............................ 90

    To the Nazarene Assembly in Philadelphia "Keep Faith in The Word of His Testimony" .............. 91

    To the Assembly in Laodicia "Do not be luke-warm!" ......................................................... 92

**CHAPTER 4** .................................................................................................................................. **94**

INTRODUCTION ................................................................................................................................ 95

REVELATION 4 RESTORED ................................................................................................................. 97

COMMENTARY ON INHERITANCE ..................................................................................................... 103

**CHAPTER 5** ................................................................................................................................ **107**

INTRODUCTION .............................................................................................................................. 108

"EYES" OR "STREAMS"? ................................................................................................................. 109

*What is all this about? How can we piece together this puzzle so that it can be understood?* ........................ 110

*The Living Water is a metaphor of The Spirit of Yahuah…* ............................................................... 111

*What are the 'Eyes' referring to?* ................................................................................................. 113

*Conclusion* ............................................................................................................................... 115

*Revelation 5:6 Error in Translation* .............................................................................................. 116

REVELATION 5 RESTORED ............................................................................................................... 117

    The Lamb Exalted ................................................................................................................ 119

**CHAPTER 6** ................................................................................................................................ **120**

INTRODUCTION .............................................................................................................................. 121

REVELATION 6 RESTORED ............................................................................................................... 123

    The First Four Seals The First Seal: The White Horse ................................................................ 123

    The Second Seal: War.......................................................................................................... 123

    The Third Seal: Famine ........................................................................................................ 124

    The Fourth Seal: Death ........................................................................................................ 125

    The Last 3 Seals The Fifth Seal: Yom Teruah – King returns for His Elect ................................... 125

    The Sixth Seal: Terror – The Day of Atonement........................................................................ 125

**CHAPTER 7** ........................................................................................................ **127**

   INTRODUCTION ................................................................................................ 128

     *The Interlude* ............................................................................................. 128

   24 ELDERS AND 12 JUDGES ............................................................................... 131

   24 ELDERS ....................................................................................................... 133

   JUDGES OVER THE 12 TRIBES ........................................................................... 134

   REVELATION 7 RESTORED ................................................................................. 135

     144,000 Sealed Servants of Yahuah ........................................................ 135

     The Great Multitude from every nation..................................................... 135

     John again describes the source of his vision... The Enoch Zodiac/Heavenly Scroll............. 136

     The Angel Reads The Heavenly Scroll to John .......................................... 138

**CHAPTER 8** ........................................................................................................ **139**

   INTRODUCTION ................................................................................................ 140

   REVELATION 8 RESTORED ................................................................................. 143

     The Seventh Seal – Completion................................................................. 143

     The First Four Trumpets ............................................................................ 144

     The Coming of the King and the Day of Yahuah ....................................... 144

**CHAPTER 9** ........................................................................................................ **146**

   INTRODUCTION ................................................................................................ 147

     *The 5 Months of Darkness*........................................................................ 148

     *Scorpion Sting Metaphor* ......................................................................... 149

   REVELATION 9 RESTORED ................................................................................. 151

     The Fifth Trumpet ..................................................................................... 151

     The Sixth Trumpet .................................................................................... 152

**CHAPTER 10** ...................................................................................................... **154**

   INTRODUCTION ................................................................................................ 155

     *Do not to write down The Mystery of the Ages*........................................ 156

   REVELATION 10 RESTORED ............................................................................... 163

     Yahusha fulfills The Heavenly Scroll......................................................... 163

**CHAPTER 11** ...................................................................................................... **167**

   INTRODUCTION ................................................................................................ 168

     *42 Months – The Battle of the Ages*......................................................... 170

     *6 x 7 = 42 the symbolic number of The Battle of the Ages* ..................... 171

     *42-Months in History* ............................................................................... 172

     *Two Olive Trees* ....................................................................................... 173

     *Two Witnesses*.......................................................................................... 174

     *Two Lampstands*....................................................................................... 180

*A "Man with a measuring rod"* ................................................................................ *182*

LET US REVIEW... THE MESSAGE IN THE STARS ............................................................ 184

REVELATION 11 RESTORED ......................................................................................... 186

    Time of the Gentiles The Battle of the Ages .......................................................... 186

    Climax of The Battle of the Ages The Two Witnesses ........................................... 187

    Fulfillment of LEO   and the Bowl of Wrath .......................................................... 188

    First 6 Trumpets and the First Resurrection   The Two Witnesses ........................ 189

    The Seventh Trumpet The Battle of the Ages is over ............................................ 190

    The King takes His Thrown in Heaven .................................................................. 190

**CHAPTER 12** ............................................................................................................. **191**

INTRODUCTION ......................................................................................................... 192

    *War in Heaven* ................................................................................................ *193*

    *The Identity of "The Dragon"* .......................................................................... *194*

    *Incarnation: The Spirit of the False Messiah* ..................................................... *198*

    *The Dragon in The Heavenly Scroll* .................................................................. *199*

    *The Dragon in History - the "Spirit" behind all false religions* ........................... *201*

FROM DAGON TO THE DRAGON THE "SPIRIT" BEHIND CHRISTIANITY... ...................... 202

    *Where did Satan come from?* ........................................................................... *204*

    *Rome = Babylon* ............................................................................................ *205*

    *The Mitre Hat* ............................................................................................... *206*

    *Nimrod was "god incarnate" Dagon in the flesh* .............................................. *209*

    *ICHTHYS - Symbol of "The Fish"* ..................................................................... *210*

    *Conclusion* .................................................................................................... *211*

THE "WILDERNESS"?   A DIVINE REHEARSAL .............................................................. 214

    *Revelation and The Greater Exodus* ................................................................ *216*

    *Do we "flee to the mountains" in fear of The Dragon?* ..................................... *217*

    *The Woman and the Wheat* ............................................................................ *218*

    *The Flood flowing forth from The Father of Lies* .............................................. *219*

    *Wings of an Eagle* .......................................................................................... *220*

    *The Seal of Protection from the flood of lies and deception* .............................. *221*

    *Temporary Dwellings?* .................................................................................... *223*

THE SIGN OF THE SON OF MAN .................................................................................. 226

    *The Sign of the Birth of Son of Man* ................................................................. *226*

    *The Sign of the Coming of The Son of Man* ....................................................... *227*

    *Yahusha is known as the Bearer of the Light of Life* ......................................... *228*

    *The brightness of his coming* .......................................................................... *229*

    *The Star Betelgeuse and the Sign in ORION* ..................................................... *231*

    *Keep watch!* .................................................................................................. *234*

REVELATION 12 RESTORED ......................................................................................... 235

    The Sign of the Birth of the Messiah .................................................................. 235

The Battle of the Ages – Age of PISCES ........................................................................ 236
Satan Thrown Down to Earth .......................................................................................... 236
The Remnant go through the Wilderness   Sukkot ....................................................... 238

**CHAPTER 13** .........................................................................................................................**240**

INTRODUCTION ............................................................................................................. 241
*Physical to Spiritual Parallels* ...................................................................................... 242
*Revived Roman Empire – The First Beast* ................................................................. 243
*The Final Kingdom that Conquers the Earth and Reigns for 42-Months* ................ 244
*Dripping in the blood of the Saints* ............................................................................ 250
*538AD-1798AD – The Papacy Reigns for 42-Months* ............................................. 251
*The Battle is with a Spiritual Kingdom* ..................................................................... 253
*The Throne in Heaven taken by force!* ....................................................................... 254
*The Mark of the Beast - X* ........................................................................................... 256
REVELATION 13 RESTORED ......................................................................................... 260
First Beast – Babylonian Demi-god ............................................................................. 260
The Second Beast – Christianity .................................................................................. 264

11 Then I saw another beast (Christianity), coming out of the Earth (Je in Latin is "Earth" or "mother Earth". SUS is pig, Jesus is the pig (beast) of the Earth. The second beast is a religion flowing forth from χℰϛ aka Jesus Christ). He (the prophet of this religion) had two horns like a lamb (Miter Hat), but he spoke like (or on behalf of) the dragon (the Spirit of Dagon). ....................................................................................................... 264

**CHAPTER 14** .........................................................................................................................**268**

INTRODUCTION ............................................................................................................. 269
*Hosts of Heaven* ........................................................................................................... 270
*End of the Age of PISCES* ........................................................................................... 271
REVELATION 14 RESTORED ......................................................................................... 273
Vision of the Divine Government ................................................................................. 273
Those found worthy to rule .......................................................................................... 274
First Angel proclaims the message   of The Heavenly Scroll ..................................... 275
The Spiritual Kingdom of   "Mystery Babylon" is destroyed .................................... 276
Those who follow the False Religion   are destroyed by fire in 1 day ....................... 276
Endure in faith in   The Word of His Testimony .......................................................... 277
The First Resurrection .................................................................................................. 277
Judgment Day Destruction of the Damned .................................................................. 278

**CHAPTER 15** .........................................................................................................................**279**

INTRODUCTION ............................................................................................................. 280
REVELATION 15 RESTORED ......................................................................................... 281
The Great Supper .......................................................................................................... 281
The Song of Moses ........................................................................................................ 282
The Seven Angels with Seven Plagues ........................................................................ 282

**CHAPTER 16** .........................................................................................................................**283**

INTRODUCTION ................................................................................................................. 284
    *3 Unclean Spirits* ........................................................................................................ 284
    *The Seven Bowls of Judgment* ................................................................................ 284
REVELATION 16 RESTORED ............................................................................................... 286
    The Seven Bowls of God's Wrath;   An allusion to the plagues of Egypt ............. 286
    The Seventh Bowl and the Temple in Heaven ........................................................ 287

**CHAPTER 17** ................................................................................................................. **288**

INTRODUCTION ................................................................................................................. 289
    *Historical Context – The Civil War between the Beast and the Woman* ................. 289
    *The 7 Kings* .............................................................................................................. 289
    *The 10 horns* ............................................................................................................ 290
REVELATION 17 RESTORED ............................................................................................... 292
    Babylon, the Prostitute (Rome),   and the Beast (Christianity) ............................ 292
    The Reformation:   The Civil War between The Beast and the Whore,   the power of the Whore is broken over the kings of Europe ............................................................................................. 293
    Protestant Christianity will later   wage war on the Lamb ................................... 293
    Explanation of the Prophetic Imagery ..................................................................... 294
    The Reformation was Yahuah's   Will to break the power of the Whore ............... 294

**CHAPTER 18** ................................................................................................................. **295**

INTRODUCTION ................................................................................................................. 296
REVELATION 18 RESTORED ............................................................................................... 298
    The Fall of Babylon ................................................................................................... 298

**CHAPTER 19** ................................................................................................................. **304**

INTRODUCTION ................................................................................................................. 305
    *Is Yahusha the "Word of God" in the flesh?* ........................................................... 306
    *King of Kings and Lord of Lords* .............................................................................. 309
REVELATION 19 RESTORED ............................................................................................... 310
    Rejoicing in Heaven .................................................................................................. 310
    The Marriage Supper of the Lamb ........................................................................... 310
    Rider on a White Horse ............................................................................................ 312

**CHAPTER 20** ................................................................................................................. **316**

INTRODUCTION ................................................................................................................. 317
    *TARURS - Great White Throne Judgment* ............................................................... 317
    The Book of the Dead is Opened ............................................................................. 318
    The Book of Life is opened ....................................................................................... 320
    *If you are not born-again, you do not live again* ..................................................... 321
REVELATION 20 RESTORED ............................................................................................... 323
    The Thousand Years .................................................................................................. 323
    The First Resurrection of the Dead ........................................................................... 323

The Defeat of Satan ....................................................................................................324
Judgment Before the Great White Throne ...................................................................324

**CHAPTER 21** ..........................................................................................................**326**

INTRODUCTION .........................................................................................................327

REVELATION 21 RESTORED ....................................................................................329
The Renewed Heaven and Earth .................................................................................329
The Day of Atonement, the Wedding Day....................................................................332
The New Jerusalem.......................................................................................................332
The Spiritual Temple made up of the Children of God .................................................332

**CHAPTER 22** ..........................................................................................................**334**

INTRODUCTION .........................................................................................................335
*The Tree of Life*.........................................................................................................*335*
Yahusha is "the Branch" that was broken off   from his own (the Jews) and planted in the ground .............335
The Nazarenes are "the Branches   flowing from The Tree of Life" .............................336
Yahusha is that Branch that sprung up from death   the Fulfillment of The Tree of Life..............336

REVELATION 22 RESTORED ....................................................................................338
The River of Life AQUARIUS Fulfilled.........................................................................338
The Conquering King Is Coming   LEO Fulfilled ..........................................................339

**APPENDIX I**.............................................................................................................**343**

**THE BATTLE OF JERICHO**.....................................................................................**343**

BATTLE OF JERICHO .................................................................................................344
*Introduction*..............................................................................................................*345*
*Summary of The Battle of Jericho*............................................................................*347*
Events foretold in the Book of Revelation ...................................................................348
The Two Witnesses - (Revelation 11 and Joshua 2:1)..................................................348
The Scarlet Thread of Redemption...............................................................................349
The 7 Seals (Revelation 8).............................................................................................349
The 7th Trumpet/shofar blast (Revelation 11) ..............................................................349
The Great Earthquake ..................................................................................................350
The Shout of the Archangel...........................................................................................351
The Appearance of The Messiah   before the Ark of the Covenant .............................351
The Rapture & Resurrection..........................................................................................352
The Messiah leading the Army of Remnant Israel   to reclaim the Earth for Yahuah ..................354
The destruction of the wicked on Earth   (the Great Supper or Day of Yahuah ..........356
The Gold/Silver Vessels................................................................................................357
The Destruction of the Earth by Fire ............................................................................358
The 1,000-year rest of the Sabbath Millennium ...........................................................358

**APPENDIX II**............................................................................................................**360**

**REVELATION AND EZEKIEL**..................................................................................**360**

*Parallels between the Book of Revelation and the Book of the Ezekiel*............................................361

**APPENDIX II** ............................................................................................................................**363**

**BOOKS BY RAV SHA'UL** ............................................................................................................**363**

Book 1 Creation Cries Out! The Mazzaroth ............................................................364

Book 2 Mystery Babylon the Religion of the Beast ............................................365

Book 3 Christianity and the Great Deception ......................................................366

Book 4 The Antichrist Revealed! ............................................................................367

Book 5 The Kingdom ..................................................................................................368

Book 6 The Yahushaic Covenant: The Mediator ................................................369

Book 7 The Law and the Pauline Doctrine ..........................................................370

Book 8 Melchizedek and the Passover Lamb ......................................................371

Book 9 'The Narrow Gate' ........................................................................................372

Book 10 The Mistranslated Book of Galatians ....................................................373

Book 11 The Nazarene ..............................................................................................374

Book 12 The Testimony of Yahuchanon ..............................................................375

Book 13 The Fall Feasts: An invitation to the Wedding ....................................376

Book 14 ........................................................................................................................377

Unlocking the Book of Revelation ........................................................................377

Book 15 Blasphemy of the Holy Spirit ................................................................378

More from Rav Sha'ul ..............................................................................................380

# *Introduction*

# What is the Book of Revelation?

# The Book of Revelation is a documented account

of what is written in the stars that must take place on Earth over what the Bible calls the "last days" which is the Age of PISCES. John is given visions as he looked up into the night sky and the angel Gabriel came to him on behalf of Yahuah and Yahusha to reveal the contents of The Heavenly Scroll. The Book of Revelation has been miSunderstood, mistranslated, and mistaught for 2000 years as the ones doing the "teaching" have rejected the very source of its message… The Heavenly Scroll.

These men and women who mislead the masses over the years are all filled with The Spirit of the False Messiah as they all worship the Beast χξς ! They are blinded to the meaning of the words of this book as prophesied on its pages, do not understand the prophetic language, and have rejected The Word of His Testimony written in the stars.

The Book of Revelation is full of symbolic, prophetic, and mysterious language. Before we get into the text of Revelation, I would like to cover some basic topics we will need to understand. In this introduction, I will cover:

- The Heavenly Scroll is the source of the Book of Revelation.

- The Revelation of The Heavenly Scroll.

- The "Glory" of Yahusha is that he fulfilled The Heavenly Scroll!

- Blessings on those who accept and curses to those deny The Heavenly Scroll…

- When do the events in Revelation transpire?

- The Word of His Testimony… is The Heavenly Scroll.

- A firm foundation in The Word of His Testimony.

- The Son of Man coming in the Clouds of Heaven.

- The Son of Man is victorious in the Battle of the Ages.

- The Sign of the Coming of The Son of Man.

- Yahuah or Yahusha? Who is the Aleph and Tav?

- The Dragon: Where did Satan come from?

- Battle of Jericho.

- Flow of the Book of Revelation.

My book **The Fall Feasts: An Invitation to the Wedding Banquet** is pre-reading for this book on Revelation. Both books cover the same events from two very distinct viewpoints. The Book of Revelation covers the duration of the Age of PISCES and the Battle of the Ages.

The Fall Feasts celebrate the return of the King and the Divine Wedding foretold in the stars. You must understand The Fall Feasts to understand the Book of Revelation.

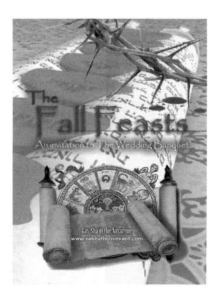

*The Fall Feasts: An invitation to the wedding banquet by Rav Sha'ul available on Amazon Books.*

# The Revelation of The Heavenly Scroll

In the Book of Revelation, we see that John is "taken to Heaven" and given visions of the "night sky". He described what he saw as a Scroll in Heaven or The Heavenly Scroll.

### Revelation Chapter 5
And I saw in the right hand of Him Who sat on the throne, a (Heavenly) Scroll written inside and on the back

This is the same "Flying Scroll" shown to Zechariah ...

### Zechariah 5:2-3
And he said to me, "What do you see (as you look into the Heavens)?" And I answered, "I see a flying Scroll!"

## The same Scroll shown to Isaiah...

### Isaiah 34:4

And all the host of Heaven (Constellations 'host stars' called Stary Hosts) shall be dissolved, and the Heavens (the stars and constellations) shall be rolled *(and read)* together as a Scroll (i.e., The Heavenly Scroll).

## The same Scroll spoken of by the Prophet Daniel:

### Daniel 4:35

"All the inhabitants of the Earth are accounted as nothing, but He does according to His will written in the host of Heaven (The Zodiac which hosts constellations. Constellations "host stars") and among the inhabitants of Earth and no one can ward off His hand Or say to Him, 'What have You done?'

## The same Scroll that Yahusha came to fulfill...

### Hebrews 10:7

""THEN I SAID, 'BEHOLD, I HAVE COME AS IT IS WRITTEN IN THE SCROLL OF THE BOOK (in Heaven) IT IS WRITTEN OF ME, I WILL DO YOUR WILL, O GOD (Matthew 6:10, written in the hosts of Heaven Daniel 4:35).'"

### Matthew 6:10

Your kingdom (declared in Heaven) come, Your will be done, on Earth as it is (written) in (the) Heaven(ly Scroll Daniel 4:35).

Right away in the Book of Revelation, John is shown The Heavenly Scroll and his book is a documentary of what he saw in the Heavens as The Heavenly Scroll was shown to him by Gabriel.

# The "Glory" of Yahuah

### Psalm 19

1 The Heavens (shamayim - 'stars') declare the glory of Yahuah; the stars proclaim the work of his hands. 2 Day after day the stars/constellations pour forth speech; night after night they reveal knowledge. 3 They have no speech, they use no words; no sound is heard from them. 4 Yet their voice goes out into all the Earth, their words to the ends of the world.

### Enoch 35:3

I blessed Yahuah of glory, who had made those great and splendid signs, that they might display the magnificence of his works to angels and to the souls of men; and that these might glorify all his works and operations; might see the effect of his power; might glorify the great labor of his hands; and bless him forever."

We see in Psalm 19 that the Sun's path along the constellations tell the story of a Bridegroom coming out of his chambers to we the Bride. This was fulfilled in Yahusha as he fulfilled The Heavenly Wedding (*the feast cycle*) laid out in the stars. This was the meaning of Yahusha's life and his joy to fulfill. It was John who was to serve as the "friend of the Bridegroom" and help prepare him. This was John's joy in his life to be the witness:

### John 3:29

28 You yourselves can testify that I said, 'I am not the Messiah, but am sent ahead of him.' 29 The bride belongs to the bridegroom (proclaimed in The Heavenly Wedding). The friend of the bridegroom stands and listens for him, and is overjoyed to hear the bridegroom's voice. That joy is mine, and it is now complete. 30 He must increase; I must decrease.

THAT.. Is the **Glory of Yahuah** that Yahusha came to fulfill, that he "had with Yahuah in the beginning"…

### Hebrews 1:3

Yahusha is the *radiance* (fulfillment of the Light of the Sun) of the glory of God (The Heavenly Scroll Psalm 19:1, Enoch 35:3)

### John 17

4 I have glorified You (he is The Glory of Yahuah Hebrews 1:3) on Earth by accomplishing the work You gave Me to do (written in Heaven Hebrews 10:7, Matthew 6:10 and Daniel 4:35). 5 And now, Father, glorify Me in Your presence (and fulfill Your Word eternally preserved in Heaven by installing me as KING) with the glory I had with You before the world existed (laid out in the stars Psalm 19:1 and Enoch 35:3).

### Hebrews 10:7

Then I said, 'Here I am--it is written about me in The Heavenly Scroll-- I have come to do your will, my Elohim! (Matthew 6:10)

### Matthew 6:10

Your kingdom (declared in Heaven/stars Matthew 4:17) come, Your will be done, on Earth as it is (written) in (the) Heaven(ly Scroll Psalm 19:1 and Enoch 35:3).

# Blessings and curses ...

In Revelation 1 we see that those who have this testimony or put their faith in the message contained in the stars are blessed.

### Revelation 1

1 The Heavenly Scroll is the revelation of Yahusha the Messiah, which Yahuah gave His Angel Gabriel to show His servants (all the prophets) what must soon take place. Yahuah made The Heavenly Scroll known by sending Gabriel to his servant John (to show him), 2 who (then John) testifies to everything he saw (in the Heavens called the Book of Revelation)—that is, the word of Yahuah (eternally preserved in The Heavenly Scroll Psalm 19, 119:89, 89:2, Daniel 4:35) and <u>The Heavenly Scroll is the testimony of Yahusha the Messiah</u>. **3 Blessed is the one who reads aloud the words of this prophecy (of The Heavenly Scroll), and blessed are those who hear it and take to heart what is written in The Heavenly Scroll, because the time is near (for its fulfillment).**

Those that deny this testimony or twist it are condemned by it.

### Romans 1 - *warning to those who deny The Heavenly Scroll*

18 **The wrath of Yahuah is being revealed from Heaven** (H8064: shamayim - the place where the stars are located i.e. the Zodiac) **against all the godlessness and wickedness of people, who suppress the truth** (of The Heavenly Scroll's message) **by their wickedness** (and worship the signs of the Zodiac, Sun, Moon, and stars Deuteronomy 3:19), 19 since what may be known about Yahuah (His Plan of Salvation) is plain to them (proclaimed in The Zodiac), because Yahuah has made it plain to them (this message goes out unto all the Earth Psalms 19, given to all mankind Deuteronomy 3:19). 20 For since the creation of the world (written in the stars at creation Rev. 13:8, 1 Peter 1:20) Yahuah's invisible qualities—his eternal power and divine nature—have been clearly seen (in the Zodiac Galatians 3:1, as Yahuah witnessed the Gospel to Abraham Genesis 15:5), being understood (the constellations are pictographs with meaning) from what has been made (in Heaven: the Sun, Moon, stars, and constellations Psalms 19, Romans 1), so that people are without excuse.

# You are living in DARKNESS!

If you have denied The Word of His Testimony (*The Heavenly Scroll*) Yahuah declares the "light/Spiritual Enlightenment of the Sun/Stars/Constellations" … <u>no longer shines in your life</u>. You live in what the Scriptures call …

## *The SHADOW OF DARKNESS...*

Which is the corrupted Babylonian Zodiac and the source of your knowledge and understanding (*even though you do not realize it*). All pagan religions stem from Babylon <u>including Christianity and Judaism</u>! The Religion of Babylon was formally transferred to Rome and became the Religion of Rome after Rome captured Babylon. Then became the foundation of Christianity and Judaism:

> **http://en.wikipedia.org/wiki/Hellenistic_religion**
> Hellenistic religion - Hellenistic religion is any of the various systems of beliefs and practices of the people who lived under the influence of ancient Greek culture during the Hellenistic period and the Roman Empire (c. 300 BCE to 300 CE). There was much continuity in Hellenistic religion: the Greek gods continued to be worshipped, and the same rites were practiced as before.

> **http://en.wikipedia.org/wiki/Hellenization**
> Hellenization - The twentieth century witnessed a lively debate over the extent of Hellenization in the Levant and particularly among the ancient Palestinian Jews that has continued until today. The Judaism of the diaspora was thought to have succumbed thoroughly to its influences. Bultmann thus argued that Christianity arose almost completely within those Hellenistic confines and should be read against that background as opposed to a more traditional (Palestinian) Jewish background

I cover more of this topic later in the book. Yahusha and the Nazarenes and all the Prophets came to shine the LIGHT on you, and you have rejected it.

> <u>Luke 1</u>
> 76 And you, my child, will be called a prophet of the Most High (for proclaiming The Heavenly Scroll/Plan of Salvation); for you will go on before the Messiah to prepare THE WAY for him (of Mikveh, Circumcision, and Offering Matthew 3:13-17), 77 to give his people the knowledge of salvation through the forgiveness of their sins (through MIKVEH called The Way), 78 because of the tender mercy of our Elohim, **BY WHICH THE RISING SUN WILL COME TO US FROM THE HEAVENLY SCROLL** (to restore The Word of His Testimony written in the stars John 1:1-3)! 79 **TO SHINE ON THOSE LIVING IN THE SHADOW OF**

**DARKNESS AND DEATH** (John 1:5), to guide our feet into the path of peace (as 'The Prince of Peace' Isaiah 6:9 to re-unite the two houses meaning of the constellation CANCER)."

### Matthew 4:15
People living in the shadow of darkness have seen a great light (as The Heavenly Scroll witnesses to all mankind Psalm 19, fulfilled in Yahusha John Chapter 1); on those living in the land of the shadow of death (corrupted Babylonian Zodiac/Incarnation), a light has dawned (The Heavenly Scroll has been fulfilled in Yahusha John Chapter 1)."...

### Malachi 4:2
'the Sun of righteousness will rise (like a Bridegroom coming out of his chambers to run the course of a wedding Psalm 19) with healing in its rays.'

### Isaiah 60:1
"Arise, shine; for your light (of the Sun) has come (been fulfilled Malachi 4:2, Luke 1:77-78, Matthew 4:15, and many more), And the glory of Yahuah (proclaimed by The Sun/Stars/Constellations Psalm 19 and Enoch 35:3) has risen upon you (who were living in the shadow of darkness of the Babylonian Zodiac called The Way of the Gentiles)."

### 2 Samuel 23:4
he dawns on them like the morning light, like the Sun shining forth on a cloudless morning.

### Psalm 67
1 Our Elohim be gracious to us and bless us, (Arise) And cause His face to shine upon us (like the Sun Luke 1:77-79) -- Selah. 2 That Yahuah's Way (The Way proclaimed in The Heavenly Scroll) may be known on the Earth (as it is "in Heaven" by the witness of the stars to all mankind Psalm 19), Your salvation has come among all nations.

### Isaiah 9:2
The people walking in darkness (the Way of the Gentiles, the Babylonian Zodiac/incarnation) have seen a great light (Luke 1:77-78, in The Heavenly Scroll as the Sun/stars witness to all mankind Psalm 19); on those living in the land of the shadow of darkness a light (the Sun/Son) has dawned (The Heavenly Scroll has been fulfilled John 1, Matthew 6:10, Hebrews 10:7)

### Isaiah 49:6
He says: "It is too small a thing for you to be my servant to restore the tribes of Jacob and bring back those of Israel I have kept (Prince of Peace CANCER). I will also make you (like/metaphor) a light (of the Sun) for the Gentiles, that my salvation may reach to the ends

of the Earth (as the Sun/stars witness to all mankind proclaiming the Plan of Salvation day after day, night after night from one end of Heaven to the other to all mankind Psalm 19)."

### Hosea 6:3
Let us acknowledge Yahuah's Handiwork (in the stars Psalm 19 and Enoch 35:3); let us press on to acknowledge Him (in creation). As surely as the Sun rises (like a Bridegroom coming out of his chambers to run the course of salvation through the ecliptic Psalm 19), he will appear (in the Heavens as 'The Son of Man riding on the clouds of Heaven ORION' as foretold in The Heavenly Scroll Matthew 16:28, Acts 7:55-56, Revelation 1:12-17, Daniel 7:13, Luke 1:77-78)

### Luke 2:32
a light (as the Sun) for revelation to the Gentiles, and the glory (the Sun/stars/constellations tell of the Glory of Yahuah Psalm 19 and Enoch 35:3) of your people Israel."

### John 8:12
When Yahusha spoke again to the people, he said, "I am the (Spiritual) light of the world (fulfillment of the Physical light of the Sun Psalm 19). Whoever follows me (walking in The Way) will never walk in darkness (the Babylonian Zodiac the foundation of every pagan religion based on incarnation) but will have the "light of life (ORION)"."

### John 12:40
39 For this reason (turning their back on The Heavenly Scroll and following The Way of the Gentiles) they were unable to believe (they fell for incarnation The Spirit of the False Messiah). For again, Isaiah says: 40 "He has blinded their eyes and hardened their hearts, so that they cannot see with their eyes (what the stars proclaim Psalm 19), and understand with their hearts (the meaning of the Light of the Sun), and turn, and I would heal them (as 'the Sun coming with healing in its wings' Malachi 4:2)." 41 Isaiah said these things because he saw Yahusha's glory (as he witnessed The Heavenly Scroll which declare the Glory of Yahuah Psalm 19 and Enoch 35:3) and spoke about Him (revealed the contents of The Heavenly Scroll and we *refused to admit it* Isaiah 48:3-7)

Yahuah declares those who deny His Handiwork in Creation, the Plan of Salvation written in The Heavenly Scroll "stiff-necked and stubborn" and no longer in covenant!

### Isaiah 48:3-6
3 I foretold the former things long ago (written in the stars on Day 4 of Creation), my mouth announced the meaning of them (the stars and constellations to my Prophets) and I made The Heavenly Scroll known (to all mankind Deuteronomy 3:19, Psalms 19, Enoch 53:5) ; then suddenly I acted, and they (the meaning of the Constellations - the Plan of Salvation written in The Heavenly Scroll i.e. The Word of His Testimony) came to pass. 4 For I knew how stubborn you were; your neck muscles were iron, your forehead was bronze. 5 Therefore I told

you these things (in The Heavenly Scroll) long ago (at Creation so that you are without excuse because Yahuah is known through His Handiwork Romans 1:20); before they happened I announced them to you (in The Heavenly Scroll) so that you could not say, 'My images brought them about (because they are written into Creation in the stars as SIGNS/CONSTELLATIONS Genesis 1:14 which come together in order as the Sun passes through them each year to proclaim The Plan of Salvation Isaiah 48:13); my wooden image and metal god ordained them.' 6 You have heard these things (that the stars proclaim day after day, night after night to all mankind as witness Psalm 19); look at them all (the meaning of the Sun/star/constellations in The Heavenly Scroll). <u>WILL YOU NOT ADMIT THEM</u> (they are *The Word of His Testimony and YOU must admit them and have that same testimony <u>Revelation 12:11</u>*)? ... 13 Surely My own hand founded the Earth, and My right hand spread out the Heavens (as a witness Psalm 19); when I summon them (the stars/constellations), they stand up together (to proclaim The Word of His Testimony). 14 Come together, all of you, and listen: Which of the idols has foretold these things (written in the stars Psalm 19, 119:89, 89:2, Daniel 4:35)?

If you deny Yahuah's eternal witness of Yahusha proclaimed by the stars to all mankind as the coming King of the Kingdom, then Scripture declares Yahuah's wrath is poured out on those "Bewitched Fools" in Galatians 3:1.

### Galatians 3:1

You foolish Galatians! Who has bewitched you (bewitched fools)? Before your very eyes (in the stars) Yahusha the Messiah was clearly portrayed as crucified (a Lamb slaughtered before the foundation of the world Revelation 13:8).

Yahuah will deny you entrance into that very Kingdom. In fact, proclaiming The Heavenly Scroll is literally <u>THE</u> Great Commission and the very message John the Baptist and brought to humanity.

### Matthew 4

16 the people living in darkness have seen a great light (The Sun is a metaphor of the Spiritual Light of the World see John 1); on those living in the land of the shadow of death, a light has dawned (The Heavenly Scroll is being fulfilled John 1) ." 17 From that time on Yahusha began to preach, "Repent, for the kingdom of (revealed in) Heaven (Shamayim 'the place in the sky where the stars are located i.e. The Heavenly Scroll) is at hand (he has come to fulfill it Hebrews 10:7)."

### Matthew 3:2

1 In those days John the Baptist came, preaching in the wilderness of Judea 2 and saying, "Repent, for the kingdom proclaimed in The Heavenly Scroll is near." 3 This is he who was spoken of through the prophet Isaiah: "A voice of one calling in the wilderness, 'Prepare The Way (Mikveh, Circumcision, and Offering) for the coming King, make straight paths for him (teach him The Way).'"

Yes! Accepting The Heavenly Scroll is not only vital to salvation, it is the foundation upon which our faith is based! It is The Great Commission to go to all nations and proclaim The Plan of Salvation written in the stars has been fulfilled by Yahusha the Messiah! It is the foundation of the Book of Revelation, what John saw, was shown, and proclaimed in his writings.

If you deny this foundation… you have missed the most basic revelation of all; the Witness of Creation.

# The Source of the Book of Revelation

### Revelation Chapter 5

And I saw in the right hand of Him Who sat on the throne (of Heaven), a (Heavenly) Scroll written inside and on the back.

We are going to take a journey into the Book of Revelation, and I am going to demonstrate that the book is the revelation of The Heavenly Scroll. We will show that John witnessed the same thing that Enoch drew (*The Enoch Zodiac*), the same exact things Ezekiel, Zechariah, Isaiah witnessed in the stars.

### Revelation 1

1 The (Heavenly Scroll is the) revelation of Yahusha the Messiah, which (The Heavenly Scroll) Yahuah gave His Angel to show His servants (all the prophets) what must soon take place (on Earth as it is written in Heaven Matthew 6:10). Yahuah made it (The Heavenly Scroll) known by sending his angel to his servant John (to reveal its contents), 2 who testifies to everything he saw (in the Heavens)—that is, the word of Yahuah (eternally preserved in The Heavenly Scroll Psalm 19, 119:89, 89:2, Daniel 4:35) and (The Heavenly Scroll) testifies of Yahusha the Messiah (*The Word of His Testimony*). 3 Blessed is the one who reads aloud the words of this prophecy, and blessed are those who hear it and take to heart what is written in The

Heavenly Scroll, because the time (of its fulfillment) is near (end of the current Age of PISCES).

The Book of Revelation is the revelation of the contents of The Heavenly Scroll as John was given insight into what must take place on Earth according to what is written in "Heaven".

### Revelation 4

1 After I was shown The Throne in Heaven I looked (into the stars), and behold, a door was opened in Heaven (he was given understanding of The Heavenly Scroll); and the first voice which I heard was (Yahuah, the Aleph/Tav), as it were, of a Shofar talking with me, which said: Come up here (in the Spirit to witness The Heavenly Scroll), and I will show you things (in The Heavenly Scroll) which must take place on Earth after this.

Then John laid out the Battle of the Ages as it would take place over the 2,000-year Age of PISCES leading up to the Second Coming when the Son of Man defeats the Dragon.

The same writer proclaimed the Light of the World was found in The Heavenly Scroll and physical light of the Sun, then that promise (*Logos means spoken promise*) was fulfilled in the flesh by Yahusha the Messiah.

### John Chapter 1

1 In the beginning (Genesis 1:1 'and Yahuah said...") was *the Spoken Promise/Plan of Salvation* (g3778 **LOGOS** ... 'Promise, thing Spoken by Yahuah'), and the *Spoken Promise*/Plan of Salvation was with Yahuah and declared His Handy Work and His Creative Acts (Psalm 19, Enoch 35:3). And the *Spoken Promise*/Plan of Salvation *exists* (g1510 **eimi** – 'exists') *Divinely* (g22316 **Theos** – 'Divinely') written in The Heavenly Scroll (Psalm 119:89, Psalm 89:2).

2 The *Spoken Promise*/Plan of Salvation *existed* (g1510 **eimi**) in the beginning with Yahuah (Spoken on Day 1 Genesis 1:1, Authored into Creation on Day 4 when He created The Heavenly Scroll Genesis 1:14-19 as SIGNS that together are The Divine Council of The Plan of Salvation Isaiah 48:13).

3 All things that were done by Yahuah in Creation were done according to the *Spoken Promise*/Plan of Salvation. And without *the Spoken Promise/Plan of Salvation*, not even one thing done by Yahuah was done (it was the 'purpose' in His Creative Acts see Ephesians 1:8-10).

4 ***The Way*** to eternal life is foretold in *the Spoken Promise/Plan of Salvation* and then ***The Way*** to eternal life was reflected by the physical light of the Sun as a

witness to all mankind in The Heavenly Scroll (Psalm 19, Isaiah 6:9-10, Isaiah 48:13, and many more).

⁵ And the Spiritual Light represented by the Sun now shines in this present spiritual darkness (Luke 1:79) and has been fulfilled on Earth as it is written in The Heavenly Scroll (Hebrews 10:7, Matthew 6:10) in Yahusha The Messiah (The Kingdom proclaimed in The Heavenly Scroll "is at hand/fulfilled" this is the Message proclaimed in the Scriptures, it is The Gospel).

⁷ He came as a witness, to testify about the (meaning of the) Light (restore The Heavenly Scroll **'the rising Sun shall come to us from Heaven'** Luke 1:78-79), so that all might believe *on account of* (g1223 **gia**) The Heavenly Scroll (that Yahusha is the one promised in the **LOGOS/DABAR**).

⁸ John was not the fulfillment of the Light of the Sun in The Heavenly Scroll, but he came to testify about the meaning of the Light of the Sun and show us ***The Way*** and that it has been fulfilled *in the flesh* (g4561 - **sarki** – *'born human to two human parents outside of any Divine Influence'*) by Yahusha the Nazarene (who was born human "likeness of sinful flesh' i.e. 'his flesh was full of sin" as all men 'prone to sin and opposed to Yahuah' and had to be Sanctified John 17:19-21 and Born-again John 3:1-21 by following ***The Way*** Romans 8:1-3).

⁹ There (in the beginning verse 1) was the *True* (g228 **true** – *'connecting (visible) fact to its underlying reality'*… the Light (**LOGOS/DABAR** called The Heavenly Scroll connects visible facts in Creation (the Sun/stars/constellations) to their underlying Spiritual Truth called a Physical to Spiritual parallel) Light which (The Heavenly Scroll) enlightens every man coming into the world (The stars proclaim The Messiah Psalm 19:4: 'Their line has gone out through all the Earth, And their utterances to the end of the world' and summoned together the stars/Sun/constellations proclaim the Plan of Salvation Isaiah 48:11-15, Enoch 35:3, Psalm 19).

¹⁰ The Heavenly Scroll exists (g1510 **eimi**) as *an ordered system* (g2889 **cosmos**) in Creation (in the beginning John 1:1), and the world *is* (g1510 **eimi**) enlightened *on account of* (g1223 **dia** – 'on account of, by reason of') The Heavenly Scroll (called The Word of His Testimony that exists Divinely written in the stars Psalm 19, Psalm 89:2, Psalm 119:89, Psalm 89:2), but the world did not know Yahuah (Who is revealed in what He Made… Romans 1 and Psalm 19, Enoch 35:3) and rejected His witness in the *stars* (h8064 **Shamayim** – 'Heaven', 'place in the sky where the stars are located' i.e. The Heavenly Scroll).

The Word of Yahuah is perfect, every book/writer is consistent in their writings when properly translated. John was sent to proclaim the Light in the Gospel of John and then again in the Book of Revelation. So, with this foundation let us approach the Book of Revelation (of The Heavenly Scroll). On the following pages we will restore the true meaning of the text. We will bring attention to The Heavenly Scroll and what it means. We will shed light on long standing mysteries, explain the mysterious symbols, creatures, and language.

We will attempt to shed light on the fulfillment of prophecies as they have been fulfilled over the entire 2,000-year age of PISCES (*the duration covered in the Book of Revelation*).

# When do the events in Revelation transpire?

In this book, we are going on the assumption the Sign of the Coming of the Son of Man is seen in the constellation ORION 3.5 years after the Sign of the Birth of the Son of Man which was fulfilled in 2017. For more information on The Sign of the Birth of The Son of Man vs. The Sign of the Coming of The Son of Man please refer to my book The Testimony of Yahuchanon.

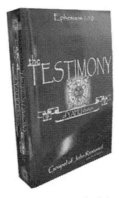

*The Testimony of Yahuchanon available on all online bookstores*

This is an "assumption" as Revelation 12 does not specify "what" occurs after the 3.5-year period. We must try and assemble the prophetic puzzle with what knowledge we have been given. Understanding that Yahuah progressively reveals knowledge over time, there may be more He has not yet shown us that will further illuminate what occurs at the end of 3.5 years (*if not the Sign of the Coming of the Son of Man*).

I put the information into graphs to illustrate the Timeline laid out in Scripture and what time period the books of Daniel and Revelation cover. Many people think these two books cover the same events and time period. This is not true. They both cover events foretold in The Heavenly Scroll as what is written in Heaven took place in their own time periods. Daniel at the end of the Age of ARIES, and John foretold the entire Age of PISCES transitioning into the Age of AQUARIUS.

# The Last Days

We read in the New Testament the writers claimed they lived in "the last days". Most people assume they were in error or even false prophets as they did not witness the coming of the King and resurrection of the dead in their lifetimes. We assume they meant literal 24-hour days in error. These men were Nazarenes which held The Heavenly Scroll as the source of their faith. In that Scroll, time is laid out in a prophetic 7-day period. This is why we celebrate The Sabbath each week, we are celebrating the Plan of Salvation written in the stars speaking of the Age of AQUARIUS the Kingdom Age in the seventh millennium.

The seven days in the stars are divided into "Ages" of two thousand years each. A prophet day is a thousand years. These men understood the Plan of Salvation and when they said "last days" they were referring to that plan in The Heavenly Scroll being the "last 2 days of PISCES". Yahusha died to usher in The Age of PISCES… the "last prophetic day"…

> **Hosea 6:2**
> After two days (Age of PISCES) he will revive us; on the third day (Age of AQUARIUS) he will restore us, that we may live in his presence (in the Kingdom/LEO).

> **2 Peter 3:8**
> But do not forget this one thing, dear friends: With Yahuah, a day is like a thousand years, and a thousand years are like a day.

The Plan of Salvation is written in The Heavenly Scroll, it is seven prophetic days made up of three full ages (*six prophetic days*) and a half an age (*one prophetic day*).

# The Sabbath Covenant
*Foretold in The Heavenly Scroll*

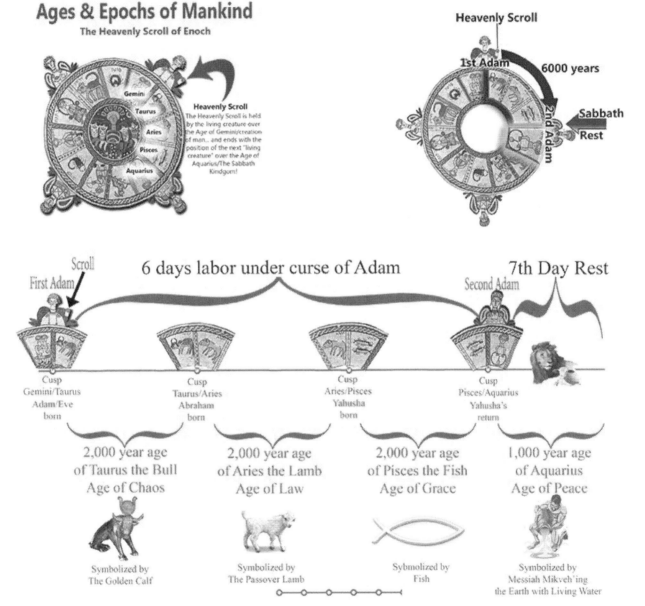

## Ages & Epochs of Mankind
The Heavenly Scroll of Enoch

**Heavenly Scroll**
The Heavenly Scroll is held by the living creature over the Age of Gemini/creation of man... and ends with the position of the next "living creature" over the Age of Aquarius/The Sabbath Kindgom!

Gemini
Taurus
Aries
Pisces
Aquarius

**Heavenly Scroll**

1st Adam — 6000 years

2nd Adam — Sabbath Rest

Scroll
First Adam

6 days labor under curse of Adam

7th Day Rest

Second Adam

Cusp
Gemini/Taurus
Adam/Eve
born

Cusp
Taurus/Aries
Abraham
born

Cusp
Aries/Pisces
Yahusha
born

Cusp
Pisces/Aquarius
Yahusha's
return

2,000 year age
of Taurus the Bull
Age of Chaos

Symbolized by
The Golden Calf

2,000 year age
of Aries the Lamb
Age of Law

Symbolized by
The Passover Lamb

2,000 year age
of Pisces the Fish
Age of Grace

Sybmolized by
Fish

1,000 year age
of Aquarius
Age of Peace

Symbolized by
Messiah Mikveh'ing
the Earth with Living Water

# End of the Age of Aries

The Last Generation ending in 70 A.D. The "Time of the End" of the Mosaic Covenant

Image property of The Sabbath Covenant Ministry www.sabbathcovenant.com by Rav Sha'ul

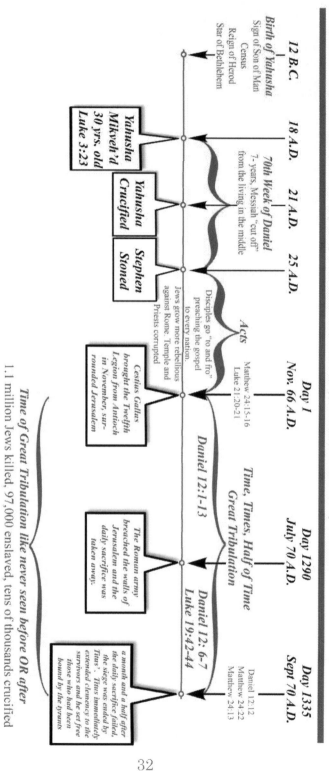

**12 B.C.**

*Birth of Yahusha*
Sign of Son of Man
Census
Reign of Herod
Star of Bethlehem

**18 A.D.**

*Yahusha*
*Mikveh'd*
*30 yrs. old*
*Luke 3:23*

*70th Week of Daniel*
7-years, Messiah "cut off"
from the living in the middle

**21 A.D.**

*Yahusha*
*Crucified*

**25 A.D.**

*Stephen*
*Stoned*

Disciples go "to and fro"
preaching the gospel
to every nation.
Jews grow more rebellious
against Rome, Temple and
Priests corrupted

*Acts*

**Day 1**
**Nov. 66 A.D.**

Matthew 24:15-16
Luke 21:20-21

Cestius Gallus
brought the Twelfth
Legion from Antioch
in November, sur-
rounded Jerusalem

*Daniel 12:1-13*

**Day 1290**
**July 70 A.D.**

*Time, Times, Half of Time*
*Great Tribulation*

The Roman army
breached the walls of
Jerusalem and the
daily sacrifice was
taken away.

*Daniel 12: 6-7*
*Luke 19:42-44*

**Day 1335**
**Sept 70 A.D.**

Daniel 12:12
Matthew 24:22
Matthew 24:13

a month and a half after
the daily sacrifice failed,
the siege was ended by
Titus'. Thus immediately
extended clemency to the
survivors and he set free
those who had been
bound by the tyrants

*Time of Great Tribulation like never seen before OR after*
1.1 million Jews killed, 97,000 enslaved, tens of thousands crucified
Jerusalem laid waste, the Temple utterly destroyed

*Daniel 9:25*
*The Anointed Ruler comes*
*there will be 7 weeks (49 years)*
*Messiah cut of 21 A.D. - 70 A.D. (49 years)*

# The Age of Pisces
## The Book of Revelation

Image property of The Sabbath Covenant Ministry www.sabbathcovenant.com by Rav Sha'ul

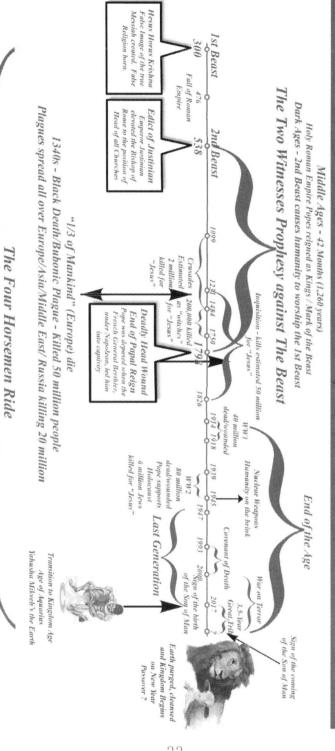

**1st Beast**
**300**

*Hesus Horus Krishna Fake Image of the true Messiah created. False Religion born.*

**476** — *Fall of Roman Empire*

**2nd Beast**
**538**

*Edict of Justinian Emperor Justinian elevated the Bishop of Rome to the position of Head of all Churches*

**Middle Ages - 42 Months (1,260 years)**
*Holy Roman Empire Popes reigned as Kings / Mark of the Beast*
**Dark Ages - 2nd Beast causes humanity to worship the 1st Beast**

### The Two Witnesses Prophesy against The Beast

*Inquisition - kills estimated 50 million for "Jesus"*

**1099**

**1291** **1484** **1750** **1798**

*Crusades Estimated 200,000 killed 2 million killed for "Jesus"*

**"1/3 of Mankind" (Europe) die**

**1340s - Black Death/Bubonic Plague - Killed 50 million people**
**Plagues spread all over Europe/Asia/Middle East/ Russia killing 20 million**

*Witches "witches" killed for "Jesus"*

**Deadly Head Wound**
*End of Papal Reign Pope was deposed when the French General Berthier, under Napoleon, led him into captivity.*

**1826**

**End of the Age**

**WW1**
*40 million dead/wounded*

**1914 1918**

*Nuclear Weapons Humanity on the brink*

**1939**

**WW2**
*80 million dead/wounded Pope supports Holocaust 6 million Jews killed for "Jesus"*

**1947** **1965** **1993**

*Covenant of Death*

**Last Generation**

*War on Terror*

**2017**

*3.5 Year Great Trib*

**2008/Sign of the birth of the Son of Man**

*Sign of the coming of the Son of Man*

*Transition to Kingdom Age Age of Aquarius Yahusha Mikveh's the Earth*

*Earth purged, cleansed and Kingdom Begins on New Year Passover ?*

### The Four Horsemen Ride

## The Beast Conquers the Earth - through death and intimidation
## Over 60,000,000 executed for "Jesus" and hundreds of millions tortured

# Battle of the Ages

*The "last days" of the Age of Pisces*

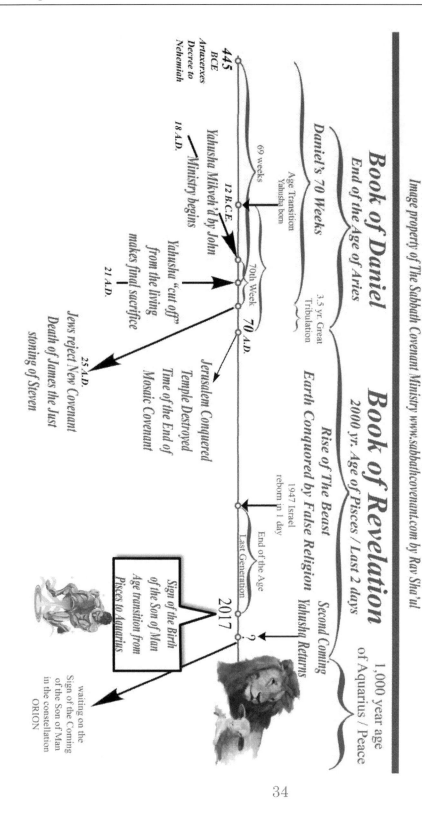

Image property of The Sabbath Covenant Ministry www.sabbathcovenant.com by Rav Sha'ul

**Book of Daniel**
*End of the Age of Aries*

**Book of Revelation**
*2000 yr. Age of Pisces / Last 2 days*

1,000 year age
of Aquarius / Peace

**Daniel's 70 Weeks**

**Rise of The Beast**
*Earth Conquered by False Religion*

**Second Coming**
*Yahusha Returns*

445
BCE
Artaxerxes
Decree to
Nehemiah

18 A.D.
Yahusha Mikveh'd by John
Ministry begins

69 weeks

Age Transition
Yahusha born

12 B.C.E.

70th Week

3.5 yr. Great
Tribulation

70 A.D.

21 A.D.
Yahusha "cut off"
from the living
makes final sacrifice

25 A.D.
Jews reject New Covenant
Death of James the Just
stoning of Steven

Jerusalem Conquered
Temple Destroyed
Time of the End of
Mosaic Covenant

1947 Israel
reborn in 1 day

End of the Age
Last Generation

2017

?

Sign of the Birth
of the Son of Man
Age transition from
Pisces to Aquarius

waiting on the
Sign of the Coming
of the Son of Man
in the constellation
ORION

34

# The Word of His Testimony

We will read as we go in Revelation about *The Word of His Testimony* which John was shown and then wrote down.

### Revelation 1

1 The (Heavenly Scroll is the) revelation of Yahusha the Messiah, Yahuah (who had The Heavenly Scroll in his hand Revelation 5:5) gave The Heavenly Scroll to His Angel to show His servants (all the prophets saw a Scroll in Heaven) what must soon take place. Yahuah made it (The Heavenly Scroll) known by sending his angel to his servant John, 2 who testifies to everything he saw (in the Heavens) — that is, the word of Yahuah (eternally preserved in The Heavenly Scroll Psalm 19, 119:89, 89:2) and (The Heavenly Scroll is) the testimony of Yahusha the Messiah (The Heavenly Scroll IS "the Word of His Testimony"). 3 BLESSED is the one who reads aloud the words of this prophecy (The Heavenly Scroll), and BLESSED are those who hear it (what the stars proclaim day after day, night after night Psalms 19) and take to heart what is written in The Heavenly Scroll (make it the Word of OUR Testimony too Revelation 12:11), because the time is near.

### Revelation 1:2,9

(Blessed are those) Who bare record of the word of God (eternally written in The Heavenly Scroll Psalm 119:89, Psalm 89:2, Daniel 4:35), and of the testimony of Yahusha the Messiah (written in The Heavenly Scroll shown to John), and of all things that he saw (written in the stars) …

It is imperative that we understand exactly what John was shown so we can then equate that to the phrase "Word of His Testimony" throughout Scripture. We must fully understand its meaning in our lives. This is because we too must have knowledge and faith in The Word of His Testimony.

In his vision, John was shown The Heavenly Scroll by Gabriel. This message written into the fabric of creation testifies of Yahusha who is the Glory of Yahuah.

### Revelation 1

1 The Heavenly Scroll is the revelation of Yahusha the Messiah, which Yahuah gave His Angel Gabriel to show His servants (all the prophets) what must soon take place. Yahuah made The Heavenly Scroll known by sending Gabriel to his servant John (to show him), 2 who (then John) testifies to everything he saw (in the Heavens called the Book of Revelation)— that is, the word of Yahuah (eternally preserved in The Heavenly Scroll Psalm 19, 119:89, 89:2, Daniel 4:35) and The Heavenly Scroll is the testimony of Yahusha the Messiah.

### Revelation 12:17

And the dragon was wroth with the woman, and went to make war with the remnant of her seed, which keep the commandments of God, and have (faith in) The Word of His Testimony (The Heavenly Scroll shown to John, and all the prophets).

### Revelation 6:9

And when he had opened the fifth seal, I saw under the altar the souls of them that were slain for the word of God, and for the testimony which they held (faith in The Heavenly Scroll Rev 12:17):

### Revelation 14:12

This calls for patient endurance on the part of the people of God who keep his commands and remain faithful to (the testimony of) Yahusha the Messiah (found in The Heavenly Scroll called The Word of His Testimony).

# A firm foundation in The Word of His Testimony

The *word* (*Greek 'LOGOS' / Hebrew 'DABAR'*) is the 'Spoken Promise' in the beginning of our Salvation.

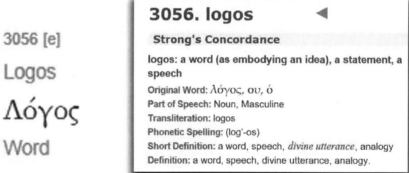

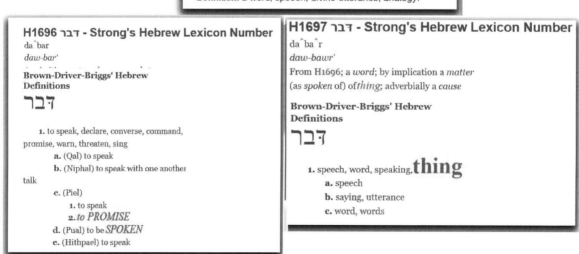

The Word of Yahuah is not just "the Torah and Prophets". In fact, it is The Heavenly Scroll, and it is preserved in the stars not on Earth.

### Psalm 89:2
I will declare that your love stands firm forever, that you have established your faithful promise (LOGOS) of salvation in The Heavenly Scroll itself.

### Psalm 119:89
Your Word (spoken promise), Yahuah, is Eternal; it Stands Firm written in The Heavenly Scroll.

### Psalm 119:105
105 Your Word (LOGOS / DABAR eternally preserved in The Heavenly Scroll Psalm 119:89) is a lamp (the Divine Council) unto my feet, and a light (revelation of the Sun/stars/constellations Psalm 19, Enoch 35:3) unto my path.

### Daniel 4:35
"All the inhabitants of the Earth are accounted as nothing, but He does according to His will written in the host of Heaven (The Zodiac which hosts constellations. Constellations "host stars)

The Torah and Prophets are based on the foundation of The Word of His Testimony written into the fabric of Creation. This Word is a light/lamp shining down from the Sun/stars/constellations written into Creation by a Loving Creator who 'promised a deliverer in the beginning'. It is His Divine Council and eternal witness to all mankind of His coming Kingdom and the King who will rule over His Creation as High Priest who is given a new name/title **Melchi Tsedek**. The Heavenly Scroll is Yahuah's Stamp over His Creation that declares that He is the Creator and that He has a plan (LOGOS/DABAR) whereby He will reconcile His Creation back to Himself through a coming anointed King and High Priest.

### Isaiah 42:5-7
5 Thus says Yahuah in The Heavenly Scroll, Who created The Heavenly Scroll and stretched out the stars and constellation (in order) to proclaim His Plan of Salvation (Isaiah 48:13), Who spread out the Earth and its offspring, Who gives breath to the people on it and revive the Spirit of those who walk in The Way of Mikveh (AQUARIUS), 6 "I am Yahuah, I have called Yahusha in The Path of Righteousness (to show My people how they can fulfill The Law and be found Righteous in My sight through Mikveh with Living Water Ezekiel 36:25), I will also hold Yahusha by the hand and watch over him to walk The Way by example (John 13:5), And I will appoint Yahusha as a covenant to the people (called The Yahushaic Covenant), As a Spiritual Light Bearer (ORION) to the Nations (fulfilling the physical light of the Sun in The Heavenly Scroll Psalm 19 Malachi 4:2 Isaiah 60:1 2 Samuel 23:4 Proverbs 4:18, Isaiah 9:2 Isaiah 30:26 Isaiah 49:6

Isaiah 60:1 Matthew 4:15 Luke 1:78 Luke 2:32 John 8:12 John 12:40), 7 To open Spiritually blind eyes, To bring out prisoners from the dungeon of The Dragon and those who dwell in darkness from the prison of human tradition and religion (Luke 42:7 Psalm 146:8 John 9:7)

### Isaiah 48:11-14
11 For My Own Sake, for My Own Sake I will do it; for how could dishonor come to My name (Yahuah)? I will not give My Glory (as Creator) to another (not even Yahusha, Yahuah ALONE sits on the Throne of Creation Isaiah 44:24)! 12 Listen to Me, O Jacob and Israel, My called; I am He; I am the Aleph, I also am the Tav (the standard of Perfection and Unity... the ONE and ONLY God John 17:3). 13 My Hand has laid the foundation of the Earth (by Himself Isaiah 44:24), and My Right Hand has spanned (authored) the Heaven (ly Scroll Psalm 19, 119:89, 89:2); when I summon the Sun/stars/constellations together (i.e. the stars and constellations contain a secret Message Enoch 6:9), they will minister together as a Divine Council to all mankind (to proclaim His Handiwork/The Messiah/Plan of Salvation Psalm 19). 14 All of you, gather yourselves together and hear (what the Sun/stars/constellations proclaim day after day, night after night Psalm 19, Enoch 35:3)!

### Isaiah 48:3-6
3 I foretold the former things long ago (written in the stars on Day 4 of Creation), My Mouth Announced them (to My Prophets who all read The Heavenly Scroll) and I made them known (to all mankind by the Word of My Testimony written in the stars Psalm 19, Enoch 35:3, given to all mankind Deuteronomy 3:19); then suddenly I acted, and the message proclaimed by the stars/constellations came to pass. 4 For I knew how stubborn you were; your neck muscles were iron; your forehead was bronze. 5 Therefore I told you these things (in The Heavenly Scroll) long ago (at Creation so that you are without excuse because Yahuah is known through His Handiwork Romans 1:20); before they were fulfilled I Announced the Plan of Salvation to you (in The Heavenly Scroll Psalm 19) so that you could not say, 'My images brought them about (because they are written into Creation in the stars as SIGNS/CONSTELLATIONS Genesis 1:14 which come together in order as the Sun passes through them each year to Proclaim The Plan of Salvation Yeshayahu/Isaiah 48:13); my wooden image and metal god ordained them.' 6 You have heard these things (that the stars Proclaim day after day, night after night to all mankind as a witness Psalm 19); look at all the stars/constellation (in The Heavenly Scroll). WILL YOU NOT ADMIT THEM (the Sun/stars/constellations are The Word of His Testimony, His Divine Council of The Plan of Salvation and the Works of His Hands Enoch 35:3)?

The prophets called this Eternal Word written in the stars The Heavenly Scroll and Divine Council. The Renewed Covenant called The Yahushaic Covenant (*the covenant that bears his name*) is based on the witness of the stars as this is the proof Yahusha is the Messiah. It is THAT "word" that he came to fulfill.

Yahuah promises that in the end, we will all know Him by His Divine Council called The Heavenly Scroll. Once we "admit it" then we all will be enlightened to the meaning of the light of the Sun/stars/constellations and know Yahuah as He (and His Chosen King the Messiah) is known through His Creation.

Below, we see Jeremiah proclaim the coming New Covenant. Where did Jeremiah get this 'knowledge'? Well, he told us right there in Chapter 31; he (*like every other Prophet*) read The Heavenly Scroll upon which The New Covenant is founded.

### Jeremiah 31:33-35

33 "But this is the covenant which I will make with the House of Israel after those days," declares Yahuah, "I will put My Law within them and on their heart, I will write it; and I will be their God, and they shall be My people. 34 "They will not teach again, each man his neighbor and each man his brother, saying, 'Know Yahuah,' for they will all know Me (from His Divine Council, 'what He created': **Romans 1**), from the least of them to the greatest of them," declares Yahuah, "for I will forgive their iniquity, and their sin I will remember no more." 35 **The New Covenant is what Yahuah declares in The Heavenly Scroll, Who gives the Sun for light (revelation) by day And the fixed order of the moon and the stars for light (revelation) by night** (knowledge is found in the light of the Sun/stars/constellations **Psalm 19**, **Enoch 35:3**), Who stirs up the sea so that its waves roar; **Yahuah author of the Heavenly hosts** (stars/constellations His Divine Council) **is His name**

### Romans 1:18-20

18 The wrath of Yahuah is being revealed from The Heavenly Scroll (the Bowl of Wrath is poured out on *The Dragon*) against all the godlessness and wickedness of people, teach unrighteousness (lies) as the Truth, 19 since what may be known about Yahuah is plain to them, because Yahuah has made it (The Heavenly Scroll) plain to them (but we rejected it and teach lies Isaiah 48:3-6). 20 For since the Creation of the world (on Day 1 when He spoke the plan into action "let there be light/Revelation of The Plan of Salvation") Yahuah's Invisible qualities — His eternal Power and Divine Nature — have been clearly seen, being understood from what has been made (as he then authored that Plan into the stars on Day 4 of Creation **Psalm 19** 'the stars proclaim the Works of His Hands' **Enoch 35:3**, 'I bless Yahuah of Glory Who made the Great and splendid Signs/Constellations, that they might proclaim the Magnificence of the Works of His Hands'), so that people are without excuse (because the Plan of Salvation is proclaimed day and night to all mankind Psalm 19 by The Heavenly Scroll).

In this book, we will demonstrate that the knowledge we must have to understand the Book of Revelation and to be saved is contained in The Heavenly Scroll! We will restore this required knowledge to the Book of Revelation and bring this book to life.

# Our testimony is '*The Word of His Testimony*'

Scripture declares we must have faith in the Word of His Testimony. The Word of His Testimony was written into the stars by the Creator in such a way that when taken together in a specific order, the star/constellation, called the "hosts of Heaven", bear witness (Psalm 19, Enoch 35:3) or testify to the Plan of Salvation through a coming King and High Priest who is Yahusha the Messiah.

### Isaiah 48:11-14

11 For My Own Sake, for My Own Sake I will do it; for how could dishonor come to My name? I will not give My Glory (as Creator) to another (not even Yahusha, Yahuah ALONE sits on the Throne of Creation Isaiah 44:24)! 12 Listen to Me, O Jacob and Israel, My called; I am He; I am the Aleph, I also am the Tav. 13 My Hand has laid the foundation of the Earth (by Himself Isaiah 44:24), and My Right Hand has spanned (authored) the Heaven (ly Scroll Psalm 19, 119:89, 89:2, Daniel 4:35); when I summon the Sun/stars/constellations together (they contain a secret Message Enoch 6:9), they will minister together as a Divine Council to all mankind. 14 All of you, gather yourselves together and hear (what the Sun/stars/constellations proclaim day after day, night after night Psalm 19, Enoch 35:3)!

What is the "*word of their (meaning our) testimony*" that defeats the Dragon/False Religion of Babylon which is based on the corrupted Zodiac!

### Revelation 12:11

They triumphed over the Dragon by the blood of the Lamb and by the word of their testimony.

It is keeping faith in The Word of His Testimony written in The Heavenly Scroll which is what John was shown and wrote down that we call the Book of Revelation. John was not writing a book, he was documenting what he was shown by the messenger in the stars!

### Revelation 1

1 The (Heavenly Scroll is the) revelation of Yahusha the Messiah, Yahuah (who had The Heavenly Scroll in his hand Revelation 5:5) gave The Heavenly Scroll to Gabriel to show His servants (all the prophets saw a Scroll in Heaven) what must soon take place. Yahuah made it (The Heavenly Scroll) known by sending Gabriel to his servant John, 2 who testifies to everything he saw (in the Heavens) — that is, the word of Yahuah (eternally preserved in The Heavenly Scroll Psalm 19, 119:89, 89:2, Daniel 4:35) and (The Heavenly Scroll is) the testimony of Yahusha the Messiah (The Heavenly Scroll IS "the Word of His

Testimony"). 3 BLESSED is the one who reads aloud the words of this prophecy (The Heavenly Scroll), and BLESSED are those who hear it (what the stars proclaim day after day, night after night Psalms 19) and take to heart what is written in The Heavenly Scroll (make it the Word of OUR Testimony too Revelation 12:11), because the time (of it fulfillment) is near.

### Revelation 12:17
And the dragon was wroth with the woman, and went to make war with the remnant of her seed, which keep the commandments of God, and have (faith in) The Word of His Testimony (The Heavenly Scroll shown to John).

### Revelation 6:9
And when he had opened the fifth seal, I saw under the altar the souls of them that were slain for the word of God, and for the testimony which they held (faith in The Heavenly Scroll Rev 12:17 which is the Word of Their Testimony Rev 12:11)):

### Revelation 14:12
This calls for patient endurance on the part of the people of God who keep his commands and remain faithful to (the testimony of) Yahusha the Messiah (found in The Heavenly Scroll called The Word of His Testimony).

We see that what John was shown in the Book of Revelation was The Heavenly Scroll. John documented the contents of that Scroll in detail as he was shown by Gabriel. The Book of Revelation is literally *The Revelation of The Heavenly Scroll's contents*!

#### Revelation 5 - *The Opening of the Scroll of the Mazzaroth*
5 Then I saw in the right hand of the one who was seated on the throne a Scroll written on the front and back (3-D Scroll of Heavenly pictographs) and sealed with seven seals (the 7 visible wandering stars were seen as seals over The Heavenly Scroll, also the 7 lampstand Heavenly Menorah).

John then describes what he sees in detail, an exact description of what Enoch drew called The Enoch Zodiac which is a picture of The Heavenly Scroll:

#### Revelation 4
1 After I was shown the Throne in Heaven, I looked into the stars and behold, a door was opened in Heaven; and the first voice which I heard was (Yahuah, the Aleph/Tav), as it were, of a trumpet talking with me, which said: Come up here (metaphorically speaking meaning Spiritually not physically), and I will show you things (in The Heavenly Scroll) which must be after this. 2 And immediately I was in the Spirit (as he looked up); and behold (in the stars), a throne was set in The Heavenly Scroll, and one sat on the throne. 3 And he who sat there had the appearance of a jasper and a sardius stone, and there was a rainbow surrounding the throne, like the appearance of an emerald.

41

*John is describing what he sees which is exactly what Enoch was shown and drew called The Enoch Zodiac. We see in the center of The Enoch Zodiac the Throne Room. On the throne is "one who's appearance is of Jasper and Sardis stone, and the throne he is sitting on is a rainbow. The Throne is surrounded by 4 living creatures and 24 elders (stars) falling before the throne. Exactly as described by Enoch, Ezekiel, John, etc.*

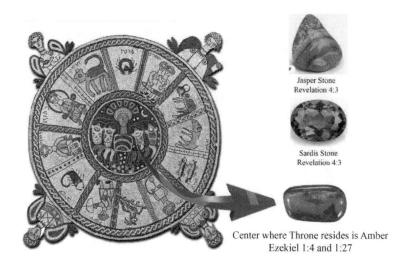

Jasper Stone
Revelation 4:3

Sardis Stone
Revelation 4:3

Center where Throne resides is Amber
Ezekiel 1:4 and 1:27

4 And surrounding the throne were twenty-four seats, and sitting on the seats I saw twenty-four elders (there are 24 stars in the center of The Enoch Zodiac above "falling before the throne" verse 10 below), clothed in white robes (stars) ; and they had crowns of gold on their heads.

5 And out of the throne proceeded lightnings, and thunderings, and voices; and there were seven lamps of fire burning before the throne, which signify and represent the complete plan of Yahuah (7-spirits/7 stars of PLAIADES... The Heavenly Menorah).

6 And before the throne there was a sea of glass, like crystal (blackness of space). And in the midst of the throne (the 4 Seraphs singing holy holy holy),and surrounding the throne (the 4 Seraphs sitting on the outer ring), were four living creatures full of eyes before and behind.

7 And the first creature (Seraph sitting on the outer ring) was like a lion (Judah/LEO), and the second creature like a calf (or Ox/Taurus/Ephraim), and the third creature had a face as a man (AQUARIUS/Rueben), and the fourth creature was like a flying eagle (Scorpio/Dan).

8 And each of the four living creatures (in the center Throne Room) had six wings (Seraphim), they were full of eyes around and within; and they did not cease day and night, saying: Holy, holy, holy, Father Yahuah Almighty, Who was, and is, and is to come.

9 And when those creatures give glory, and honor, and thanks, to Him who sat on the throne, to Him Who lives forever and ever, 10 The twenty-four elders (seen as stars) fall down before Him Who sat on the throne (the 24 stars surrounding the throne in the middle are falling before Him who sites on the throne),

*Notice in the Throne Room (center of the Enoch Zodiac) there are exactly 24 stars and they are "falling before/under the Rainbow Throne" upon which sits The Son of Man the color of Sardis Stone! With 4 living creatures singing Holy, Holy, Holy!*

## The Heavenly Scroll is what John "saw and described" that is "the testimony of Yahuah that Yahusha is the Branch"!

John literally describes The Enoch Zodiac (*Enoch's drawing of The Heavenly Scroll*) in great detail above. THAT is the "Word of His Testimony" that we ALL must have faith in. With the context of all of Revelation added back into Chapter 1, we have the proper interpretation below:

### Revelation 1

1 The (Heavenly Scroll is the) revelation of Yahusha the Messiah, which Yahuah gave His Angel to show His servants (all the prophets) what must soon take place. Yahuah made it (The Heavenly Scroll) known by sending his angel to his servant John, 2 who testifies to everything he saw (in the Heavens)—that is, the word of Yahuah (eternally preserved in The Heavenly Scroll Psalm 119:89) and (The Heavenly Scroll is) the testimony of Yahusha the Messiah (The Word of His Testimony). 3 Blessed is the one who reads aloud the words of this prophecy, and blessed are those who hear it and take to heart what is written in The Heavenly Scroll, because the time is near.

# And Idiom for The Word of His Testimony

In the Book of Revelation, John was shown "the Son of Man coming in the clouds of Heaven" and described what he saw written in The Heavenly Scroll. "The Son of Man coming in the clouds of Heaven" is <u>an idiom</u> for The Heavenly Scroll as ORION represents The Son of Man and the "clouds of Heaven" is seen as The Milky Way Galaxy. The Scroll speaks of Yahusha who is represented by ORION coming in the clouds of Heaven. We see John begin reading The Heavenly Scroll:

### <u>Revelation 1</u>
4 John, to the seven churches which are in Asia: Grace to you and peace from Him who is and who was and who is to come, and from the seven Spirits who are before His throne, 5 and from Yahusha the Messiah, the true and faithful witness (of The Heavenly Scroll Matthew 4:16-17), the firstborn from the dead (CAPRICORNUS), and the ruler over the kings of the Earth (LEO). To Him who loved us and washed us (AQUARIUS) from our sins in His own blood (LIBRA), 6 and has made us kings and priests to His God and Father (Yahuah), to Him (Yahuah) be glory and dominion forever and ever. Amen. 7 Behold in The Heavenly Scroll, He (ORION) is coming with (the) clouds (of Heaven the Milky Way), and every eye will see Him (The Sign of the Coming of The Son of Man), even they who pierced Him (CAPRICORNUS). And all the tribes of the Earth will mourn because of Him. Even so, Amen.

12 And I turned to see (in The Heavenly Scroll) the voice that spoke with me (Yahuah had spoken, identified Himself as Aleph/Tav, the Father). And having turned (he didn't see Yahuah), I saw (in The Heavenly Scroll) a golden seven lamp lampstand (7 classical planets also seen as the seals over The Heavenly Scroll, it is The Heavenly Menorah); 13 And in the midst of the seven-lamp lampstand (in The Heavenly Scroll) One like the Son of Man (ORION), clothed with a garment (of the High Priest) down to the feet (tallit - Psalms 110:3) with a

girdle of gold about His chest (chest plate of the High Priest). 14 The hair of His head was white like wool (John begins describing the constellation ORION), as white as snow; and His eyes were as a flame of fire; 15 And His feet glowed like bronze which had been fired in a furnace; and His voice sounded like many (Living) waters (*AQUARIUS*).

16 And in His (ORION's) right hand He had seven stars (PLAIADES); and out of His mouth went a sharp, two-edged sword (the sword of ORION, a metaphor of the Word of Yahuah); and His face was like the Sun (the Sun is a metaphor of the Messiah see Psalms 19) shining in its strength. 17 And when I saw Him, I fell at His feet as though dead (literally "scared to death" so to speak).

We see these 7 stars and ORION mentioned on several occasions in scripture, as Yahuah witnessed the gospel to His prophets, who described The Heavenly Scroll in detail. We see ORION and the 7 stars mentioned by Amos, whose prophetic understanding was guided by The Heavenly Scroll. PLAIADES brightest of all constellations and easily seen in the "Heavens or Heavenly Scroll".

### Amos 5:8
Yahuah who made the PLAIADES (7 stars) and ORION (the Son of Man)

### Job 9:9
Yahuah is the Maker of the Bear (Ursa Major) and ORION, the (7 stars of) PLAIADES and the constellations of the south.

### Revelation 14:14-20
"And I looked (in the Heavens), and behold a white cloud, and upon the cloud (Milky Way) one sat like unto the Son of Man (ORION), having on his head a golden crown, and in his hand a sharp sword."

In Amos, we see a clear reference to the "Heavens" or The Heavenly Scroll having an effect on the "foundations on the Earth"

### Amos 9:6
Yahuah builds His lofty palace in the Heavens (Mazzaroth/Heavenly Scroll) and sets its foundation on the Earth (the Heavens and Earth are intimately connected, what is portrayed in the Heavens, plays out on Earth).

46

# The Son of Man is victorious

Before going any further, let us review the contents of The Heavenly Scroll:

## *The Heavenly Scroll*

### Story Told through major constellations

*VIRGO*: A young maiden will give a virgin birth (*the Branch will open her womb and be the firstborn and heir*) to a beautiful glorious and righteous branch. The seed of the woman will be

a man of humiliation to rise to be the desire of nations and will become exalted first as shepherd (*High Priest/Spring Feasts*) then as harvester (*Conquering King/Fall Feasts*). *LIBRA*: The scales demand a price to be paid of this seed (*he must pay the dowry with his life*), the wood of the sacrifice to carry; the victim will be slain and purchase a crown. *SCORPIO*: There is a conflict between the seed and the serpent leading to a struggle with the enemy; the enemy is vanquished. *SAGITTARIUS*: The double-natured seed (*King and High Priest*) triumphs as a warrior

and pleases the Heavens, builds fires of punishment, casts down the
dragon. *CAPRICORNUS*: Eternal life comes from his death, he's the Arrow of Yahuah, he is pierced, yet springs up again in abundant life. *AQUARIUS*: He pours out "living water" from on high, humanity drinks of the Heavenly river and the faithful live again, he is the deliverer of the good news (*Gospel*), Carrying the wood of the sacrifice over the Earth. *PISCES*: The Redeemer's people multiplied, supported and led by the Lamb, The Bride is exposed on Earth, the Bridegroom is exalted. *ARIES*: The Lamb is found worthy, the Bride is made ready, Satan is bound, the strong man triumphs. *TAURUS*: The conquering Ruler comes, the sublime vanquisher, to execute the great judgment, he is the ruling Shepherd King. *GEMINI*: The Marriage of the Lamb, the enemy is trodden down, the Prince comes in great Glory. *CANCER*: The great Bride, the two Houses of Judah and Israel are united, they are brought safely into the kingdom. *LEO*: The Lion King is aroused for rending, the Serpent flees, the Bowl of Wrath is upon him, his Carcass is devoured. The Lion of the tribe of Judah rules as King.

### Story Told through minor constellations called Decans

A ***virgin*** Maiden is the mother of an Infant Prince who is half mortal and half god (***Centaur***) and who will grow up to be the Good Shepherd (***Herdsman***). He is the Redeemer who will pay the price of sin (***Balance***) through his suffering (***Cross***) as a sacrifice (***Beast***) in order to win the Crown. He will be the great Healer who will crush sickness and death (***Scorpion***). He is the Savior (***Archer, Hercules***) who slays the Dragon, resulting in great rejoicing (***Harp***). He is also the Goat (***Sea Goat***) sacrificed on the Altar, but then resurrecting (***Dolphin***). He is the messenger of his Father (***Eagle and Arrow***). He is the Master Teacher (***Waterman***), who pours out knowledge and blessings on his church (***Southern Fish***), carrying it upward (***Flying Horse***) to someday be glorified (***Swan***). He is the Ram who breaks the Bands of Death, and the Hero who looses the chains of hell which bind and shackle both the House of Israel and House of Judah (***Fishes***) to the awful Sea Monster. The Hero is also the Bridegroom who then marries his Bride (***Princess***). He is enthroned as the King and the glorified Bride becomes his Queen. At the beginning of the Millennium, Yahusha reigns as King and King of the Kingdom of Yahuah (***Bull***). As the royal Hunter he destroys the harlot (***Hare***) who has perverted religions and governments worldwide, and he executes judgment on the wicked (***River***). He is both the High Priest and King (***Twins***). He who comes in power to destroy the great harlot (***Hare***) at the Second Coming (***Big Dog***) is also he who came in meekness and allowed himself to be slain by her at the First Coming (***Little Dog***). He is the Deliverer (***Crab***) who leads the dead up out of hell (***Ship***) and delivers his flocks (***Big and Little Bears***). As the millennial King (***Lion***), he permanently overcomes the fleeing ***Water Serpent***, who suffers the ***Cup of the wrath*** of God, and whose corpse is eaten by birds of prey (***Raven***).

With that foundation, let us now reveal the meaning of these Scriptures in context. In Revelation 5 and Daniel 7 we see the Son of Man is victorious over the False Messiah and The Dragon in The Battle of the Ages.

### Revelation Chapter 5

1 And I saw in the right hand of Him Who sat on the throne, a (Heavenly) Scroll written inside and on the back (Scroll made up of 3D Heavenly "signs"/pictographs), sealed with seven seals (7 classical planet).

2 And I saw a mighty malak proclaiming with a loud voice: Who is worthy to open the (Heavenly) Scroll, and to release its seals? 3 And no one in Heaven, nor in Earth, neither under the Earth was able to open the (Heavenly) Scroll, neither to look at it. 4 And I wept bitterly, because no one was found worthy to open and to read the (Heavenly) Scroll, neither to look upon it.

5 But one of the elders said to me: Do not weep! Behold (in The Heavenly Scroll, the pictograph of LEO, the last sign in the Plan of Salvation written in the stars), the Lion of the

tribe of Yahdah, the Root of David, has overcome (the Dragon, DRACO/SERPENS/SCORPIO... the meaning behind the constellation LEO and OPHIUCHUS) to open the (Heavenly) Scroll and to release its seven seals (7 stars of *PLAIADES*).

6 And I looked (into the stars), and behold (in The Heavenly Scroll), in the middle of the throne room and the four living creatures, and in the midst of the elders, stood a Lamb as though it had been slain, having complete power and complete knowledge and understanding, which signify and represent the complete plan of Yahuah (the 7 Spirits/7 stars of *PLAIADES*) sent forth into all the Earth.

7 And he came and took The Heavenly Scroll out of the right hand of Him Who sat upon the throne. 8 And when he had taken the (Heavenly) Scroll, the four living creatures and twenty-four elders fell down before the Lamb, each one of them having a harp (LYRA), and golden bowls full of incense (Crater), which are the prayers of the saints. 9 And they sang a new song, saying: You are worthy to take the (Heavenly) Scroll, and to open its seals (ARIES); for You were slain (LIBRA), and have redeemed us to Yahuah by Your blood out of every tribe, and language, and people, and nation (PISCES); 10 And have made us kings and priests to our Father (CANCER); and we will reign upon the Earth (LEO);.

11 And I looked, and I heard the voice of many malakim (he was looking at the stars) surrounding the throne, and the (4 living) creatures, and the (24) elders; and the number of them (the stars in the sky which represent malakim/angels) was ten thousand times ten thousand, and thousands of thousands, 12 Saying with a loud voice: Worthy is the Lamb Who was slain to receive power, and riches, and wisdom, and strength, and honor, and glory, and blessing!

13 And every creature which is in Heaven, and on the Earth, and under the ground, and such as are in the sea, and all that are in them, I heard saying: Blessing, and honor, and glory, and power belongs to Him Who sits on the throne (Yahuah still on the throne at that time), and to the Lamb (the Prince of Peace who is not sat on the throne until the very end), forever and ever! 14 And the four living creatures said: HalleluYahuah! And the twenty-four elders fell down and worshiped Him Who lives forever and ever (Yahuah).

# Who is the Aleph and Tav?

In the Book of Revelation, we see the use of two titles:

1. Alpha and Omega (Aleph and Tav in Hebrew)
2. First and Last

These two titles are used interchangeably for both the Father and the firstborn son. Leading us to blaspheme the Holy Spirit in the process believing in the Spirit of the False Messiah which is incarnation. See my book Blasphemy of the Holy Spirit for more on this topic.

*Blasphemy of the Holy Spirit by Rav Sha'ul.*
*Available on all online bookstores.*

The Truth is that these titles are not interchangeable! The Hebraic Mindset and meaning of Aleph and Tav has been twisted into Greek through Hellenism. The Greek and the English translators have even altered the scriptures and written into them "Alpha and Omega" in two places to build into Scripture the Spirit of the False Messiah. They made it look as though Yahusha claimed to be Yahuah and said he was the Aleph and Tav, when he never made such a claim… anywhere! Then they added "first and the last" as if Yahuah claimed that title.

*Excerpt from The Fall Feasts: An invitation to the wedding by Rav Sha'ul*

The Greek phrase "Alpha and Omega" is misleading, as it does not carry forward the Hebraic mindset behind the Aleph and Tav! What the Bible translators did not realize (*or they rejected*) is that each individual Hebrew letter can be a word or phrase unto itself, with a specific meaning. This is clearly pointed out by Fabre d'Olivet in his book, The Hebraic Tongue Restored. Dr. d'Olivet in which he gives clear, precise explanations of the meanings of each individual Hebrew letter, and what they point out or declare. On page 98 of his book, Dr. d'Olivet also states that knowing that each Hebrew letter has a meaning of its own, is the key to understanding the Scriptures. In reference to the letters Aleph and Tav, Dr. d'Olivet gives clear proof that these two letters make statements in their own right.

Aleph

The first letter in the Hebrew alphabet, as Dr. d'Olivet points out from The Hebraic Tongue Restored on pages 95 and 287, stands for unity.

א A.–This first character of the alphabet, in nearly all known idioms, is the sign of power and of stability. The ideas that it expresses are those of <u>unity...</u>

א A. First character of the alphabet in nearly all known idioms. In its hieroglyphic acceptation, it characterizes <u>unity</u>, the central point, the <u>abstract principle of a thing</u>. As sign, it expresses <u>power, stability, continuity.</u>

51

Tav

On pages 98 and 465 of this book, Dr. d'Olivet clearly points out that the letter TAV, the last letter of the Hebrew alphabet, means and stands for perfection.

> ת TH. Sign of reciprocity: image of that which is mutual and reciprocal. Sign of signs. Joining to the abundance of the character ר, to the force of the resistance and protection of the character ט, the idea of <u>perfection</u> of which it is itself the symbol.
>
> ת TH. This character as consonant, belongs to the sibilant sound. As grammatical sign in the Hebraic Tongue, it is that of <u>sympathy and reciprocity</u>; joining, to the abundance of the character ר , to the force of <u>resistance and protection</u> of the character ט, the idea of <u>perfection</u> and necessity of which it is the emblem.

Incredible as it may sound, both single letters Aleph and Tav, are in themselves Hebrew words that have specific meanings. As Clark, in his Commentary, and the writers of The Anchor Bible have shown, the Alpha and Omega should have been written: the Aleph and the TAV.

<u>The Anchor Bible, Revelation Volume 38, page 379</u>, gives us the explanation of this phrase.

> *the Alpha and the Omega. The Hebrew would be aleph and taw, probably standing respectively for Urim and Thummim, the sacred lots of the high priest used to determine the will of God, and also meaning all "encompassing."*

<u>Adam Clarke, in his Commentary, Volume 6, page 971</u>, agrees that Alpha and Omega are Aleph and Tav in Hebrew, as the Scriptures were Hellenized and twisted into Greek to remove all Hebrew flavor and meaning.

> *[The beginning and the ending.] That is, as Aleph or Alpha is the beginning of the Alphabet, so am I the author and cause of all things; as TAV or Omega is the end, or*

*last letter of the Alphabet, so am I the end of all things, the destroyer as well as the establisher of all things*

Tav     Aleph

# The Aleph and Tav in Scripture

The phrase "Alpha and Omega" is written four times in the King James Version of the Scriptures (*which is the foundation of most English Bibles*). However, this phrase should only have been written two times. It was added to the Scriptures twice, in order to infer that it is Yahusha the Messiah Who is "Alpha and Omega". This needs to be corrected as it has given rise to justifying The Spirit of the False Messiah that Yahuah came to Earth as a man named Jesus. Even those who have come out of "Babylon" and come to know the true name of the Messiah, are still stuck in idolatry worshipping a man who died above Yahuah as "God-incarnate" which is forbidden (*Romans 1*).

We have all been taught erroneously, that it was "Jesus" speaking in the Book of Revelation. This is not true… it was "the Messenger of Yahuah" speaking to Yahuchanon who is Gabriel, showing Yahuchanon what must take place on Earth as it was written in The Heavenly Scroll. Gabriel was delivering a message from Yahusha and Yahuah.

> It is Gabriel who is "the messenger of Yahuah" that is his role. Like Michael is to defend Israel, and Yahusha is to minister before the Golden Altar. It was Gabriel who was sent to show John the meaning of The Heavenly Scroll. The same role he played in the lives of Daniel, and Zechariah (John's father). It is Gabriel who "stands in the presence of Yahuah" who is sent to speak to Yahuah's Prophets:

> **<u>Luke 1:19</u>**
> The angel said to him, "I am *<u>Gabriel</u>*. I stand in the presence of Yahuah, and I have been sent to speak to you and to tell you this good news.

**Daniel 8:16-18**

16And I heard the voice of a man between the banks of Ulai, and he called out and said, "*Gabriel*, give this man an understanding of the vision." 17So he came near to where I was standing, and when he came I was frightened and fell on my face; but he said to me, "Son of man, understand that the vision pertains to the time of the end."

**Daniel 9:21**

while I was still in prayer, *Gabriel*, the man I had seen in the earlier vision, came to me in swift flight about the time of the evening sacrifice.

**Revelation 1**

1 The revelation from Yahusha the Messiah, which God (Yahuah) gave him to show his servants what must soon take place. Yahuah made it known by sending His angel Gabriel to his servant John, 2 who testifies to everything he saw (in The Heavenly Scroll)—that is (The Heavenly Scroll), the word of Yahuah and the testimony of Yahusha the Messiah (The Heavenly Scroll is Yahuah's testimony of Yahusha Psalms 19). 3 Blessed is the one who reads aloud the words of this prophecy, and blessed are those who hear it and take to heart what is written in it, because the time is near.

We see further confirmation that it is the Messenger of Yahuah speaking not Yahusha as it continues... and the Messenger says He is bringing words from both Yahuah and Yahusha...

**Revelation 1**

4 Yahuchanon to the seven churches that are in Asia: Grace to you and peace from Him (Yahuah) who is and who was and who is to come (the Eternal Almighty), and from the seven spirits who are before his throne, 5 **and** (in addition to Yahuah) from Yahusha the Messiah the (true) faithful witness (*Immanuel)*, the firstborn of the dead (he is NOT the Eternal Almighty, Yahusha is the first created of all eternal creation), and the ruler of kings on Earth (not King of Creation, that is Yahuah. Yahusha is the proxy King over the Earth).

We must be faithful to study the Book of Revelation, because the Messenger speaks (as a proxy) for both Yahuah and Yahusha. The messenger identifies "who" he is speaking for each time the Messenger speaks! We are going to examine each place in Scripture where it is taught that Alpha and Omega was used by Yahusha, and we are going to prove it was Yahuah speaking through His Messenger, not Yahusha speaking directly. Let's look at Revelation Chapter 1, and continue to reveal 'who is who' and who is speaking when:

**Revelation 1**

5 (the Messenger gives Glory where Glory is due, first to Yahusha) To him who loves us and has freed us from our sins by his blood (speaking about Yahusha), 6 and has made us to be a

kingdom and priests to serve his (Yahusha's) God and Father (clearly Yahuah is Yahusha's "God and Father"!)— (now to Yahuah, the God and Father) to Him be glory and power for ever and ever! Amen.

7 (Now, Yahuah speaks from His throne, and testifies about Yahusha. Yahuah tells Yahuchanon to behold the constellation ORION, which represents the Messiah in The Heavenly Scroll) **"Look (at ORION), he is coming with the clouds (of Heaven, the Milky Way),"**

*ORION see in "Heaven" rides on the Milky Way (clouds of Heaven)*

and "every eye will see him, even those who pierced him (ORION is a pictograph of the Messiah in The Heavenly Scroll)"; and all peoples on Earth "will mourn because of him." So shall it be! Amen. 8 (Yahuah still speaking) "I am the Alpha and the Omega," says the Yahuah Elohim, "who is, and who was, and who is to come, the Almighty."

This Scripture cannot be any clearer than it is. This is Yahuah speaking about Himself. "Lord God" is always Yahuah Elohim in scripture, He is the only everlasting, Almighty True God, Yahusha is the first created son (verse 5)!

### John 17:3
Now this is eternal life: that they know you (Father, Yahuah), the only true God, and (come to You in covenant with) Yahusha the Messiah, whom You have sent (as prophesied in The Heavenly and Earthly Scrolls).

### Isaiah 45:5
I am Yahuah, and there is no other, besides me there is no God!

Now, Alpha and Omega are written again in Revelation 1:11 in the King James Version. This is where the translators ADDED to the words of this book. It is a violation of Yahusha and Yahuah's instruction to add or subtract from the Book of Revelation! So let us continue with verse 9 of Revelation in the King James Version Bible, I underlined the words added.

### Revelation 1 – King James Version
9 I John, who also am your brother, and companion in tribulation (*tribulation began 2000 years ago*), and in the kingdom and patience of Jesus Christ, was in the isle that is called Patmos, for the word of God, and for the testimony of Jesus Christ. 10 I was in the Spirit on Yahuah's day, and heard behind me a great voice, as of a trumpet, 11 Saying, <u>I am Alpha and Omega, the first and the last: and</u>, What thou seest, write in a book, and send it unto the seven churches which are in Asia; unto Ephesus, and unto Smyrna, and unto Pergamos, and unto Thyatira, and unto Sardis, and unto Philadelphia, and unto Laodicea.

The words above underlined were added to this part of scripture. It is very sad when even Yahoo answers knows more about the attempt to build "incarnation" into our Bibles that most of us on Facebook who claim to know "Yahuah"!

## https://answers.yahoo.com/question/index?qid=20090321082439AAALmXM

"Some Trinitarians in the past thought that it was a good idea to add words to the Bible, in order to help bolster the unscriptural Trinity doctrine. One of the places they added words was in Revelation 1:11. The inserted words are "I am the alpha and the omega, the beginning and the end." This phrase is not found in the most ancient extant Greek manuscripts. Most modern biblical scholars are sure that these words aren't original - the UBS's Greek New Testament version 4 doesn't even mention it as a rejected reading. Nowhere does the Bible associate the words "Alpha and the Omega" with Jesus Christ. That title belongs to Jehovah, and Jehovah alone. Some do, though, associate "Alpha and the Omega" with Jesus in Revelation chapter 22. In verse 13, God says he is the Alpha and the Omega. Then, in verse 16, it appears that it is Jesus who has been talking. However, the words "I Jesus" is the writer's indication that the speaker has just changed. This was very common in the writings of ancient times, since they did not use quotations marks, or any punctuation at all. An example of this occurring is in Revelation chapter 1, when God says he is the Alpha and the Omega in verse 8, but then the writer indicates a change in speaker in verse 9 by writing "I John." Since no one thinks that Yahuchanon is God because of theses verses, why do some think Jesus said "Alpha and the Omega" in chapter 22? Trinitarian bias.

Nowhere in scripture did Yahusha say that he was the Aleph Tav or Alpha and Omega. He said he was "the first and the last" referring to "firstborn from the grave" and that he is the "beginning and ending" of the Plan of Salvation written in stars. It has been proven by textual critics that the oldest Greek manuscripts did not contain that statement in Revelation 1:11, it was added to promote "incarnation"! Revelation 1:11 Saying, "I am Alpha and Omega, the first and the last" these characters, which were repeated here, (because Yahuah used them in Revelation 1:8); are not found in the Alexandrian copy, the Complutensian edition, the Vulgate Latin, Syriac, and Ethiopic versions of Revelation.

**NOTE:**
To understand Revelation, you must shed the light of The Heavenly Scroll on the book. Please watch my video teaching proving John was shown The Heavenly Scroll by Yahuah ... I cover Daniel, Ezekiel, and John in my video series here:

https://www.youtube.com/channel/UCVLZgChmeSa78Mo7b228sjQ

So let me continue with Revelation Chapter 1, with verse 9 the way it was actually written in the Greek manuscripts:

**Revelation 1**
9 I, John, your brother and companion in the suffering and kingdom and patient endurance that are ours in (covenant with) Yahusha, was on the island of Patmos because of the word of Yahuah and the testimony of Yahusha (proclaimed in The Heavenly Scroll). 10 On the Day of Yahuah, I was in the Spirit (being shown The Heavenly Scroll), and I heard behind me a loud voice like a Shofar (Yahuah speaking, His voice is like a loud Shofar blast Hebrews 12:19), 11 which said: *"Write on a Scroll what you see and send it to the seven churches: to Ephesus, Smyrna, Pergamum, Thyatira, Sardis, Philadelphia and Laodicea."* 12 And I turned to see (in The Heavenly Scroll) the voice that spoke with me (Yahuah had spoken, identified Himself as Aleph/Tav, the Father verse 8). And having turned (he didn't see Yahuah), I saw (**in The Heavenly Scroll**) a golden seven lamp lampstand (7 classical planets also seen as the seals over The Heavenly Scroll); 13 And in the midst of the seven lamp lampstand (in The Heavenly Scroll / stars) One like the Son of Man (constellation ORION represents the Son of Man in The Heavenly Scroll), clothed with a garment (of the High Priest) down to the feet (tallit - Psalms 110:3) with a girdle of gold about His chest (chest plate of the High Priest Zachariah Chapter 3, Yahusha was consecrated High Priest by Yahuah and adorned the garments of the High Priest). 14 The hair of His head was white like wool (John begins describing the constellation ORION), as white as snow; and His eyes were as a flame of fire; 15 And His feet glowed like bronze which had been fired in a furnace; and His voice sounded like many (Living) waters (reference to the Water Bearer of AQUARIUS). 16 And in His (ORION's) right hand He had

seven stars (constellation PLAIADES - Amos 5:8, Job 9:9, Rev. 14:14-20); and out of His mouth went a sharp, two-edged sword (the sword of ORION, a metaphor of the Word of Yahuah); and His face was like the Sun (the Sun is a metaphor of the Messiah see Psalms 19) shining in its strength. 17 And when I saw Him, I fell at His feet as though dead (literally "scared to death" so to speak). Then he (the Angel of Yahuah now speaks for Yahusha after showing Yahuchanon ORION, the Son of Man) placed his right hand on me and said (speaking for Yahusha, represented by ORION, the Messengers says): *"Do not be afraid. I am the First* (born from the grave) *and the Last* (the end all be all of the Plan of Salvation). 18 *I am the Living One; I was dead, and now look, I am alive for ever and ever! And I hold the keys of death and Hades"*.

Notice Yahusha did not say "Alpha and Omega", nor did he say "Aleph and Tav", he said "I am the first and the last"! So in Revelation Chapter 1, it is Yahuah (*The Aleph and Tav*) speaking through His Messenger to Yahuchanon, until Yahuah directs John's attention to the constellation ORION. Then, as ORION, Yahusha (*the First Born from the Grave, i.e. First and the Last*) speaks through the Messenger to John. In other words, Yahusha told Yahuchanon not to be afraid, for He was alive forevermore. Yahusha did not identify Himself by that title Alpha and Omega (*Aleph/Tav*) he said he was the first born of eternal creation and the last indicating his preeminence.

Then, the phrase Alpha and Omega is again written in Revelation 21:6-7, which is speaking of Yahuah.

> **Revelation 21:6-7, KJV**
> 6 And He said unto me, It is done. I am Alpha (*Aleph*) and Omega (*Tav*), the beginning (**Unity**) and the end (**Perfection** - not the firstborn from the dead vs. 5). I will give unto him that is athirst of the fountain of the water (Yahusha, AQUARIUS the Water Bearer) of life freely. 7 He that overcometh will inherit all things (as Yahuah gives an inheritance through His first born son Yahuah); and I will be his Father (Yahuah is the Father of all His sons including Yahusha), and he shall be My son.

Yahuah is the Father Who is doing the speaking in this prophecy. The words "beginning", and "end" are Hellenized twisting of the meaning of Aleph and Tav. It should read "I am Aleph and Tav, Unity and Perfection". This is where the twisting come in because Yahusha is "the beginning and end, first and the last" of eternal creation. Yahuah is Eternal period. By putting in Alpha and Omega the translating the meaning of those Hellenized words instead of Aleph Tav, they made it look as through both Yahuah and Yahusha claimed the same title!

Now, we come to the second Scripture in which the literal words Alpha and Omega were added, in order to say that Yahusha is the Alpha and Omega. This Scripture is Revelation 22:13. Revelation 22:16 undeniably states that these are Yahusha's words.

**Revelation 22:12-17, KJV**
12 And behold, I come quickly, and my reward is with me, to give every man according as his work shall be. 13 [117][I am Alpha and Omega] the beginning and the end the first and last. 14 Blessed are they that do his commandments, that they may have right to the tree of life, and may enter in through the gates into the cities. 15 For without are dogs, and sorcerers, and whoremongers, and murderers, and idolaters, and whosoever loveth and maketh a lie. 16 I Jesus have sent mine Angel, to testify unto you these things in the Churches. I am the root and the offspring of David, and the bright and morning star. 17 And the Spirit and the Bride say, Come. And let him that heareth, say, Come. And let him that is athirst, come. And whosoever will, let him take the water of life freely.

The King James has a footnote number 117, which I put in red in verse 13. The footnote of this Bible, shows that the Alexandrian (NU) and the Vatican (M) texts omit the phrase, Alpha and Omega.

117 NU-Text and M-Text read "the First and the Last, the Beginning and the End".

Tav    Aleph

# Conclusion

Yahuah claimed the titles Aleph and Tav which means Unity and Perfection. The translators mistranslated and Hellenized the scriptures to say "Alpha and Omega" then used the definition of those Greek words to say "Beginning and Ending" which is the title of Yahusha. Then added "Aleph and Tav" to the scriptures where Yahusha is speaking, twisting the meaning of the words in the Book of Revelation! Then we are taught that it is only Yahusha (*Jesus*) speaking the entire time, when in fact it is the Angel of Yahuah speaking in proxy for both Yahuah and Yahusha!

Well, you might say, "What difference does it make that those three little words were added to this Scripture in Revelation 22:13?" Never before has there been a true understanding of what Yahuah actually said when He identified Himself as the Unity and Perfection (*Aleph and Tav*). Since we know that Yahuah said that He Unity and Perfection (*not first and last*) in Revelation 21:6, let us thoroughly study the Scriptures to come to Yahuah's truth.

In Revelation 1:8, the Being Who is speaking identifies Himself as the Almighty, Who we all know is Yahuah. Following is an exact copy of this Scripture from The Concordant Version of the Sacred Scriptures, which one can see differs greatly from the more modern Greek Interlinear:

Almost all English versions of the Bible render Revelation 1:8 in the same way the King James Version is translated.

### Revelation 1:8, KJV
I am Alpha and Omega, ~~the beginning and the ending~~ (added), saith Yahuah, which is, and which was, and which is to come, the Almighty.

By merely leaving this text as it is written, a tremendous understanding has been lost. However, if these two Greek letters are researched in detail, one will readily see that Yahuah is revealing much more about Himself than just being "the beginning and the end" because he is Aleph and Tav in Hebrew!

In the Greek alphabet, the letter alpha is the first letter, and omega is the last letter. However, in the Hebrew Language, in which even the so-called New Testament Scriptures are now known to have been originally written, the letter aleph is the first letter, and the letter TAV is the last.

It is an admitted fact by the Biblical scholars that Revelation 1:8 should say in Hebrew:

*I am the ALEPH and the TAV*

Getting back to the beginning of this teaching, we defined the meaning of the Aleph and the Tav. Yahuah was saying:

*I am UINITY and PERFECTION (Perfect Unity)!*

Yahusha claimed to be the firstborn from the dead... the first (of eternal creation) and the last (preeminent among the sons of Yahuah)

### Colossians 1:15-20

15 He is the image of the invisible Yahuah (not Yahuah), the firstborn of all (eternal) creation (of the resurrection Luke 20:36). 16 For by Yahuah all things were created, in Heaven and on Earth, visible and invisible, whether thrones or dominions or rulers or authorities—all things were created through Yahuah and for Yahusha. 17 And Yahuah is before all things (The Creator), and in Yahuah all things hold together. 18 (now he changes subject) And Yahusha is the head of the body, the church. Yahusha is the beginning (first and last), the firstborn from the dead, that in everything (Yahuah created) Yahusha might be preeminent (first and the last). 19 For in Yahusha all the fullness of Yahuah's Spirit was pleased to dwell (full of the Holy Spirit), 20 and through Yahusha, Yahuah would reconcile to Himself all things, whether on Earth or in Heaven, making peace (between the two houses) by the blood of his cross (Yahuah would reconcile creation in covenant with Yahusha, and call out a Remnant family from among The House of Israel and The House of Judah)

*End of Excerpt*

# Was Yahusha the essence of Unity and Perfection?

Below is the meaning of preeminence:

**pre·em·i·nence**
> noun: pre-eminence; plural noun: pre-eminences; noun: preeminence; plural noun: preeminences
>> 1. the fact of surpassing all others; superiority.

Yahusha claimed to be the "end all be all" of Yahuah's plan and creation, not the Aleph and Tav (Unity and Perfection), that title belong to Yahuah! Whenever anyone attempted to imply that he was "perfection/Tav" Yahusha stopped them in their tracks…

### Mark 10

17As Yahusha was setting out on a journey, a man ran up to Him and knelt before Him, and asked Him, "Good Teacher, what shall I do to inherit eternal life?" 18 And Yahusha said to him, "*Why do you call Me good? No one is good except Yahuah alone* (*who alone is UNITY and PERFECTION*).

Yahusha "came in the flesh" which is the Hebrew word 'sarki'

g4561 'sarki' - Thayer: 2a) the body of a man 2b) used of natural or physical origin, generation or relationship 2b1) born of natural generation 4) the flesh, denotes mere human nature, *__the Earthly nature of man apart from divine influence, and therefore prone to sin and opposed to God__*.

Yahusha was born disobedient and imperfect, he was perfected through discipline in a life on Earth

### Hebrews 5:8-9 NKJV

8 though He was a Son, yet He learned Obedience (to Yahuah) by the things (discipline) which he suffered (for disobedience). 9 And having been perfected (through discipline and suffering called 'sanctification' John 17:19-21), he became (was not born that way) the author of (or forefather of) Everlasting Life to all who obey him (and follow his Righteous example 1 Peter 2:21).

### John 17:19-21

"And for their sakes I sanctify myself (Yahusha had to be perfected through sanctification, he is The Way we all follow), that they also might be sanctified through the truth (by following his example which is the True Way that leads to Eternal Life *John 14:6*). Neither pray I for these alone, but for them also which shall believe on me through their word (enter into covenant with him as the Bride); That they all may be one (family); as you, Father, are in (covenant with) me (to be adopted then begotten as Your first born-again son), and I in (covenant with) you (crying out Abba Father *Galatians 4:6*), that they also may be one in (covenant with) us (and adopted then begotten too): that the world may believe that you hast sent me (to prove The Way works where Yahuah perfects our sinful flesh and forgives our iniquity and remembers our sin no more through Mikveh)."

### Hebrews 2

11 For both He who sanctifies (Yahuah) and those who are sanctified (Yahusha and the rest of

the sons) are all from one Father; for which reason Yahusha is not ashamed to call them brothers

Yahusha was not "perfect" from birth. He was perfected!

### Hebrews 7:28

28 For The Law appoints as High Priests men who have weakness, but the Word of The Oath, which came after The Law, appoints the Son who has been perfected forever.

# The Dragon
# Where did Satan come from?

In the Book of Revelation, we see that False Religion of Babylon later known as Christianity is called The Dragon. To fully understand this book we must understand why Christianity is The Dragon also called The Beast. It has fulfilled ever prophecy of this book! I address this topic in my book **Christianity and the Great Deception**.

*Excerpt from my book Christianity and the Great Deception...*

The etymology of the name "Satan" is directly connected to Leviathan. Sa-TAN and Levia-TAN both are derived from the word TANeem (*sea creature*) which is plural. The singular of Taneem is TAN. Sa-TAN and Levia-TAN are simply later versions of the Taneem god Dagon later known as The Dragon as the word Dagon evolved over time.

It is Dagon the Dragon that is the Spiritual source behind the Christian Church the Religion of Babylon (*Rome formally transferred the religion of Babylon to Rome*). Any Sunday/Christmas/Easter/Trinity/Jesus church is the Religion of Babylon founded on The Spirit of the Dragon. The Pope and priesthood of the Catholic Church is the high priest and priests of Dagon the Dragon in disguise (*not a very good disguise actually*).

The Priests of Dagon even to this day wear the "fish hat" called a Mitre Hat. They have dictated Christian theology world-wide including Protestant Theology from the City of Rome for 1500 years. Every fundamental doctrine of the Christian Church such as Sunday worship, Christmas, Easter, The Trinity, abolishment of The Law, pagan holidays, etc. were all Papal Edicts not found in Scripture. They violate clear explicit commands in Scripture, so we are taught "Jesus did away with the Law" to sell this lie.

# Rome = Babylon

Rome is actually called "Babylon" in The Bible because it embodied the same Mystery Religion of Babylon.

### 1 Peter 5:13
The church that is at Babylon (speaking of the church in Rome), elected together with you, saluteth you; and so does Marcus my son

It is a matter of historical fact that the Mystery Religion of Babylon was literally and FORMALLY transferred from Babylon to Rome (when Rome conquered Babylon) ....

"When Attalus, the Pontiff and King of Pergamos died, in B.C. 133, he bequeathed the headship of the "Babylonian Priesthood" to Rome. When the Etruscans came to Italy from Lydia, (the region of Pergamos), they brought with them the Babylonian religion and rites.

They set up a Pontiff (High Priest of Dagon the Dragon) who was head of the priesthood. Later the Romans accepted this Pontiff as their civil ruler. Julius Caesar was made Pontiff of the Etruscan Order in B.C. 74. In B.C. 63, he was made "Supreme Pontiff" of the "Babylonian Order," thus becoming heir to the rights and title of Attalus, Pontiff of Pergamos, who made Rome his heir by will. Thus, the first Roman Emperor became the head of the "Babylonian Priesthood," and Rome the successor of Babylon. Each successor to Emperor from that point forward held the title Pontifus Maximus literally The High Priest of the Babylonian Cult of Sol Invictus which was simply another incarnation of Mithraism stemming from the worship of Tammuz in Babylon. The Pope of Rome now carries forward that High Priesthood as Pontiff.

The Roman Empire began their official recognition of Sun worship during the time of Aurelian when he instituted the cult of "Sol Invictus". There is virtually no difference between the cult of Sol Invictus and that of Mithraism or for that matter Catholicism/Christianity. All later versions of The Mystery Religion of Babylon the Great Whore. In the year 307 A.D. Emperor Diocletian, a Sun Worshipper, was involved in the dedication of a temple to Mithra, and was responsible for the burning of Holy Scripture (the Hebrew originals that is why we don't have any today) which made it possible for later emperors to formulate Christianity, and thus began the Roman version of the "Universal Christo-pagan Mystery Religion." After the reign of Diocletian, the Roman Emperor Constantine (the creator of modern-day Christianity) maintained the title "Pontifus Maximus" the high priest of paganism and remained a worshipper of Apollo (Apollo is Tammuz in the Greek culture). His coins were inscribed: "SOL INVICTO COMITI", which is interpreted as "Committed to the Invincible Sun". During his reign, pagan Sun worship was blended with the worship of the True Creator (called syncretism), and officially titled "Christianity" by the (less than holy) Roman Empire and its' official church the (less than holy) catholic (universal) church.

Cybele, the Phrygian goddess, known to her followers as "the mother of god", was closely related to the worship of Mithra. Just as Mithraism was a man's religion, the worship of Cybele was practiced by women. The priests of Mithra were known as "Fathers" and the Priestesses of Cybele as "Mothers". After baptism into the Mysteries of Mithra, the initiate was marked on the forehead with an X. The sign of the cross formed by the elliptic and the celestial equator was one of the signs of Mithra. Sunday (Deis Solis), the day of the Sun, was considered by Mithraist a sacred day of rest. December 25th (the birthday of Mithra) was celebrated as the birth of the Sun, given birth by the "Queen of Heaven" – "Mother of god." The Mithraists celebrated a mithraic love feast. This feast consisted of loaves of bread decorated with crosses with wine, over which the priest pronounced a mystic formula. Mithra was considered mediator between god and man (another "Demi-God" or "God in the Flesh"). All of which, originated in Babylon as a religion based on the corrupted Zodiac.

This is the true origin of Christianity! Once we fully understand what "Christianity" actually is, what it is based on, and where it came from, then we can begin to understand why Christianity abolished the Law of Yahuah, abolished His Sabbath Day, and changed the sacrifice of the Passover Lamb to the Easter Pig. Every one of the above moves (not commanded by Yahuah) were made by the Pope of Rome… The High Priest of Dagon… The Dragon.

*End of Excerpt*

# Flow of the Book of Revelation

The Book of Revelation does not flow sequential, one chapter does not necessarily follow the previous. Some chapters happen concurrently. The Seals, Trumpets and Bowl Judgments happen at the same time in a very short period of time over a 10-day period once the seals are opened and The Heavenly Scroll is revealed.

That 10-day period is called The Days of Awe between the 6th Trumpet sounding on Yom Teruah (*Feast of Trumpets*) and Yom Kippur (*Day of Atonement*). The "Day of Yahuah" is the last event to take place on Earth on Yom Kippur. The Feast of Tabernacles (*Sukkot*) tells of how His Chosen are taken on wings of an Eagle to the wilderness where Yahusha spread his tabernacle over us in protection during this 10-day period if Tribulation.

> ### Revelation 2:10
> Do not be afraid of what you are about to suffer. I tell you, the devil will put some of you in prison to test you, and you will suffer persecution for ten days. Be faithful, even to the point of death, and I will give you life as your victor's crown.

The Book of Revelation is not a 7-year period as taught in Christian circles (*there is no 7-year period in the Book of Revelation*). Below is an introduction to the Book of Revelation:

- *Chapter 1* - is John's commission and revelation from Gabriel of the meaning behind The Heavenly Scroll.

- *Chapter 2-3* - is Yahusha's warning to all of us to endure in the faith and not compromise giving us specific examples of how we will be led astray using the 7 assemblies of Nazarenes in John's time as examples.

- *Chapter 4* - is describing The Enoch Zodiac called The Heavenly Scroll with The Throne in Heaven in the middle to establish the source of the revelation.

- *Chapter 5* - All of Chapter 5 occurs and is showing us what takes place after the 7th Trumpet sounds.

- *Chapter 6* - "the first four Seals" occur over the Age of PISCES and can be proven in historical accounts dating back 2000 years. The Age of PISCES is the Age of Tribulation on Earth (*the last days*) as the False Religion came to power and bathed itself in the blood of the Nazarenes and people of Earth. The Fifth Seals is Yom Teruah when the King returns for those who have died in The Age of PISCES. The Sixth Seal is Yom Kippur (*The Day of Atonement*) called The Great and Terrible Day of Yahuah when those left on Earth are "sacrificed" to atone. The 7th Seal is a period.

- *Chapter 7* - "The 144,000 Sealed Servants" are those sealed over the 2,000-year Age of PISCES as the first four Seals are broken. The number 144,000 is symbolic of the number of perfect government (*12x12*).

- *Chapter 8* - is the first 4 Trumpets that begin sounding on Yom Teruah (*Trumpets*) and take us to The Day of Yahuah (*Atonement - Yom Kippur*) when a massive sacrifice of atonement is made on Earth.

- *Chapter 9* - is the 5th and 6th Trumpet that occur concurrently with the prior 4 Trumpets. Trumpets 1-6 are blown during the 10-days of Tribulation rehearsed each year during the 10 Days of Awe between Yom Teruah and Yom Kippur.

- *Chapter 10* - is the 7th Trumpet sounded on Yom Kippur. After Yahusha makes atonement, the 7th Trumpet sounds and Yahusha is revealed as the fulfillment of The Heavenly Scroll. This is the same event Daniel witnessed in Daniel chapter 7 as The Son of Man is judged alongside The Dragon (*False Messiah*). Yahuah anoints the Son of Man the King over The Kingdom and fulfillment of The Heavenly Scroll.

- *Chapter 11* – A description of The Battle of the Ages and the revelation of The King who defeats the Dragon and wins the Age-old battle described in the Book of Revelation that occurs during the "last days" or rather the 2 prophetic days of PISCES.

- *Chapter 12* – The duration of The Battle of the Ages. Begins with the birth of the Messiah (sign of the birth of the son of man), then Satan is thrown down to Earth and wages war on those who follow the Messiah. The faithful who keep The Word of His Testimony written in the stars "love their lives not, even unto death". The remnant "woman/Bride" is given renewed strength (*wings of an eagle*) and are brought through the "wilderness" (*Sukkot*) and into the Kingdom.

- Chapter 13 – Identity of the first and second beast and of The False Messiah.

- Chapter 14 – The Bride is revealed on Earth, the damned judged by fire, The Great Harvest is harvested

- Chapter 15 – The Great Supper … the inhabitants of Earth who fight against the King of Kings are destroyed. The 7 plaques are released.

- Chapter 16 - The 7 bowls of wrath are poured out over Earth. The 3 unclean spirits are identified and destroyed. The judgements are complete, and the attention is turned on Babylon the Great Whore.

- Chapter 17 – Babylon the Great is identified. Civil war within the Beast, the Beast destroys Babylon.

- Chapter 18 - Basically, in Chapter 17, the "head" is cut-off followed by the death of the body in Chapter 18. Chapter 17 is dealing with the Spiritual entity of Babylon while Chapter 18 deals with the commercial/political entity.

- Chapter 19 – The Battle of the Ages ends, Mystery Babylon defeated. Yahusha emerges from the fray covered in blood riding a white horse and he is called The Fulfillment of the Word (found in The Heavenly Scroll).

- Chapter 20 – The Age of AQUARIUS begins, Yahusha the Water Bearer mikveh's the Earth to cleanse it from the Battle of the Ages. Fallen humanity is destroyed along with the Dragon, the False Messiah, and the False Prophet. The First Resurrection occurs as Yahusha builds The 3rd and Final Temple of Yahuah.

- Chapter 21 – After the Earth is Mikveh'd clean by The Water Bearer with living water, it becomes a "new creation" (just as we do when we are Mikveh'd). New Jerusalem (the sons of Yahuah) descend back to Earth to rule over it.

- Chapter 22 – The River of Life flows freely over the New Earth and the sons of God live eternally.

# *Chapter 1*

# Introduction

With the knowledge that this book in the Bible is the Revelation of The Heavenly Scroll, I will put the entire book back into context of that source. Revelation begins with that very thing, John telling us the source of his writing is The Heavenly Scroll.

Chapter 1 is John's commission and revelation from Gabriel of the meaning behind The Heavenly Scroll. John declares that the angel Gabriel is sent to him on behalf of both Yahuah and Yahusha. Gabriel speaks on their behalf in the first person as their "power of attorney" so to speak. That is the definition of "Angel" they are elohims:

> **Divine Ruler/Judge/Representative** – h430 'elohim' Thayer's – "1 plural in number. a. rulers, judges, either as <u>divine representatives at</u> <u>sacred places or as reflecting divine majesty</u> <u>and power</u>"

So, Gabriel comes to John to speak for Yahuah and Yahusha as their representative given the "divine majesty and power" to speak in the first person for them. This has caused confusion as many people (*and most teachers*) do not comprehend this simple concept. They see Gabriel speaking for Yahuah then later as Yahusha and presto… "Yahuah is Yahusha" and the blind lead the blind off the cliff of Blasphemy. We have Gabriel speaking for Yahuah and thinking it is Yahuah speaking directly to John we conclude that John "saw the Father" which is not possible, or that Yahuah is Yahusha, or that Yahusha is an "angel" … all lies.

The translations we use today employ passive voice "him, he" not identifying who is doing the speaking by name further confusing the Scriptures. This is the work of The Spirit of the False Messiah to confuse the issue and imply "Yahuah is Yahusha".

**<u>Side Note</u>**:
Another scheme of the Spirit of the False Messiah to confuse us is who sits on the Throne in Heaven. We are not taught that Yahuah sat on the Throne in Heaven until <u>AFTER</u> Yahusha completes the message contained in the stars (*crowned as King in the very end, LEO*). We read of this event in Daniel Chapter 7. Until then Yahusha is the Prince of Peace with no throne and Yahuah is King. Then Yahusha inherits the Throne in Heaven and is crowned King by his Father Yahuah. So, at times, Yahuah is described on the Throne in Heaven, and other times John is given a vision of the future when Yahusha sits on the Throne in Heaven. We are not taught this distinction in an effort again to imply "Yahuah is Yahusha" because they both sit on the throne. Yahuah is the King of Creation

as The Creator. Yahusha is the King OVER Creation as the head of the government called the Kingdom of Yahuah. This difference cannot be overstated and is one not made by so-called "teachers" today. Filled with the Spirit of the False Messiah they use the fact there are two Kings who sit on the same throne at different times to claim Yahuah is Yahusha.

It is The Heavenly Scroll that is where the revelation of Yahusha the Messiah is found as The Heavenly Scroll is *The Word of His Testimony*. We see references to "the words of this book" and assume it is speaking of the Book of Revelation. This is not the case; it is referring to The Heavenly Scroll which is revealed in the vision John wrote down. This is an important distinction.

# Revelation 1 Restored

1 The Heavenly Scroll is the Revelation of Yahushua the Messiah (Revelation 5:1, Revelation 4:1),

> ### Revelation 5
> 1 And I saw in the right hand of him who sat on the throne, a (Heavenly) Scroll written inside and on the back (Scroll made up of 3D Heavenly "signs"/pictographs), sealed with seven seals (7 classical planet).
>
> ### Revelation 4
> 1 After I was shown the Throne in The Heavenly Scroll, I looked into the stars and behold, a door was opened in Heaven; and the first voice which I heard was (Yahuah, the Aleph/Tav), as it were, of a shofar talking with me, which said: Come up here (Spiritually not physically), and I will show you things (in The Heavenly Scroll) which must be after this.

which is *the testimony Yahuah gave to Yahusha*, to show his servants things which must shortly come to pass (on Earth as it is written in The Heavenly Scroll John 17:4, Hebrews 10:7, Matthew 6:10, Psalm 19, 119:89, 89:2, Daniel 4:35); and Yahusha sent and signified the revelation through Yahuah's messenger Gabriel (Revelation 8:2, Luke 1:19, Daniel 8:16-18, Daniel 9:21) in a vision to his servant Yahuchanon.

> It was Gabriel who spoke with John not Yahusha as is taught in error; Gabriel was to show John the meaning of the stars/constellations on Yahusha's behalf just like Gabriel did with Daniel, Zechariah, etc.. Yahusha is The Royal High Priest and ministers before the Golden Altar, not running around delivering messages/visions. That is Gabriel's role. John did not "see Yahusha" he witnessed ORION in The Heavenly Scroll when visited by Gabriel.

2 Yahuchanon testified to the word of Yahuah (eternally preserved in The Heavenly Scroll, Psalm 19, 119:89, 89:2, Daniel 4:35) which is the **Testimony of Yahusha the Messiah** (The Word of His Testimony), and to all things that he saw (in a vision). 3 Blessed is he who reads, and those who hear the words of this prophecy (found in The Heavenly Scroll) and keep those things which are written in The Heavenly Scroll (and make The Heavenly Scroll the "word of their testimony" Revelation 12:11, Revelation 14:12); for the time is at hand (end of the Age of PISCES - Matthew 28:20).

### Revelation 12:11
They triumphed over the Dragon by the blood of the Lamb and by the word of their testimony (remaining faithful to The Word of His Testimony - Revelation 14:12).

### Revelation 14:12
This calls for patient endurance on the part of the people of Yahuah who keep His commands and remain faithful to (the testimony of) Yahusha the Messiah (found in The Heavenly Scroll called The Word of His Testimony).

## Yahusha's word to the Seven Congregations of Nazarenes

4 - Yahuchanon, to the seven assemblies in the province of Asia: Grace and peace to you from Yahuah who is and was and is to come and from the seven spirits (Love, Wisdom, Understanding, Knowledge, Counsel, Might and Reverence) before Yahuah's throne (seen as The Heavenly Menorah and represented by the Menorah before the Altar).

5 - And from Messiah Yahusha, the faithful (and true) witness (meaning of the title *'Immanuel'*), the first born from the (physically) dead, and ruler of the kings of the Earth. Praise be to Yahusha who loves us and has released us from (the penalty of death for) our sins (through marriage covenant consummated) by His blood (Sacrifice to show us *The Way*). 6 - Who has made us (Nazarenes) to be a Kingdom (of Tzadok i.e., righteous) priests to Yahusha's God and Father - to *Yahuah* be the glory and power forever and ever! HalleluYahuah.

7 – Behold in The Heavenly Scroll Yahusha is coming with the clouds (John is reading The Heavenly Scroll where ORION, the Son of Man, comes in the clouds of Heaven/Milky Way), and every eye will see him (the Sign of the Return of the Son of Man in the constellation ORION) even those who pierced Yahusha (all throughout history have seen ORION coming in the clouds of Heaven in the Fall each year in The Heavenly Scroll). And all the tribes will mourn because of Yahusha. So shall it be! HalleluYahuah. 8 - "I am the Aleph (Unity) and the Tau (Perfection)," says Yahuah Elohim, who is and was and is to come (Y-H-V-H Exodus 3:14).

# John's vision of
# The Heavenly Scroll

9 - I, John, your brother and partner in the tribulation and (the future) kingdom (of Yahuah) and **perseverance** (during these last days on **"wings of an eagle"** Chapter 12) that are (promised) in (covenant with) Yahusha; was on the island of Patmos because of (persecution for) the Word of Yahuah and my testimony (found in The Heavenly Scroll) about Yahusha (proclaiming The Word of His Testimony as his own).10 - On Yahuah's day (the Sabbath) I was in the Spirit,

> Everything from this point forward Yahuchanon sees in the realm of the Spirit not the physical realm. He is being shown the meaning of the stars and constellations and what is proclaimed in them called The Heavenly Scroll which is The Word of His Testimony.

and I heard behind me a loud voice resembling a Shofar blast (Yahuah speaking, His voice is like a loud Shofar Hebrews 12:19), 11 - saying, "Write in a small (Earthly) Scroll what you see (in The Heavenly Scroll) and read it to the seven assemblies: to Ephesus, Smyrna, Pergamum, Thyatira, Sardis, Philadelphia and Laodicia.

12 - Then I turned to see the voice that was speaking with me (hoping to "see" Yahuah). And having turned (he didn't see Yahuah as he would have died Exodus 33:20), I saw seven golden lampstands/Menorah (in The Heavenly Scroll. The seven spirits of Yahuah represent the complete plan of Yahuah). 13 - And among the lampstands was one resembling the Son of Man (constellation ORION) dressed (as Royal Zadok High Priest) in a long robe (made of fine white linen) with a golden sash around Yahusha's chest. 14 - The hair of his (ORION's) head was white resembling wool, as white as snow and his eyes resembled a blazing fire. 15 – his feet resembled polished bronze (color of the Enoch Zodiac) refined in a fiery furnace (by being sanctified, John

17:19-21, by fire, the Word of Yahuah - Jeremiah 23:29) and resembled the roar of much Living Water (AQUARIUS).

16 – He (ORION) held in his right hand (the) seven stars (of the PLAIADES) and a sharp double-edged sword (of ORION) came from Yahusha's mouth. His face resembled the (physical) Sun shining at its brightest (the Sun is a metaphor of The Messiah Psalm 19)

17 - When I saw him, I fell at his feet like a dead man (he was "scared to death"). But he (the Son of Man) placed His right hand on me and said, "Do not be afraid. I am the first and the last (the firstborn of the dead Revelation 1:5, and the last faithful and true witness - Revelation 19:11).

18 - The living one (firstborn of eternal creation upon resurrection - Colossians 1:15). I was dead (completely ceased to exist), and behold, now I am alive forever and ever (being risen by Yahuah)! And I hold the keys of death and of the grave. 19 – Therefore write down the things you have seen (perceived in a vision) and the things that are (in this present Age of PISCES), and the things that will happen after this (The end of the age of PISCES, beginning of the age of AQUARIUS).

## *The Keys to The Kingdom Revealed*

20 – This is the mystery (key) of the seven stars (of the PLAIADES - a metaphorical representation of Yahuah's seven spirits) you saw in my (ORION's) right hand and of the seven golden lampstands (Heavenly Menorah): The seven stars (of the PLAIADES) are the guardians (Strong's 5894) of the seven (spiritual perfection) assemblies, and the seven lampstands (seven spirits represented in the Menorah) are the seven assemblies.

# Chapter 2

# Introduction

Yahusha encourages all of us to endure in the faith and not compromise. He gives us specific examples of how we will be led astray using the 7 assemblies of Nazarenes in John's time:

- Yahusha instructs the church of Ephesus to repent finding them guilty of abandoned their first love, or the love they once had.

- Yahusha instructs the church of Smyrna to warn them of ten days of tribulation that may cost them their lives or imprisonment.

- Yahusha instructs the church of Pergamum to repent finding them guilty of following the doctrines of Balaam and the Nicolaitans.

- Yahusha instructs the church of Thyatira to repent finding them guilty of following the teachings of the prophetess Jezebel.

These are all examples of how we would all be led astray by the False Religion and world system over the course of the last days (*Age of PISCES*). With each example and instruction to the churches, Yahusha identifies himself by ORION in The Heavenly Scroll.

Now let us learn some basic precepts from which to build a foundation for understanding this book.

# Call his name *Immanuel*

In recent years, I have noticed going around social media the accusation that the Messiah's name is not Yahusha (or even Jesus, Yeshua, or Yahshua) but Immanuel. The following verse is used to justify this claim:

### Isaiah 7:14
Therefore the Lord Himself will give you a sign: Behold, the virgin will be with child and will give birth to a son, and will call Him Immanuel.

### Matthew 1:23
"The virgin will conceive and give birth to a son, and they will call him Immanuel".

These same verses are used to justify the doctrine of Incarnation as it is said "Yahuah came to Earth as a sinful man" that is why the Messiah's name is Immanuel which is said to mean "God is with us". Is this true? Or is Immanuel a title with deeper meaning having nothing to do with incarnation?

We read in Revelation Chapter 3 Yahusha claim the title "Amen" which means "true and faithful witness".

### Revelation 3:14
And unto the angel of the church of the Laodiceans write; These things saith the Amen (aman), (meaning) the faithful and true witness, the beginning of the (eternal) creation of Yahuah (firstborn of the dead);

Is there any link between Immanuel and the Amen? A connection that would bring Scripture back into agreement, resolve these issues with Immanuel implying incarnation and give us greater insight into the Messiah's role?

"Immanuel" is a Hebrew name with meaning that gives glory to Yahuah. It, like his other titles (names) such as Yahusha and Elijah, is a contracted sentence name. In this case it is a contraction of Imman – u – El, and as such, can be a "title" not just a name. In Hebrew it is a contracted form of the English sentence "*Faithful and True Witness of Yahuah*". It does not mean "*God is with us*" as it taught in the false Christian Church.

The word "aman" is the root in Hebrew of eman, or iman (the beginning of Immanuel)'? Aman it is the same word and there are three ways of writing it in Hebrew; aman(u), amen(u) and iman(u). The word trail (with Strong's numbers) is: Aman (H6004), Amen (H543) and Iman (H5973). There is also emune(ah), which means "I am one of them that are faithful and peaceable". We must, in the case of Hebrew, study the word trail to come to a full understanding of a "sentence name" or "title" such as Immanuel:

**Strong's H-6005**. *'Immanuw'el, im-maw-noo-ale'*;
from {A.}H-5973 and {B.}H-410 with suff. pron. ins.; with us (is) God; Immanuel, a typ. name of Isaiah's son:--Immanuel.

**Strong's H-5973**. *'im, eem*;
from H-6004; adv. or prep. with (i.e. in conjunction with ), in varied applications; spec. equally with; often with prep. pref. (and then usually unrepresented in English):-- accompanying, against, and, as (X long as), before, beside, by (reason of), for all, from (among, between), in, like, more than, of, (un-) to, with (-al).

**Strong's H-410**. *'el, ale*;
short. from H-352; strength; as adj. mighty; espec. the Almighty (but used also of any deity):--God (god), X goodly, X great, idol, might (-y one), power, strong. Comp. names in "-el."

**Strong's H-6004**. *'amam, aw-mam'*;
a prim. root; to associate; by impl. to overshadow (by huddling together):--become dim, hide;

**Strong's H-539** ʻ*aman aw'man;*
Primary root word; properly, to build up or support; to foster as a parent or nurse; figuratively to render (or be) firm or faithful, to trust or believe, to be permanent or quiet; morally to be true or certain; once (Isa. 30:21; interchangeable 541) to go to the right hand:--hence, assurance, believe, bring up, establish, + fail, be faithful (of long continuance, stedfast, sure, surely, trusty, verified), nurse, (-ing father), (put), trust, turn to the right.

**Strong's H-352**. *'ayil, ah'-yil;*
from the same as H-193; prop. strength; hence anything strong; spec. a chief (politically); also a ram (from his strength); a pilaster (as a strong support); an oak or other strong tree:- -mighty (man), lintel, oak, post, ram, tree.

**Strong's H-193.** *'uwl, ool;*
from an unused root mean. to twist, i.e. (by impl.) be strong; the body (as being rolled together); also powerful:--mighty, strength.

So, ame(a)nu'el, imanu'el and emune'el all are *Immanuel* and together give us the full meaning. It's like how Yahushua, Yahshua, and Yahusha are all the same name, but sometimes the placement of the vowels vary.

"I" is often pronounced with the YEH sound. In fact, those that call themselves Ethiopian Jews say Amanu'el, which (to them) means "to have faith in Elohim, my faith is in EL, Amen (Amon, Imam, Magnet, Faith)" and claim this was a literal name for Yahusha, even citing Revelation 3:14 not realizing it was his title. "Name" in Hebrew also means "title".

### Revelation 3:14
And unto the angel of the church of the Laodiceans write; These things saith the Amen (aman), (meaning) the faithful and true witness, the beginning of the (eternal) creation of Yahuah (firstborn of the dead);

The word "aman" defines itself there – a "faithful and true witness" of Yahuah". It is not just given to the Messiah, or Isaiah's son, but Yahuah Himself is also called "faithful and true". Moses and Samuel were called faithful witnesses they are "Immanuel", as are many others.

Immanuel is a title and not a literal name (*much like Elijah is a title*) - even though the prophecy has been misapplied and the word mistranslated as "god with us" in order to promote the church's falsely claimed position of Yahusha's deity. Discernment tells us, however, that Yahusha WAS an Aman'el, and any other person who is faithful to Yahuah's two witnesses (*The Heavenly and Earthly Scrolls*) is also an Aman'el.

# Revelation 2 Restored

## *To the Nazarene Assembly in Ephesus, don't compromise your first love*

1 - To the angel of the Nazarene assembly in Ephesus write: He who holds the seven stars (of the PLAIADES) in his (ORION's) right hand and walks among seven golden lamp lampstand (Heavenly Menorah in The Heavenly Scroll) says:

2 - I know your (righteous) works, your labor and your patience. I know that you cannot tolerate those who are evil, and you have tested and exposed as liars those who falsely claim to be apostles (false teachers/pastors filled with The Spirit of The False Messiah/Incarnation and promote pagan influence).

3 - Without growing weary you have persevered and endured many things for the sake of (the covenant that bears) My Name (The Yahushaic Covenant).

4 - But I have this against you: You have abandoned your first love (the love of Yahuah and keeping His Commandments overtime was replaced by the love of Venus in all her forms. This is applicable to modern society today in the west with its infatuation with sex and pornography).

5 - Therefore keep in mind how far you have fallen (from the loving devotion to Yahuah through The Yahushaic Covenant) repent (and turn back to your first love) and perform the (righteous) deeds you did at first (keeping the intent of the Law). But if you do not repent, I will come to you and remove your lampstand from its place (destroy their witness before men).

6 - But you have this to your credit: You hate the (unrighteous) works of the Nicolaitans (who used sex in the act of worship – sexual idolatry) which I also hate.

7 - He who has an (a spiritual) ear, let him (spiritually) hear what the spirit (of Yahuah) says too the assemblies (as their sin was passed down to us Jeremiah 8:8). To the one who is victorious (over the lies and false doctrines passed down to us), I will grant the right to eat from the tree of life (in covenant with Yahusha who is the tree of eternal life) in the midst of the garden of Yahuah (Yahuah is the gardener of His House - John 15:1).

### John 15:1
"I am the true vine (tree of life), and my Father is the gardener".

## *To the Nazarene Assembly in Smyrna,*
## *Endure Persecution and Slander*

8 - To the angel of the Nazarene assembly of Smyrna write: These are the words of the first (born of the dead) and the last (True and Faithful Witness), who (physically) died and returned to (everlasting) life (CAPRICORNUS/ORION).

> **Revelation 3:14**
> And unto the angel of the church of the Laodiceans write; These things saith the Amen (aman), (meaning) the True and Faithful Witness, the beginning of the (eternal) creation of Yahuah (firstborn of the dead).

> **CAPRICORNUS**
> Eternal life comes from his death, he's the Arrow of God (*ORION*), he is pierced, yet springs up again in abundant life.

9 - I know your tribulations and your (physical) poverty --- though you are rich (Spiritually in His Kingdom)! And I am aware of the slander against you of those who falsely claim to be Yahudites but are in fact a Synagogue of Satan (Religious Jews at time, the False Religion at the end of PISCES).

10 - Do not fear what you (Nazarenes) are about to suffer (for My Righteousness). Look (mentally discern the meaning of The Heavenly Scroll), the devil is about to throw some of you into (metaphorical) prison to test you (your faith) and you will suffer tribulation for ten days (Days of Awe, The Day of Yahuah). Be faithful even onto death, and I will give you the crown of life.

11 - He who has an (a spiritual) ear let him hear what the spirit says to the assemblies. The one who is victorious (over persecution and slander for His Name's Sake) will not be harmed by the second death (decree at the Great White Throne Judgement).

## *To the Nazarene Assembly in Pergamum*
## *'Overcome the Dragon'*

12 - To the angel of the assembly in Pergamum write: These are the words of the one (Son of Man) who holds the double-edged sword (of ORION).

13 - I know where you live where the throne of Satan sits. Yet you have held fast to (the Covenant that bears) My Name and have not denied your faith in Me, even in the day when My faithful witness Antipas was killed among you (for his testimony concerning Me), where Satan (the Dragon) dwells.

14 - But I have a few things against you, because some of you hold to the teaching of Baalam, who taught Balak (a Moabite king) to put a stumbling block before the Yisraelites so they would eat food sacrificed to idols (Zeus, Jupiter, Apollo, Osirus, Horus, Hesus Krishna, Jesus Christ, etc.) and commit sexual immorality (Spiritual adultery by worshiping these false gods).

15 - In the same way (like Balak) some of you also hold to the teaching of the Nicolaitans (incorporating sex into the false worship).

> A common view holds that the Nicolaitans held the antinomian heresy of 1 Corinthians 6, although this has not been proved. One scholar who espouses this interpretation, John Henry Blunt, maintains that the comparison between the Nicolaitans and Balaam "proves that the fornication spoken of is not that crime under ordinary circumstances, but fornication connected with religious rites"… *John Henry Blunt M.A., F.S.A., ed. (1874). Dictionary of Sects, Heresies, Ecclesiastical Parties, and Schools of Religious Thought. London: Rivingtons.*

16 - Therefore repent (of these abominations)! Otherwise, I will come to you (as ORION) shortly (riding the clouds of Heaven) and wage (spiritual) war against them with the double-edge sword (of ORION in) my mouth (as foretold in The Heavenly Scroll where The Son of Man battles the Serpent/Dragon).

*Son of Man battling The Serpent crushing the head of the "enemy" while being struck in the heel depicted in The Heavenly Scroll as revealed to Adam in Genesis 3:15*

17 - He who has an (a spiritual) ear let him hear what the spirit says to the assemblies. To the one who is victorious (over the Dragon/False Religion) I will give the hidden manna (hidden secrets found in The Heavenly Scroll Enoch 9:6 and Matthew 13:11, Knowledge of Yahuah, and reveal the Mystery Language Deuteronomy 29:29). I will also give him a white (Righteous) stone (to be laid atop the chief cornerstone - Messiah Yahusha 1 Peter 2:5) inscribed with a new name/title, known only to the one who receives it (those in The Yahushaic Covenant are "living stones" in the construction of the final Spiritual Temple 1 Peter 2:5, each has its own role in the body defined by his title Ephesians 4:16).

## *To the Nazarene Assembly in Thyatira*
## *"Overcome the Dragon"*

18 - To the angel of the Nazarene assembly in Thyatira write: These are the words of the Son of Yahuah whose eyes are resembling a blazing fire (reference to ORION) and whose feet (have walked The Way) resemble polished (fine finished) bronze.

19 - I know your deeds, your love, your faith, your service, your perseverance -- and your latter deeds are greater than your first.

20 - But I have this against you: You tolerate that women Jezebel (Semaramis/Ishtar/Virgin Mary), who calls herself a prophetess (The Pope speaks blasphemies Revelation 13:5-6 on behalf

of/for Hesus/Jesus the final incarnation of Tammuz) By her (false trinity) teaching she misleads My servants (errant Yisrael) to be sexually immoral (by committing physical and spiritual adultery with her i.e. Christianity by the worshiping and following of Mystery Babylon - the False Trinity) and to eat food sacrificed to idols (Ham on Easter i.e. a pig on Ishtar Day which is the abominable sacrifice on the altar that desecrates the Temple of Yahuah called The Way of the Gentiles)

21 - Even though I have given her time (the Age of PISCES) to repent of her immorality (Spiritual Adultery prostituting out the worship of the One and ONLY True God Yahuah to a host of gods in the form of the pagan trinity), she is unwilling.

22 - Behold, I will cast her onto a bed of (Spiritual) sickness and those (Christians) who commit adultery with her (bearing the Mark of the Beast) will suffer great tribulation unless they repent of her deeds.

23 - Then I will strike her children (Spiritual Fruit - begotten by the Spirit of the False Messiah/Incarnation) dead, and all the assemblies will know that I am the one (High Priest and Judge) who searches (the Intent of their) minds and hearts and I will repay each of you according to your deeds.

24 - But I say to the rest of you in Thyatira, who do not hold to her (idolatrous) teaching and have not learned the so called deep things of Satan (the Dragon): I will place no further burden upon you.

25 - Nevertheless, hold fast to what you have until I come.

26 - And to the one who is victorious (over The Dragon) and continues in my work (to fulfill the Great Commission proclaiming the fulfillment of The Heavenly Scroll) until the end (of their life), I will give authority over the nations.

> **Revelation 12:17**
> And the dragon was wroth with the woman, and went to make war with the remnant of her seed, which keep the commandments of God, and have (faith in) The Word of His Testimony (The Heavenly Scroll shown to John).

> **Revelation 12:11**
> They triumphed over the Dragon by the blood of the Lamb and by the word of their testimony.

27 - he (context is still speaking of he that is victorious over the Dragon) will rule them (the nations) with an iron scepter and shatter them like pottery -- just as I have received authority from my Father (to rule with an Iron Scepter).

28 - And I (Yahusha speaking) will give him that overcomes (the Dragon) the morning star (the authority of the Son of Yahuah to rule as Kings and Priests Revelation 1:6)

### Revelation 1
6 and Yahusha has made us kings and priests to his God and Father to him be glory and dominion forever and ever.

29 - And he who has an (a spiritual) ear let him (spiritually) hear what the spirit (of Prophecy) says to the assemblies (of Nazarenes).

# *Chapter 3*

# Introduction

Yahusha's warning to all of us to endure in the faith and not compromise continues in this chapter:

- Yahusha judges the church of Sardis for being "dead" or unaware of things to come, whose works are not perfect before God.

- Yahusha encourages the church of Philadelphia to persevere with what little strength they have; to hold fast so that no one takes their crown.

- Yahusha instructs the church of Laodicea to repent from investing in material riches that make them miserable; rather, invest in the refined gold of Him who has overcome.

- We rule with Yahusha on Thrones in Heaven

# The Center of the Enoch Zodiac – The Throne in Heaven

Before Yahusha defeats the Dragon at the end of the Age of PISCES, he is NOT yet the King of Kings. He is the Prince of Peace until Yahuah crowns him King and "sits Yahusha on Yahuah's Throne". We read this in verse 21.

> 21 - To the one who is victorious (over the Dragon/Spirit of the False Messiah) I will grant the right to sit with me on my throne (and rule as King under my authority), just as I overcame (the Dragon) and sat down with my Father on His throne

This has caused much confusion as false teacher abound who claim "Yahuah is Yahusha" because it is Yahuah described as sitting on the Throne in Heaven in much of Revelation. Other times it is Yahusha as John is given a vision after he is sat on the Throne in Heaven. We must keep the context of all these prophetic books. The same issue arises in books like Daniel, it is not until Daniel 7 that we see Yahuah crown Yahusha and give him authority and power to rule sitting on Yahuah's Throne in Heaven.

# Revelation 3 Restored

## *To the Nazarene Assembly in Sardis*
## *"Faith without Works is Dead Works"*

1 - To the angel of the assembly of Sardis write: These are the words of the one (Yahusha) who holds the seven spirits (complete knowledge) of Yahuah and the seven stars (reference to ORION the Son of Man). I know your works; You have a reputation for being (spiritually) alive, yet you are dead (in your works Hebrews 6:1 lacking faith in The Word of His Testimony).

2 - Wake up and strengthen what (works) remain, which was about to die (without faith); for I have found your deeds incomplete (you have works without faith - James 2:17) in the sight of my God.

3 - Remember, then, what you have received (The Word of His Testimony) and (spiritually) heard (the stars proclaim Psalm 19:4). Keep (faith in The Word of His Testimony - Revelation 12:11) and repent (of your lack of faith). If you do not wake up (pay attention to the signs in The Heavenly Scroll - Genesis 1:14) I will come resembling a thief (at a time when you least expect it - 1 Thessalonians 5:2) and you will not know the hour when I will come upon you (because you have rejected The Heavenly Scroll - Jeremiah 8:7-9).

> **Jeremiah 8:7-9**
> 7 But My people do not know the ordinance of Yahuah (Eternally preserved in the stars - Psalm 119:89). 8 How can you say, we are wise men (h2450 chakam - 'astrologers' and know 'the secrets preserved in The Heavenly Scroll which men were striving to learn' - Enoch 6:9), And the Word of Yahuah's Testimony (that Yahusha is The Branch foretold in The Heavenly Scroll) is with us? But behold, the 'lying pen of the scribes' has made My Word (LOGOS/DABAR - 'Spoken Promise in the beginning' Eternally preserved in The Heavenly Scroll - Psalm 19, 119:89, 89:2, Daniel 4:35) into a lie (by removing The Word of His Testimony). 9 The wise men (h2450 chakam – 'astrologers') are put to shame (for twisting The Heavenly Scroll into Incarnation the 'Mystery' of the Babylonian Zodiac called The Way of the Gentiles - Romans 1), They are dismayed (by the constellations/stars/Sun to worship them - Jeremiah 10:2 – "Do not learn the way of the nations/corrupted Babylonian Zodiac and do not be dismayed at the signs/constellations/stars of The Heavenly Scroll") and caught (in idolatry - Deuteronomy 4:19 – "When you look to the Heavens and see the Sun, moon, and stars—all the stars in the sky—do not be led astray to bow in worship to them and serve them."); Behold, they have rejected the Word of My Testimony (The Heavenly Scroll), And what kind of wisdom (Spiritual Understanding of The Plan of Salvation written in the stars which proclaim

The Glory of Yahuah - Psalm 19:1, which is Yahusha - Hebrews 1:3, and declare His Handiwork - Psalm 19 and Enoch 35:3 - and many more Scriptures) do they have (because the Scriptures are literally based on The Heavenly Scroll/Plan of Salvation/LOGOS written in the stars at Creation which is what Yahusha came to fulfill - Hebrews 10:7 and Matthew 6:10)?

4 - But you do have a few people in Sardis who have not soiled their (wedding) garments (laying with the Whore of Babylon), and because they are worthy (walked The Way) they will walk with me in white (righteous garments).

5 - Like them (who have not soiled their wedding garments), he who overcomes (dead works with faith in The Word of His Testimony - Revelation 14:12)

> **Revelation 14:12**
> This calls for patient endurance on the part of the people of God who keep his commands (do good works) and remain faithful to (the testimony of) Yahusha the Messiah (found in The Heavenly Scroll called The Word of His Testimony).

will be dressed in white (wedding garments). And I will never blot out his name from the Book of Life, but I will confess his name before my Father and His angels.

6 - He who has an (a spiritual) ear, let him (spiritually) hear what the spirit (of Prophecy) says to the assemblies (of Nazarenes).

## *To the Nazarene Assembly in Philadelphia*
## *"Keep Faith in The Word of His Testimony"*

7 - To the angel of the assembly in Philadelphia write: These are the words of the one who is (the) holy (faithful) and true (the meaning of ***Immanuel***), who holds the key (rightful heir to the house) of David (Yahusha was a descendent of David on both sides of his family tree).

8 - I know your deeds. Behold, I have placed before you an open (Heavenly) door (to understanding The Heavenly Scroll), which no one (including Satan) can shut. For you only have a little strength, yet you have kept My Word (Word eternally preserved in The Heavenly Scroll - Psalm 19, 119:89, 89:2, Daniel 4:35) and have not denied (the Covenant that bears) My Name (The Yahushaic Covenant).

9 - Behold those who belong to the accuser who claim to be those who worship Yahuah but are liars instead, I will make them (these usurpers) come and bow down (be humbled) at your feet (you will rule them with a rod of iron - Revelation 2:27), and they will know that I love you.

10 - Because you have kept The Word of My Testimony faithfully and endured with much patience, I will also keep you from the hour of testing (Day of Yahuah) that is about to come upon the whole world to test (with judgments) those (not covered by The Blood of the Lamb) who dwell on the Earth.

11 - I am coming soon (end of the Age of PISCES - Matthew 28:20). Hold fast to what you have (faith in The Word of His Testimony, proclaimed in The Heavenly Scroll) so that no one (false teachers filled with The Spirit of the False Messiah who deny The Word of His Testimony in the stars) will take your crown (of Life).

12 - The one who is victorious (over the Dragon through faith in The Word of His Testimony) I will make a pillar (Spiritual Living Stone - 1 Peter 2:5) in the Temple (body of believers) of My God, and He (Yahuah) will never again leave that Temple. Upon him (the victorious over the Dragon) I will write the Name of My God (YHVH), and the name of the city of My God (New Yerusalem) which comes down from Shamayim, and my new name/title (Melchizedek means Ruling High Priest, we all become *Melchi Tsedek*).

13 - He who has an (a spiritual) ear (understands the Intent/Spirit of My Torah), let him (spiritually) hear what the spirit says to the assemblies (the heart and mind of Yahuah's children).

## To the Assembly in Laodicia
## "Do not be luke-warm!"

14 - To the angel of the Nazarene assembly in Laodicia write: These are the words of the amen (which means), the faithful and true witness (Immanuel), the object (heir) of Yahuah's creation (which is to be given Yahusha as an inheritance). 15 - I know your deeds; you are neither cold nor hot. How I wish you were one or the other! 16 - So because you are lukewarm neither hot nor cold - I am about to vomit (remove) you (your name) out of My mouth (and **not** proclaim it before Yahuah as His heir - Revelation 3:5).

17 - You say 'I am (physically) rich; I have grown wealthy and need nothing; (self-righteous) But you do not realize that you are wretched (heart and mind sick with unrighteousness) pitifully poor (in wisdom), (spiritually) blind and naked (your sin is exposed to Yahuah, you are not covered by The Blood of the Lamb by walking *The Way*). 18 - I counsel you to buy from me gold (Salvation) refined by (the) fire (His Spirit - Matthew 3:11) so that you may become rich with white (wedding) garments so that you may be clothed (covered by the Blood of the Lamb) so that your

shameful nakedness (sin) is not exposed, and healing ointment to anoint your (Spiritual) eyes so that you may see (with your mind). 19 - Those I love, I rebuke and discipline; therefore be zealous (for the Word of His Testimony) and repent (of your dead works). 20 - Behold, I stand at the door (of your heart and mind) and knock. If anyone (spiritually) hears and opens the door (to their heart and mind - the Temple of Yahuah), I will come in and dine (at the Altar) with him and he with me (as Priests on the sacrifice of Atonement - Leviticus 6:26 - as we shall "eat the body and drink the blood" of the sacrifice metaphorically - John 6:54).

21 - To the one who is victorious (over the Dragon/Spirit of the False Messiah) I will grant the right to sit with me on my throne (and rule as King under my authority), just as I overcame (the Dragon) and sat down with my Father on His throne (John is reading The Heavenly Scroll as Daniel was shown in Daniel 7).

> **Daniel 7** – *Daniel's Vision of The Heavenly Scroll*
> 13 I saw in the night (sky) visions (of The Heavenly Scroll, like I said he was laying down at night looking at the stars), and behold (the constellation ORION), One like the Son of man came riding with the clouds of Heaven (the Milky Way), and (the Son of Man/ORION and the Dragon) came to the Ancient of days (Yahuah, who had taken His seat to judge between them), and they (both) were brought together before Yahuah (to declare who was the fulfillment of The Heavenly Scroll, the books had been opened). 14 And there was given Him (the Son of Man) ruling authority, and glory, and a kingdom, that all peoples, nations, and languages should obey Him; His government is an everlasting government, which will not pass away; and His kingdom is one which will not be destroyed (message behind the pictograph of LEO). 15 I, Daniyl, was grieved in my spirit within my body, and the visions (of The Heavenly Scroll) that passed through my mind (as he studied the Enoch Zodiac) troubled me (as he lay on his bed at night, looking up at the stars, he was not dreaming, he was writing these down as Yahuah gave him understanding as he said in verse 1). 16 I came near to one of those who stood by and asked him the truth of all this (what do these constellations mean?). So he told me, and revealed the interpretation of these things to me (revealed the meaning behind the Heavenly pictographs).

22 - He who has an (a spiritual) ear, let him (spiritually) hear what the spirit (of Prophecy) says to the seven Nazarene assemblies.

# *Chapter 4*

# Introduction

Now that Yahusha has warned the Elect for the coming Age using the Nazarene Assemblies during the time John wrote Revelation as examples, John is given a vision of The Throne in Heaven. John literally described the diagram Enoch drew after his vision. The same diagram described by Isaiah and Daniel.

Chapter 4 is describing The Enoch Zodiac called The Heavenly Scroll. He describes The Throne in Heaven in the middle to establish the source of his revelation.

- The Heavenly throne with a rainbow around it, having the One seated in it, is revealed.

- Twenty-four surrounding thrones seated with twenty-four crowned elders appear.

- The four living creatures present themselves: each having six wings full of eyes, one having the face of a lion, another as a calf, the third as a man, and the last as an eagle.

The first vision is that of entering Heaven and seeing the Throne in Heaven in the center of The Heavenly Scroll (*Enoch Zodiac Revelation 4:1–6*).

In Revelation, The Throne in Heaven is described as "having the appearance like that of jasper and a throne with a rainbow-like halo as brilliant as emerald". Around Yahusha's throne are twenty-four other thrones, on which sit elders in white robes. From the throne come thunder and lightning and, in front of the throne, the author sees seven candlesticks and a sea of crystal.

What is all this symbolism? What is it exactly that John was given a vision of by Gabriel? He was shown the same thing Enoch was when he "went to Heaven" and returned to draw what he saw called the Enoch Zodiac. Enoch witnessed the same color scheme as John.

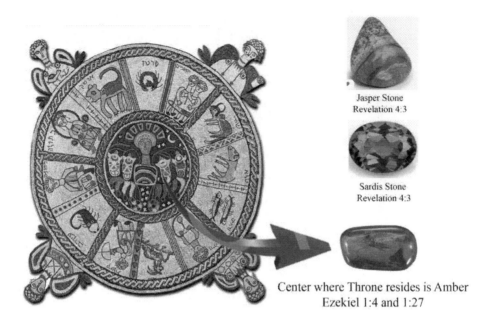

Jasper Stone
Revelation 4:3

Sardis Stone
Revelation 4:3

Center where Throne resides is Amber
Ezekiel 1:4 and 1:27

Like Enoch, Isaiah, Ezekiel, and others, John witnesses four creatures which have six wings and are covered in eyes (*Revelation 4:6–11*) called Seraphim. The Seraphim are giving thanks to Yahuah and, whenever one of them bows down to worship Yahuah, the twenty-four elders (*Enoch illustrated with stars*) around Yahusha's throne bow down to worship Yahuah.

In this chapter, John describes in great detail the "source" of his revelation and knowledge: The Heavenly Scroll. The same source used by Enoch, Noah, Moses, Ezekiel, Daniel, Jeremiah, Sha'ul, Yahusha, Zechariah and every other prophet. For more in this topic, please read my book Creation Cries Out! The Mazzaroth:

*Creation Cries Out! The Mazzaroth by Rav Sha'ul available on all online bookstores.*

# Revelation 4 Restored

1 - After this I beheld in my vision (Strong's 2372 - behold, envisioned in visions - in this case John was looking to mentally digest the Stars/Heavenly Scroll as all his prophet were instructed - Ezekiel 3:3, Revelation 10:9)

### Ezekiel 3:3
Then he said to me (as I gazed into the Heavens), "Son of man, eat this (Heavenly) Scroll I am giving you and fill your stomach with it." So I ate it, and it tasted as sweet as honey in my mouth.

### Revelation 10:8-9
8 Then the voice that I had heard from Heaven spoke to me once more: "Go, take the (Heavenly) Scroll that lies open in the hand of the angel who is standing on the sea and on the land." 9 So I went to the angel and asked him to give me the little Scroll. He said to me, "Take it and eat it."
and saw a door standing open in The Heavenly Scroll.

### Isaiah 22:22
And the key to "The house of David" will I (Yahuah) lay upon his (Yahusha's) shoulder; so he shall open (the door to Heaven), and none shall shut; and he shall shut, and none shall open.

And the voice I (spiritually) heard (was Yahuah - the Aleph and the Tav) speak to me (in my vision) resembling a shofar was saying, "*Come up here and I will show you what must happen* (on Earth as proclaimed in The Heavenly Scroll Matthew 6:10) *after these things*" (over the Age of PISCES).

### Hebrews 10:7
Then I said, 'Here I am--it is written about me in The Heavenly Scroll-- I have come to do Your Will, my Elohim! (Matthew 6:10)

### Matthew 6:10
Your Kingdom (declared in Heaven Matthew 4:17) come, Your Will be done, on Earth as it is written in The Heavenly Scroll (Psalm 19, 119:89, 89:2, Daniel 4:35).

### Psalm 89:2
I will declare that your love stands firm forever, that you have established your faithful promise (LOGOS / DEBAR) of salvation in The Heavenly Scroll itself.

**Psalm 119:89**
Your Word (LOGOS / DEBAR), Yahuah, is Eternal; it Stands Firm written in The Heavenly Scroll.

**Psalm 119:105**
105 Your Word (LOGOS / DABAR eternally preserved in The Heavenly Scroll - Psalm 119:89) is a lamp (the Divine Council, we as His Bride are to keep our Lamps lit by keeping The Word of His Testimony - Isaiah 48) unto my feet, and a light (revelation of the Sun/stars/constellations - Psalm 19, Enoch 35:3) unto my path (The Heavenly Scroll is 'the Path of Righteousness' called The Way - Isaiah 42:5-7).

**Daniel 4:35**
"All the inhabitants of the Earth are accounted as nothing, but He does according to His will written in the host of Heaven (The Zodiac which hosts constellations. Constellations "host stars")

2 - At once I was in the spirit (everything John saw was not physical, but Spiritual, a mental vision) and I saw a throne standing in the midst of The Heavenly Scroll, with someone (the Son of Man) seated on it. 3 - The one seated (on the throne in the middle of The Enoch Zodiac) looked like jasper and Sardis stone, and <u>a rainbow that gleamed like an emerald encircled the throne.</u>

**Revelation 7:9**
9 After this I looked (before the Throne in Heaven), and behold, a great multitude that no one could number, from every nation, from all tribes and peoples and languages, standing before the throne (represented by the rainbow) and before the Lamb, clothed in white robes, with palm branches in their hands.

*The Rainbow Throne represents all skin colors that the Chosen Few were called out of every nation.*

4 - Surrounding the throne (in Heaven) were twenty-four other thrones and on these thrones sat twenty-four elders (represented by the 24 stars in the throne room of the Enoch Zodiac) dressed in white wedding garments with golden crowns on their heads (Gold = salvation - Revelation 3:18).

### Revelation 3
18 - I counsel you to buy from me gold (Salvation) refined by (the) fire (His Spirit Matthew 3:11) so that you may become rich with white (wedding) garments so that you may be clothed (covered by the Blood of the Lamb) so that your shameful nakedness (sin) is not exposed, and healing ointment to anoint your (Spiritual) eyes so that you may see (with your mind).

5 - From the throne came flashes of lightning, and rumblings, and peals of thunder. Before the throne were seven lamps of fire (the Heavenly Menorah). These are the seven spirits (perfect Knowledge) of Yahuah.

6 - And before the throne was something like a sea of glass, as clear as crystal. (Strong's 5193 - to be translucent – John was looking at black "space" in the Heavens), And in the center of the throne (were 4 Seraphs singing holy holy holy),

*4 living creatures singing "Holy, Holy, Holy" around the Rainbow Throne with 24 stars falling before the throne. Son of Man sitting on throne with fire/lightening emanating from his face.*

and surrounding the throne, were four living creatures (Seraphs sitting on the outer ring. There are 4 inside and 4 outside total 8) full of Spiritual insight (figuratively speaking of the mind's eye G3788 ophthalmos) before (or foresight G1715. Emprosthen) and After (G3693. Opisthen).

*4 living creatures surrounding the throne on the outer ring*

They were covered with eyes in the front and back (foresight and hindsight, all-seeing). 7 - The first living creature (on the outer ring surrounding the throne room) was like a lion (Yahudah), the second like an Ox (Ephraim), the third had the face like a man (Reuben), and the fourth was like an eagle in flight (Dan).

8 - And each of the four living creatures (called Seraphim) had six wings (2 pointing up, 2 covering their body, and 2 pointing down) and was covered with eyes all around and within

(again, full of spiritual insight). Day and night, they never stop saying: "Holy, Holy, Holy, is Yahuah Elohim, who was and is and is to come!" (Y-H-V-H)

*6-Winged Seraph*

6 Wings (3 sets)

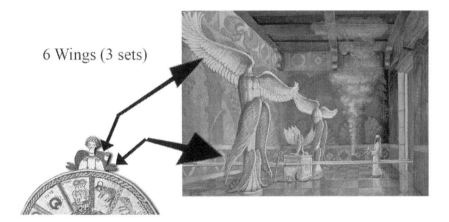

*6 winged Seraphs in The Heavenly Scroll. Seraphs around the throne (altar) on Earth.*

*8 total Seraphim in the Holy of Holies. 4 by the altar, 2 painted on the ceiling behind the altar, and 2 on the veil. The Holy of Holies is patterned after The Throne in Heaven (The Heavenly Scroll).*

9 - And the (8) living creatures give glory, honor, and thanks to the one seated on the throne (Messiah Yahusha) who lives forevermore (is the firstborn of the dead Revelation 1:5).

10 - The twenty-four elders (represented by the 24 falling stars in the Enoch Zodiac) fall down before the one (Yahusha) seated on the throne (in Heaven) and they worship (bowed in respect of his authority as their King Strong's g4352 - "do obeisance/respect") him who (now immortal) lives forevermore (post resurrection, firstborn of the dead). They cast their crowns before the throne, saying:

11 - "You are worthy, our King and elohim (Strong's h430 - Diving Representative of Yahuah's power)" to receive glory and honor and power (from Yahuah), and _because_ (Strong's g3745 – "because") of you all things were created; (as an inheritance Ephesians 1, Romans 8:17) because of Yahuah's will for you, they exist, and came to be (for you as an inheritance)."

# Commentary on Inheritance

We see in verse 11 that it was Yahuah that created the Universe, and it was by His Will and Word they exists (*Genesis 1:1 "Yahuah SAID "let there be light"*). Yahuah created the Universe as a loving Father so that He could give something, an inheritance, to His future children. The firstborn from the dead in that future family is Yahusha to whom the inheritance was given. Yahuah is "love" and "love" can only be expressed through giving! To fully express His love for His family, Yahuah had to give them an inheritance.

### Ephesians 1

8 Wherein (covenant with Yahusha) He (Yahuah) hath abounded toward us (Love) in all wisdom and prudence; 9 Having made known (His Love) unto us (from the beginning written in the stars/The Heavenly Scroll) the mystery of His will (to beget a family), according to His (Yahuah's) good pleasure which He hath purposed (in The Heavenly Scroll/Logos/Dabar) in (the full image of) Himself (He is begetting a family and is the Father of Elohim, the One True Living God - *Matthew 17:3*): 10 That in the dispensation of the time of fulfillment of The Heavenly Scroll (4th prophetic day as foretold in The Heavenly Scroll and the prophets) He (Yahuah) might gather together (again) in one all things in (covenant with Yahusha the) Messiah, both which are in Heaven (The Kingdom of Yahuah), and which are on Earth; even in Him(self, Yahuah will reconcile creation through the sacrifice of His Son *Colossians 1:20*): 11 In (covenant with) whom (the first born Son, Messiah Yahusha) also we (too) have obtained **AN INHERITANCE** (as sons of YHVH, we inherit the Universe THROUGH Yahusha as co-heir *Romans 8:17*), being predestinated according to **THE PURPOSE** of Yahuah (from the beginning written into creation called The Heavenly Scroll, what John saw in Revelation, to beget a family to rule His Creation) who works all things after the counsel of His own will (the Dabar/Logos called The Divine Council. All that was done was done according to His predestined purpose/plan and *Psalms 19* 'the stars declare the Works of His Hands'): 12 That we (sons of Yahuah) should be to the praise of His glory, who first trusted in Messiah Yahusha (as our Mediator who showed us The Way and fulfilled The Heavenly Scroll/Logos/Dabar/Spoken Promise from the beginning John Chapter 1).

### Romans 8:17

16 The Spirit Himself testifies with our spirit that we are Yahuah's children (we are given an earnest guarantee after Mikveh and we are filled with the fullness of deity - Ephesians 3:19). 17 And if (we walk The Way) we are children, then (after being born-again) we are heirs: heirs of Yahuah and **CO-HEIRS** with Yahusha — if indeed we suffer with him, so that we may also be glorified with him (in the resurrection to share in his inheritance).

## Hebrews 1

1 In the past Yahuah spoke to our ancestors through the prophets (not Yahusha because he did not yet exist) at many times and in various ways (via The Heavenly Scroll and through proxies/elohims), 2 but in these last days (at the time of fulfillment/fullness of time the 4th Prophetic Day as laid out in The Heavenly Scroll) he has spoken to us by his Son (who fulfilled the Logos/Dabar/Heavenly Scroll in the flesh John 1), whom Yahuah APPOINTED HEIR OF ALL THINGS (after he was risen divine), and ON ACCOUNT OF whom also Yahuah made the universe (as an inheritance to give to Yahusha verse 1). 3 The Son is the radiance of Yahuah's glory (fulfillment of The Heavenly Scroll, the Sun's radiance proclaims THE GLORY of Yahuah - Psalms 19:1) and the exact representation of his being (after being resurrected, the first born of the dead, the first of the resurrection, the first fruits of the grave, the first of eternal creation), sustaining (ruling over... Daniel 7, Isaiah 9:6, LEO) all things by his powerful word (he is seated as KING, the Right Hand of Yahuah and rules in Righteousness). AFTER he had provided purification for sins (by defeating death), THEN (not at creation) he sat down at the right hand of the Majesty in The Heavenly Scroll (took his rightful place on the Throne in Heaven Daniel 7). 4 So he BECAME as much superior to the angels (as he inherited the Universe from his Father) as the name/reputation/title he has INHERITED (he is not Creator of the Universe, he is HEIR through inheritance) is superior to theirs (he is the Melchi Tsedek, Ruling High Priest).

## Galatians 4

4 What I am saying is that as long as *AN HEIR* is underage, he is no different from a slave, although he owns the whole estate. 2 The heir is subject to guardians and trustees until the time set by his father. 3 So also, when we were underage, we were in slavery under the elemental spiritual forces of the world. 4 But when the time of fulfillment of The Heavenly Scroll had come, Yahuah sent his Son, born of a woman, born under the law, 5 to redeem those under the curse of the law (the Death Decrees), that we might receive adoption to sonship. 6 Because you are his sons, Yahuah sent the Spirit of his Son into our hearts (after our Mikveh and we are born-again), the Spirit who calls out, "Abba, Father." 7 So you are no longer a slave (to the fear of death), but Yahuah's child; and since you are His child, Yahuah has made you ALSO (with Yahusha the firstborn) *AN HEIR* (to Creation).

In many of the verses above in your English Bibles it reads as if it was through Yahusha that the Universe was created. Yahusha being the "Word made flesh" that holds together creation, a Divine Emanation from the Father. This is a pagan philosophy and totally untrue and contrary to Scripture.

If you look at the word the translators chose to translate as "through" as if *Yahusha* created the Universe (*instead of heir of Yahuah, The Creator, through **inheritance***) we see that the word translated "through", in fact, means "***on account of***" or *"because of"* or *"for the sake of"*. This word choice is consistent with The Plan of Salvation as Yahuah created the Universe <u>on account of Yahusha</u> because of His Purpose to beget a family and will to that family an inheritance. It is THROUGH INHERITANCE that Yahusha rules the Universe as I will prove it was given him as his inheritance as the first-born son of The Father who alone is THE CREATOR.

The word translated *'through'* is the preposition *'dia'* g1223 below:

## ◀ 1223. dia ▶

### Strong's Concordance

**dia: through, on account of, because of**
Original Word: διά
Part of Speech: Preposition
Transliteration: dia
Phonetic Spelling: (dee-ah')
Short Definition: through, on account of
Definition: (a) gen: through, throughout, by the instrumentality of, (b) acc: through, on account of, by reason of, for the sake of, because of.

Which word the translators should have used for 'dia' should have been determined based on Yahuah's <u>PURPOSE in Creation</u> and dictated by context of what is written in Scripture and revealed in the Logos/Dabar (*written in the stars*) which is the Plan of Salvation. However, the translators where pagan Greeks and Hellenized the Scriptures to conform to their Greek Philosophy and ignored The Plan of Salvation, **denied** The Heavenly Scroll, abolished the words of His Prophets, and twisted the Scriptures… all to mistranslate the word "dia" to elevate a man who died as God above Yahuah.

We know in Daniel Chapter 7 that Yahusha, the firstborn of the DEAD not creation, comes before Yahuah "the Ancient of Days" at the end of The Age of PISCES beginning of AQUARIUS after fulfilling the pictograph of LEO. Yahusha is <u>THEN</u> given his inheritance! He did not create the Universe it was created by Yahuah as an inheritance to give to him or "on account of Yahusha" as His firstborn son.

### Daniel 7

13 "I kept looking in the night visions (he was looking at the stars/constellations in The Heavenly Scroll), and behold (in The Heavenly Scroll), with the clouds of Heaven One

(ORION) *like* a Son of Man (ORION represents the Messiah in The Heavenly Scroll) was coming, (now Daniel reads the message in The Heavenly Scroll) And He (ORION/The Messiah) came up to the Ancient of Days (POST resurrection after he had come back as Conquering King to subdue all Kingdoms, defeat The Dragon, and reconcile Creation back to his Father) And Yahusha (the PRINCE of Peace not yet King) was presented before Yahuah (to be crowned King). 14 "And to Him (Yahusha) was given (by Yahuah as an inheritance) dominion (the Universe), Glory and a kingdom (he was seated at the Right Hand of Yahuah over the government that will govern Creation), that all the peoples, nations and men of every language might serve Him. His dominion (As King over the Government that governs creation) is an everlasting dominion which will not pass away; and His kingdom is one which will not be destroyed (*Isaiah 6:9* and *LEO*).

# *Chapter 5*

# Introduction

Now that John has described The Heavenly Scroll as the source of his vision, he is shown what must take place on Earth as it is written in "Heaven". All of Chapter 5 occurs and is showing us what takes place after the 7th Trumpet sounds.

- A book/Scroll secured by seven seals is revealed in the right hand of Him/the One (God) who sits on the throne (*Revelation 5:1*).

- It is made known that only "The Lion that is from the Tribe of Judah" (*Revelation 5:5*) is worthy to open this book/Scroll.

- The Lamb, with seven horns and seven eyes, takes the book/Scroll from Him who sits on the throne (*Revelation 5:6–7*).

- The Lamb Fulfills The Heavenly Scroll and is Found Worthy to Open It

- All Heavenly beings sing praise and honor The Lamb (*Revelation 5:9*).It is only at this point, that Yahusha is given his inheritance and seated on The Throne in Heaven by our Father. Let first go over some precepts needed to understand and properly translate this chapter.

# "Eyes" or "streams"?

In this chapter we see a reference to "eyes":

### Revelation 5:6

Then I saw a Lamb, looking as if it had been slain, standing at the center of the throne, encircled by the four living creatures and the elders. The Lamb had seven horns and seven eyes, which are the seven spirits of God sent out into all the Earth.

What is meant by this imagery? To understand the meaning of "eyes" which is a mistranslation in context, we need to consult "context" found in Zechariah. In Zechariah 3:10 and Revelation 5:6 the translators used the word "eyes" erring in context. What is the "rock with 7 eyes" in Zechariah Chapter 3?

### Zechariah 3:9

See, the stone I have set in front of you Yahusha! There are seven eyes on that one stone, and I will engrave an inscription on it,' says Yahuah Almighty, 'and I will remove the sin of this land in a single day.'

What is Yahuah talking about? What "rock"? We see that in the book of Joshua (*son of Nun and successor to Moses*) that a rock was set before Israel as a witness to the covenant with Yahuah, to re-affirm the Covenant Law:

### Joshua 23

25 On that day Joshua made a covenant for the people, and there at Shechem he reaffirmed for them decrees and laws. 26 And Joshua recorded these things in the Book of the Law of Yahuah. Then he took a large stone and set it up there under the oak near the holy place of Yahuah. 27 "See!" he said to all the people. "This stone will be a witness against us. It has heard all the words Yahuah has said to us. It will be a witness against you if you are untrue to your Elohim." 28 Then Joshua dismissed the people, each to their own inheritance.

These rocks are metaphorically speaking of "**a solid foundation, a rock-solid witness**". Before we can begin to interpret properly what the rock with 7 eyes is speaking of, we must first firmly establish that Zechariah Chapter 3 is speaking of The Messiah... The Branch!

Most "teachers" will not touch this prophecy because it clearly says, "**see High Priest Yahusha, I have forgiven your sin!**" They cannot reconcile that one statement with the clear evidence that this prophecy is speaking of the coming Messiah being consecrated Eternal High Priest of the

House of Zadok by Yahuah personally! So, let us first establish a foundation from which to approach this most important of all Prophecies. Where our Messiah is consecrated High Priest directly by the Father and enters into The Yahushaic Covenant on our behalf as our Mediator!

In Zachariah Chapter 3, the end result of this covenant that Yahuah and Yahusha enter into is that Yahusha makes the final sacrifice "**for his brothers** (*John 15:13*)" as required in The Heavenly Scroll and further elaborated in The Spring Feasts. He must die and pay the dowry for his Bride with his life. Yahuah then makes a promise to Yahusha… He speaks in the Mystery Language of "*7 eyes on one stone*" that is "*put before him*" or rather "*what lies ahead of him*" … being his destiny. It is a "*stone of destiny*", so to speak, and where the idea of such a stone to coronate Kings originated. Yahuah then declares He will remove the sin of the land in one day.

This was laid out in the stars on Day 4 of Creation Week:

---

**CAPRICORNUS**: Eternal life comes from his death, he's the Arrow of God, he is pierced, yet springs up again in abundant life. **AQUARIUS**: He pours out "living water" from on high, humanity drinks of the Heavenly river and the faithful live again, he is the deliverer of the good news (Gospel), Carrying the wood of the sacrifice over the Earth. **PISCES**: The Redeemer's people multiplied, supported and led by the Lamb, The Bride is exposed on Earth, the Bridegroom is exalted.

---

# What is all this about? How can we piece together this puzzle so that it can be understood?

In context, Yahuah is directly referencing the "effects" of Yahusha's sacrifice by tying it to removing sin; which defeats death leading to resurrection as laid out in the pictogram of Capricorn. Yahusha, then, is laid as "The Chief Cornerstone" of the final Temple after fulfilling The Heavenly Scroll.

**Ephesians 2:20**
built on the foundation of the apostles and prophets, with Yahusha the Messiah himself as the chief cornerstone.

That "stone" embodies perfection (*number 7*) of the 7 Spirits of Yahuah (*perfect word or revelation*).

### Isaiah 11:2-3
The Spirit of Yahuah will rest on Him (he is NOT Yahuah, he was an anointed teacher), including the Spirit of Yahuah (that Yahusha came in the flesh as a human being not a demi-god), and the Spirits of wisdom, of understanding, of counsel, of might, of knowledge and of fear of Yahuah, here are represented the seven Spirits, which are before the throne of Yahuah (he was filled with The Ruach and the 7 Spirits of perfection upon Mikveh Colossians 2:9).

### Isaiah 61:1
The Spirit of Yahuah is upon me (after he was Mikveh'd Matthew 3:16), Because Yahuah has anointed me (as High Priest in the desert just after his Mikveh). To bring good news to the afflicted; He has sent me to bind up the brokenhearted, To proclaim liberty to captives And freedom to prisoners; (Luke 4:18)

### Luke 4:18
"The Spirit of Yahuah is on me (he was anointed by Yahuah, he was not Yahuah), because He has anointed me to proclaim good news to the poor (Isaiah 61:1). He has sent me to proclaim freedom (from the Law of Sin and Death) for the prisoners (held captive by fear of death Hebrews 2:14-15) and recovery of sight for the (Spiritually) blind, to set the oppressed (by human rules and traditions) free!

# The Living Water is a metaphor of The Spirit of Yahuah...

### Isaiah 44:3
For I will pour water on the thirsty land, and streams on the dry ground; I will pour out my Spirit on your offspring, and my blessing on your descendants.

Yahusha is the fulfillment of AQUARIUS in The Heavenly Scroll, he is the one who Mikveh's the Earth with Living Water.

### Isaiah 44
2 Thus says Yahuah who made you And formed you from the womb, who will help you, 'Do not fear, O Jacob My servant; And you Jeshurun whom I have chosen. 3 For I will pour out water on the thirsty land And streams on the dry ground (AQUARIUS); I will pour out My Spirit on

your offspring And My blessing on your descendants; 4 And they will spring up (into Eternal Life CAPRICORNUS) among the grass Like poplars by streams of water.'...

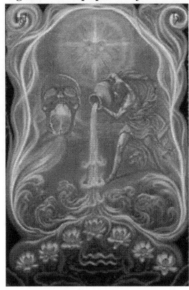

These 7 Spirits are seen in The Heavenly Scroll as The Heavenly Menorah before the Throne. "Fire" is a metaphor of the Word of Yahuah (*Jeremiah 23:29*), and 7 flames burning (*a Menorah*) is a metaphor of the PERFECT Word of Yahuah burning eternally in... The Heavenly Scroll!

### Psalm 119

88 Revive me according to Your lovingkindness, So that I may keep the testimony of Your mouth (written in The Heavenly Scroll). Lamedh. 89 Forever, O Yahuah, Your word is written in (the) Heaven(ly Scroll).

### Psalm 89:2

For I have said, "Lovingkindness will be built up forever; In the Heaven(ly Scroll) You will establish Your faithfulness."

# What are the 'Eyes' referring to?

"Eyes" is a mistranslation in this context. Eyes could also be translated "fountains" or "springs" of living water, which is more appropriate in the context of Yahusha, who is the Living Water Bearer AQUARIUS and whoever drinks of his cup, STREAMS of Living Water flow (*John 4:14*).   The word translated as "eyes" in this case is *h5869* 'ayin'.

◀ **5869. ayin** ▶

**Strong's Concordance**

ayin: an eye

Original Word: עַיִן
Part of Speech: Noun
Transliteration: ayin
Phonetic Spelling: (ah'-yin)
Short Definition: eyes

*NASB Translation*

appearance (4), appeared* (1), before (3), broad (1), concern* (1), confidence (1), disdained* (1), displease* (2), displeased* (4), disregard* (1), eye (68), eyebrows* (1), eyelids* (1), eyes (372), eyesight (1), forehead* (5), generous* (1), glares* (1), gleam (3), humble person* (1), knowledge (1), like* (1), look (4), look* (3), looked* (3), looks* (1), maliciously* (1), notice (1), outward appearance (1), own eyes (1), please* (3), pleased* (14), pleases* (1), prefer* (2), presence (8), saw* (1), see (1), see* (1), seem (1), seemed* (1), selfish* (1), sight (277), sight* (1), sleep* (1), sparkles* (1), sparkling (1), spring (1), surface (4), think (2), thought (1), watch (1), watch* (1), whatever you like* (1), wish* (2), yourselves (2).

**Brown-Driver-Briggs**

II. עַיִן **noun feminine spring** (of water)

**Strong's Exhaustive Concordance**

affliction, outward appearance, before, think best, color, conceit, be content

Probably a primitive word; an eye (literally or figuratively); by analogy, a fountain (as the eye of the landscape) -- affliction, outward appearance, + before, + think best, colour, conceit, + be content, countenance, + displease, eye((-brow), (-d), -sight), face, + favour, fountain, furrow (from the margin), X him, + humble, knowledge, look, (+ well), X me, open(-ly), + (not) please, presence, + regard, resemblance, sight, X thee, X them, + think, X us, well, X you(-rselves).

Notice another usage of this word is "streams/fountains/springs" of living water!

**John 4:14**
but whoever drinks the water I give them will never thirst. Indeed, the water I give them will become in them a spring of living water welling up to eternal life."

---

Yahusha is...
## "the perfect rock which serves as the Chief Cornerstone of the final Spiritual Temple; from which 7 streams (perfect expression of Yahuah's Spirits) of living water flow" the fulfillment of AQUARIUS the Water Bearer

---

This is in fulfillment of the physical shadow of Moses striking the rock and living water came gushing out to satisfy the thirst in the land.

**Numbers 20:11**
Then Moses raised his arm and struck the rock twice with his staff. Water (not 'eyes') gushed out, and the community and their livestock drank.

**John 7**
37 On the last and greatest day of the feast of Sukkot, Yahusha stood up and called out in a loud voice (to all of Israel, that he is the fulfillment of AQUARIUS the Water Bearer), "If anyone is thirsty, let him come to Me and drink. 38 To the one who believes in Me (that I am the fulfillment of The Heavenly Scroll), it is just as the Scripture has said: 'Streams of living water (not 'eyes') will flow from within him.'"

# Conclusion

So, the proper translation of Zachariah's prophecy, IN CONTEXT, with the Mystery Language interpreted is:

> **Zechariah 3:9**
> See, the stone I have set in front of (a witness to your destiny) Yahusha! There are seven fountains of Living Water on that one (Chief Corner) stone, and I will engrave an inscription on it (I will personally witness)', says Yahuah Almighty, *'and I will remove the sin of this land in a single day'* (the day Yahusha fulfills his end of the agreement and gives his life and is set as the Chief Cornerstone of the 3rd Temple in fulfillment of The Heavenly Scroll, this is the fundamental "promise" throughout scripture to be fulfilled in The Yahushaic Covenant).

Yahusha had to walk the path of The Branch laid out in The Heavenly Scroll where the Groom pays the dowry for his Bride with his life to redeem her from death. This Plan of Salvation laid out in The Heavenly Scroll was then later revealed and rehearsed in the Feast Cycle as *Passover*!

So, after Yahusha gave his life to fulfill his role as The Branch on Passover at the end of the Age of ARIES (*the Lamb*) as a "lamb that was slaughtered" foretold in the stars on Day 4 of Creation Week... Yahusha became The Chief Cornerstone of the Final Spiritual Temple, by which all the sons of Yahuah inherit eternal life as they drink from the fountains of living water that flow forth from that rock.

# Revelation 5:6 Error in Translation

We find the same error in translation in Revelation 5:6 where Yahusha is "is given complete power as The Lamb with 7 Streams of Living Water" meaning he is The King, LEO, and fulfillment of The Heavenly Scroll AQUARIUS.

What is the proper translation and meaning of Revelation 5:6 in light of what I have just shown and context of The Heavenly Scroll?

### Revelation 5:6

6 - Then I saw a lamb (Yahusha) who appeared to have been pierced, standing in the center of the throne (room of the Enoch Zodiac) encircled by four living creatures (singing Holy, Holy, Holy) and the elders (Represented by the 24 falling stars in the throne room). The Lamb had seven (*complete*) horns (*power*; Strong's g2768 - *a horn as a symbol of power*) and seven fountains of living water ('eyes' is not correct, in Hebrew it is Strong's h5869 - it is seven fountains of living water as in Zechariah Chapter 3:9), which represent the seven spirits of Yahuah poured out (like living water) onto all the Earth (AQUARIUS).

# Revelation 5 Restored

1 - Then I saw a (Heavenly) Scroll in the right hand of the one (who fulfilled it, the Messiah Yahusha) seated on the Throne in Heaven. (Yahusha fulfilling The Heavenly Scroll is seen in Daniel Chapter 7) The Scroll had writing on both sides (a 3D Scroll of Heavenly pictographs) and was sealed with seven seals.

2 - And I saw a mighty messenger (of Yahuah) proclaiming in a loud voice, "*who is worthy to break the seals and open The Heavenly Scroll?*" 3 - But no one in the stars or on Earth or under the Earth was able to open The Heavenly Scroll or look inside it.

4 - And I began to cry with despair, because no one was found worthy to open The Heavenly Scroll and interpret inside it (only he who fulfills it is worthy to open and read it).

5 - Then one of the elders said to me, "*Do not weep! Behold the Lion of the tribe of Yahudah, the root of David, has triumphed* (meaning of constellation LEO) *to open The Heavenly Scroll and* (break) *its seven seals.*

6 - Then I saw a lamb (Yahusha) who appeared to have been pierced, standing in the center of the throne (room of the Enoch Zodiac) encircled by four living creatures (singing Holy, Holy, Holy) and the elders. (Represented by the 24 falling stars in the throne room)

The Lamb had seven (*complete*) horns (*power*; Strong's g2768 - *a horn as a symbol of power*) and seven fountains of living water (eyes is not correct, in Hebrew it is Strong's h5869 - it is seven fountains of living water as in Zechariah Chapter 3:9), which represent the seven spirits of Yahuah poured out (like living water) onto all the Earth (AQUARIUS).

7 – The messenger came and took The Heavenly Scroll from the right hand of the one (Yahusha) seated on the throne.

8 - When he had taken the Scroll, the four living creatures (in the throne room) and the twenty-four elders (the 24 stars falling in the throne room) fell down (to pay homage, respect to the King) before the Lamb. Each one had a harp (constellation LYRA),

and they were holding golden bowls full of incense, which are the (righteous) prayers of the saints. 9 - And they sang a new song: "Worthy are you (Yahusha) to take The Heavenly Scroll and open its seals (reveal the message), because you (fulfilled The Heavenly Scroll when you) were slain, and by Your blood (shed to consummate the Marriage Covenant) You purchased for Yahuah (as children-in-law), those from every tribe (skin color) and tongue and people and nations (illustrated by the rainbow throne).

*The rainbow throne represents the Elect from every tribe among all nations.*

10 -You have made them to be Kings (Melchi) and (Zadok) priests (we serve the Ruling High Priest in the Order of Melchizedek) to serve our Eloah, and they will reign upon the Earth (for 1,000 years)."

## *The Lamb Exalted*

11 - Then I looked (mentally understood) as I heard the voices of many angels and living creatures and elders encircling the throne, and their number was myriads of myriads and thousands of thousands (John is looking at the stars).

12 - In a loud voice they said: "*Worthy is the Lamb* (Yahusha) *who was slain to receive power and riches and wisdom and strength and honor and glory and blessing* (from Father Yahuah as an inheritance).

13 - And I (spiritually) heard every creature in the stars, and on Earth, and under the Earth, and in the sea, and all that is in them (every living thing ever created by Yahuah), saying: To **Yahuah** who sits on the throne (over Creation), and to the Lamb (Proxy King Yahusha who sits at Yahuah's Right Hand on the Throne over The Kingdom that will govern Creation), be praise and honor and glory and power Forever and ever. 14 - And the four living creatures (surrounding the Throne in Heaven) said, "*HalleluYahuah*," *and the elders* (represented by the 24 stars) *fell down and worshiped* (Yahuah Elohim and Yahusha the Messiah).

*4 "living creatures" saying HalleluYahuah, the 24-stars falling before the throne*

# *Chapter 6*

# Introduction

The first four Seals occurred over the Age of PISCES and can be proven in historical accounts dating back 2000 years. The Age of PISCES is the Age of Tribulation on Earth (*the last days*) as the False Religion came to power and bathed itself in the blood of the Nazarenes and people of Earth. These seals representing war, death, and famine have all been inflicted upon mankind over the "last days" of PISCES as I will show.

The Fifth Seals is Yom Teruah when the King returns for those who have died in The Age of PISCES. The Sixth Seal is Yom Kippur (*The Day of Atonement*) called The Great and Terrible Day of Yahuah when those left on Earth are "sacrificed" to atone.

- The first seal is broken, and the first of the four living creatures introduces a *white horse* whose crowned rider, equipped with a bow, goes out to conquer.

- The second seal is broken, and the second of the four living creatures introduces a *red horse*, whose rider wields a great sword, goes out to take peace from the Earth. Humanity is consumed with war and conquest.

  Note: I originally had added every conflict in human history over the Age of PISCES as an Appendix to this book to illustrate the point. That Appendix added 400 pages to this book literally thousands of battles fought. I removed that Appendix for obvious reasons. Please refer to the link below to illustrate the fact that peace was taken from the Earth over the Age of PISCES:

  https://en.wikipedia.org/wiki/Lists_of_battles

- The third seal is broken, and the third of the four living creatures introduces a *black horse*, whose rider carries a pair of scales, which represent famine.

- The fourth seal is broken, and the fourth of the four living creatures introduces a *pale horse* comes out, whose rider has the name *Death* and *Hades* follows him. Given authority to kill with wars and famine and disease and wild animals.

- The fifth seal is broken revealing the souls of those who had been slain for the "Word of Yahuah".

- The sixth seal is broken, "and there was a great Earthquake; and the Sun became black as sackcloth made of hair, and the whole moon became like blood; and the stars of the sky fell to the Earth. The sky was split apart, every mountain and island were moved out of their places." Mankind hides themselves in the caves and mountains acknowledging the presence of *Him* who sits on the throne and the wrath of the Lamb.

# Revelation 6 Restored

### *The First Four Seals*
### *The First Seal: The White Horse*

1 - Then I watched (as I looked up at the stars) as the Lamb (Yahusha) opened one of the seven seals (over The Heavenly Scroll) and I heard one of the four living creatures (surrounding the throne) say in a thunderous voice, "Come!" 2 - So I envisioned a white horse, and its rider had a bow (Strong's H935 – 'To besiege'). And he was given a crown (of righteousness), and he rode out to overcome and conquer (the Dragon called The Battle of the Ages).

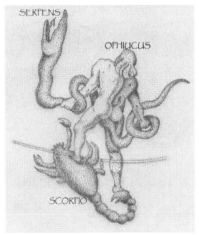

*Ophiuchus represents the Son of Man battling The Serpent, crushing its head while it strikes his heal. This is The Battle of the Ages*

## *The Second Seal: War*

3 - And when the Lamb opened the second seal, I heard (Spiritually) the second living creature say, "Come!" 4 - And another horse went forth. It was bright red (fire, Yahuah's Judgement, SAGGITARIUS)

> **SAGITTARIUS**: The double-natured seed (*King and High Priest*) triumphs as a warrior and pleases the Heavens, builds fires of punishment, casts down the dragon

and its rider was granted permission to take peace from the Earth and to make men slay one another. And he was given a great sword (the double-edged sword of ORION to "cast down the Dragon").

## The Third Seal: Famine

5 - And when the Lamb opened the third seal, I heard the third living creature say "Come." Then I envisioned a dark horse (Strong's H2821 – 'withhold light i.e., Spiritual knowledge, to be dark, cause Spiritual darkness' called The Dark Ages when The False Religion conquered the known world) and its rider held in his hand a pair of scales (John was interpreting LIBRA in The Heavenly Scroll).

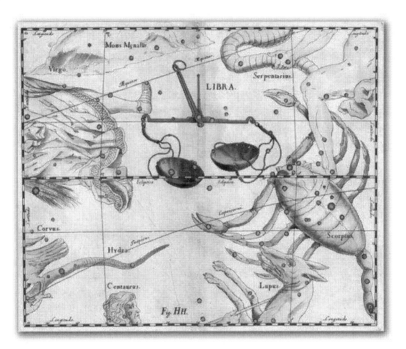

6 - And I heard what sounded like a voice (Yahusha) from (The Throne in Heaven) among the four living creatures saying "A measure of wheat for a denarius, and three measures of barley for a denarius; but do not hurt the oil (the anointed) and wine (chosen bloodline those with the seal of YHVH on their forehead).

## The Fourth Seal: Death

7 - And when the Lamb opened the fourth seal (over The Heavenly Scroll), I heard the voice of the fourth living creature say "Come!" 8 - I looked and envisioned an ashen horse; It's riders name was death, and sheol (the eternal grave) followed close behind. And (each) of the 4 horses were given authority over a fourth of the Earth to kill by sword, famine, and plague, and by the beasts of the Earth.

## The Last 3 Seals
## The Fifth Seal: Yom Teruah – King returns for His Elect

9 -And when the Lamb opened the fifth seal (over The Heavenly Scroll) I saw under the (Rainbow) alter the souls (Yahuah's remembrance recorded in the Book of Life) of those who had been slain for the Word of Yahuah and for the testimony (The Word of His Testimony) they upheld (that Yahusha fulfilled The Heavenly Scroll - Hebrews 10:7, Matthew 6:10)).

10 - And they (the slain Nazarenes) cried out (not literally, this is a vision of The Book of Life, they had not yet been resurrected) in a loud voice, *"How long, O King, holy and true, until you judge (TAURUS) those who live on the Earth and avenge our blood?"*

> TAURUS: The conquering Ruler comes, the sublime vanquisher, to execute the great judgment, he is the ruling Shepherd King.

11 - Then each of them (Yahusha had Shepherded TAURUS) was given a white (wedding) garment (as The Bride of the Messiah) and told to rest (metaphorically sleep in the grave) a little while longer, until the complete number of their fellow servants (Nazarenes), their brothers, were (physically and metaphorically) killed, just as they had been (physically and metaphorically) killed (for the Word of Their Testimony).

## The Sixth Seal: Terror – The Day of Atonement

12 - And when I saw the Lamb open the sixth seal (over The Heavenly Scroll), there was a great Earthquake (Revelation 16:18) and the Sun withheld its light resembling a sackcloth of goat hair, and the whole moon turned blood red (to reveal The Sign of the Son of Man a bright light in the constellation ORION).

13 - And the stars of the sky fell to the Earth resembling unripe figs dropping from a tree shaken by a great wind (at the Sign of the Son of Man - Matthew 24:29-31).

> **Matthew 24**
> 29 Immediately after the tribulation of those (10) days (of Awe): 'The Sun will be darkened, and the moon will not give its light; the stars will fall from the sky, and the powers of the Heavens will be shaken.' 30 At that time the sign of the Son of Man will appear in The Heavenly Scroll (ORION), and all the tribes of the Earth will mourn. They will see (ORION) the Son of Man coming on the clouds of Heaven, with power and great glory. 31 And He will send out His angels with a loud trumpet call (Feast of Trumpets), and they will gather His elect from the four winds, from one end of the Heavens to the other....

14 - The Heavens receded resembling a Scroll being rolled up (to be read by the Son of Man) and every mountain and island was moved from its place.

15 - Then the kings of the Earth, the nobles, the commanders, the rich, the mighty, and every slave and free man hid in the caves and among the rocks of the mountains.

16 - And they (the unrighteous) said to the mountains and the rocks, "Fall on us and hide us from the face of the one (Yahusha) seated on the Throne in Heaven, and from the wrath of the Lamb.

17 - For the Great Day of their wrath has come (Great and Terrible Day of Yahuah as prophesied - Joel 2:31, Zephaniah 1:14-18), and who is able to withstand it?

> **Joel 2**
> 28 And it shall come to pass afterward, that I will pour out my spirit upon all flesh (AQUARIUS); and your sons and your daughters shall prophesy, your old men shall dream dreams, your young men shall see visions: 29 And also upon the servants and upon the handmaids in those days will I pour out my spirit. 30 And I will shew wonders in the Heavens and in the Earth, blood, and fire, and pillars of smoke. 31 The Sun shall be turned into darkness, and the moon into blood, before the great and terrible day of Yahuah comes. 32 And it shall come to pass, that whosoever shall call on the name "Yahuah shall be saved" (Yahusha means "Yahuah shall be saved").

# Chapter 7

# Introduction

In the last Chapter 6, John has seen the effects on mankind of the Battle of the Ages during the Age of PISCES. That Battle begins to turn going into Chapter 7 beginning with a short break in the action.

## The Interlude

Revelation 7 is a pause between the sixth and seventh seals during which John sees a throng of people before the throne of Yahuah too many to count, loudly proclaiming "Salvation belongs to our God Yahuah, who sits on the throne, and to the Lamb Yahusha" (*Revelation 7:10*).

We are given an inside look at Yahuah's Grace and Salvation during the time of "tribulation on Earth" where this Earth is judged for violating the Everlasting Covenant of the Sabbath and breaking His Laws.

> **Isaiah 24**
> 4 The Earth mourns and withers; the world languishes and fades; the exalted of the Earth waste away. 5 The Earth is defiled by its people; they have transgressed the laws; they have overstepped the decrees and broken the everlasting covenant. 6Therefore a curse has consumed the Earth, and its inhabitants must bear the guilt; the Earth's dwellers have been burned, and only a few survive....

The winds that blow from the 4 corners are Yahuah's judgment of the Earth, and the four angels are restrain or hold back the judgment until Yahuah's special servants can be sealed on their foreheads for protection, of which there are 144,000. "The 144,000 Sealed Servants" are those sealed over the 2,000-year Age of PISCES as the first four Seals are broken. The number 144,000 is symbolic of the number of perfect government (*12x12*).

- Yahuah's breath/Spirit/wind is withheld from blowing His Inspiration on the Earth

- The sealed servants of Yahuah set apart before the destruction of the Earth.

- 144000 is the total number given, this number like the rest of this vision is a VISION and symbolic.

- Twelve thousand from each tribe are sealed: from Judah, Reuben, Gad, Asher, Naphtali, Manasseh, Simeon, Levi, Issachar, Zebulun, Joseph, and Benjamin.

- A great multitude who came out of the Great Tribulation present themselves in white robes, with palm branches in their hands.

Concerning the 144k, this number represents the perfect number from each of the 12 tribes of Israel chosen for the Kingdom of Yahuah. Only a "very few" find the narrow gate (*which is properly keeping Passover as Yahusha set the example and overcoming the Dragon*).

### Matthew 7

13 Enter through the narrow gate. For wide is the gate and broad is the way that leads to destruction, and many enter through it (Revelation 21:7). 14 But small is the gate and narrow the way that leads to life, and only a few find it (those that overcome the Dragon Revelation 21:7). 15 Beware of false prophets. They come to you in sheep's clothing, but inwardly they are ravenous wolves....

It is these that have overcome The Dragon by believing in and keeping The Word of His Testimony as their own...

### Revelation 12:11

They triumphed over him by the blood of the Lamb and by the word of their testimony (which is keeping The Word of His Testimony found in the stars... faith in Yahusha see Revelation 2:13); they did not love their lives so much as to shrink from death.

### Revelation 6:9

And when the Lamb opened the fifth seal (of The Heavenly Scroll), I saw under the (rainbow) altar (in The Heavenly Scroll) the souls of those who had been slain for the word of God (preserved in the stars Psalm 119:89, Psalm 89:2) and for the testimony (of Yahuah's written in the stars) they had upheld (or "held fast" Revelation 2:13, Hebrews 10:23, Hebrews 3:6, to The Plan of Salvation written in The Heavenly Scroll).

### Revelation 7:14

"Sir," I answered, "you know." So he replied, "These are the ones who have come out of the great tribulation; they have washed their robes and made them white in the blood of the Lamb.

The number 144,000 is not literal it is a physical to spiritual parallel of perfection 12x12, like the number of disciples (*12*). There are many more than 144,000. Relative to the number of humans ever created (*about 15 billion*) whatever the actual number is it is a very small remnant.

The number 12 represents governmental perfect. Yahusha came to establish the Kingdom of Yahuah which is a divine government, his choosing 12 disciples was symbolic of setting up the kingdom... 144,000 is symbolic of those who inhabit His Kingdom. For more information on the number 144, please see:

http://www.biblestudy.org/bibleref/meaning-of-numbers-in-bible/12.html

# 24 Elders and 12 Judges

There is speculation that the 24 Elders could be the 24 Kings over Israel. I reject that list because many of those kings were pagan rebellious men who would not have been raised by Yahuah but instead were judged for their idolatry against Him. They would NOT live eternally to sit on those coveted seats/thrones and would not have been awarded crowns by Yahuah to rule by the side of the King Yahusha. They were guilty of Spiritual Fornication with those pagan deities, the worst of crimes against the Kingdom. We read in ***The International Standard Bible Encyclopedia***:

> Star-worship seems to have been an enticement to Israel from the first (Deuteronomy 4:19; 17:3; Amos 5:26; compare Acts 7:42,43), <u>but this idolatry attained special prominence in the days of the later kings of Judah.</u> The name of Manasseh is particularly connected with it. This king built altars for "all the host of Heaven" (*worshipping the Signs of the Zodiac*) in the courts of the temple
>
> > **Kings 21:3-5**
> > 3 For he rebuilt the high places which Hezekiah his father had destroyed; and he erected altars for Baal and made an Asherah, as Ahab king of Israel had done, and worshiped all the host of Heaven and served them. 4 And he built altars in the house of Yahuah, of which Yahuah had said, "In Jerusalem I will put My name 5 For he built altars for all the host of Heaven in the two courts of the house of Yahuah."
>
> Josiah destroyed these altars, and cleansed the temple from the idolatry by putting down the priests and burning the vessels associated with it.
>
> > **2 Kings 23:4-5**
> > Then the king commanded Hilkiah the high priest and the priests of the second order and the doorkeepers, to bring out of the temple of Yahuah all the vessels that were made for Baal, for Asherah, and for all the host of Heaven; and he burned them outside Jerusalem in the fields of the Kidron, and carried their ashes to Bethel. And he did away with the <u>idolatrous priests whom the kings of Judah had appointed to burn incense in the high places</u> in the cities of Judah and in the surrounding area of Jerusalem, also those <u>who burned incense to Baal, to the Sun and to the moon and to the constellations and to all the host of Heaven</u> (constellations of the Zodiac)

These idolatrous Kings caused Israel to be judged and taken into captivity, they were not even blessed on Earth and the thrones they were given were in most cases taken away along with their children's crowns! Ultimately the entire line of Kings was suspended due to their idolatry against the Most High. They were not later honored in the seats reigning next to Yahusha.

Below are those I believe are Elders in the Kingdom of Yahuah. Those raised eternal to sit on the 24 thrones with Crowns of Gold on their heads with positions of respect and authority in the Kingdom next to Yahusha the King. The list below represents those few men in history who have shaped our faith, heard directly from Yahuah, many gave their lives for His Truths. They are His Prophets and Signatories to His Covenants:

# 24 Elders

1. Isaiah - Prophet
2. Jeremiah - Prophet
3. Ezekiel - Prophet
4. Daniel - Prophet
5. Elijah - Prophet
6. Samuel - Prophet
7. Enoch - Prophet
8. Hosea - Prophet
9. Joel - Prophet
10. Amos - Prophet
11. Obadiah - Prophet
12. Jonah - Prophet
13. Micah - Prophet
14. Nahum - Prophet
15. Habakkuk - Prophet
16. Zephaniah - Prophet
17. Haggai - Prophet
18. Zechariah - Prophet
19. Malachi - Prophet
20. Adam – Signatory to the Adamic Covenant
21. Noah – Signatory to the Noahic Covenant
22. Abraham – Signatory to the Abrahamic Covenant
23. Moses – Signatory to the Mosaic
24. David – Signatory to the Davidic Covenant

# Judges over the 12 tribes

1.  John the Baptist

2.  Peter

3.  Andrew

4.  James the Just

5.  Philip

6.  Bartholomew

7.  Matthew/ Levi

8.  James, son of Alpheus

9.  Thomas

10.  Simon

11.  Jude Thaddeus

12.  Sha'ul or Judas the Sicarii (this is Yahusha's decision to make)

# Revelation 7 Restored

## 144,000 Sealed Servants of Yahuah

1 - After this I saw four angels (the first Four Trumps of Revelation 8) standing at the four corners (Strong's G1137 – a secret place i.e., 4 cardinal points of The Heavenly Scroll) holding back its four winds (the Ruach) so that no wind would blow (Yahuah does not breath His Spirit on His creation) on land or sea or any tree (for 5 months - Revelation 9).

2 - And I saw another angel ascending from the east, with the seal (Yahuah's Name and the Shema) of the Living God. And the angel called out in a loud voice to the four angels (the first four trumps of Revelation 8) who had been given power to harm the land and the sea.

3 - *"Do not harm the land or sea or trees until we have sealed the foreheads* (minds) *of the servants of Yahuah* (with the Shema, denial of incarnation. This is how we are saved in 'the wilderness' from the Dragon).

4 - And I heard the number of those who were sealed 144,000 from all the (12) tribes of Yisrael. 5 From the tribe of Judah 12,000 were sealed, from the tribe of Reuben 12,000, from the tribe of Gad 12,000, 6 from the tribe of Asher 12,000, from the tribe of Naphtali 12,000, from the tribe of Manasseh 12,000, 7 from the tribe of Simeon 12,000, from the tribe of Levi 12,000, from the tribe of Issachar 12,000, 8 from the tribe of Zebulun 12,000, from the tribe of Joseph 12,000, from the tribe of Benjamin 12,000.

## The Great Multitude from every nation

9 - After this I envisioned a multitude too large to count, from every nation and tribe and people and tongue standing before the throne (represented by the colors of the rainbow) wearing white (wedding) robes and were holding palm branches (symbolic of triumph) in their hands. 10 - And they cried out in a loud voice: "Salvation to our God, who sits on the throne (of creation) and to the Lamb (Proxy King Yahusha who

sits on the throne over the Kingdom that will govern Creation at the Right Hand of the Creator),

*John again describes the source of his vision...*
*The Enoch Zodiac/Heavenly Scroll*

11 - And all the angels (represented by stars in the sky) stood around the throne and around the elders (represented by the twenty-four stars in the Enoch Zodiac throne room falling before The Rainbow Throne) and the four living creatures (surrounding The Rainbow Throne).

*24 stars "falling" before the rainbow throne,*
*4 living creatures singing "holy, holy, holy"*

And they (elders represented by the 24 stars in the center of the Enoch Zodiac above) fell face down before the throne and worshiped Yahuah. 12 - Saying, *"Hallelu Yahuah! Blessing and glory and wisdom and thanks and honor and power and strength to our God forever and ever! Hallelu Yahuah."*

136

13 - Then one of the elders addressed me: "*These in white* (fine linen wedding) *robes*", he asked, "*who are they, and where have they come from?*" 14 - "*Sir.*" I answered, "*you know.*" So he replied, "*These are the ones* (Chosen Few) *who have come out of the great tribulation* (Age of PISCES*); they have washed their robes* (through Mikveh) *and made* (their robes) *white* (Righteous*) in the blood* (sacrifice) *of the Lamb* (walking with Him in The Way i.e. the Doctrine of Righteousness). 15 - *For this reason* (because they walked The Way), *they are before the throne of Yahuah and serve Him day and night in Yahuah's temple* (the body of His Elect who are living stones sat upon The Chief Cornerstone Yahusha*); and the one seated on the throne* (in Heaven) *will dwell* (g4637 – dwell) *among, together, and within* (g1909 – together/within)

# 4637. skénoó

*Word Origin*

from skéné

*Definition*

to have one's tent, dwell

*NASB Translation*

dwell (3), dwelt (1), spread His tabernacle (1).

## ◀ 1909. epi ▶

*NASB Translation*

about (4), above (2), after (2), against (41), among any (2), around (2), basis (4), because (2), because* (2), bedridden* (1), before (24), besides (1), beyond (1), certainly* (2), chamberlain* (1), charge (1), concerning (4), connection (1), embraced* (2), extent* (2), further* (3), inasmuch* (1), onto (1), over (57), passenger* (1), point (1), referring (1), time (3), together (7), toward (5), truly* (2), under (1), under* (1), view (1) within (1).

*them* (the Temple of Yahuah is the body of his elect, Yahusha dwells in that Temple ministering at the altar of their heart - Revelation 21:22, 1 Cor 3:16, Hebrews 10:19).

16 - *Never again will they hunger,* (for My righteousness - Matthew 5:6) *and never will they thirst,* (for Living Water - John 7:38) *nor will the Sun beat down on them, nor any scorching heat* (of Tribulation - Daniel 12:1, Revelation 7:14).

## The Angel Reads The Heavenly Scroll to John

17 - *For the Lamb* (Yahusha*) in the center of the throne* (in Heaven) *will be their* (the Chosen Elect i.e. Nazarene's) *shepherd* (TAURUS). (The Great Shepherd) *Yahusha* (Hebrews 13:20-21, TAURUS) *will lead them to springs of living water* (represented by AQUARIUS in The Heavenly Scroll) *and Yahuah will wipe away every tear from their eyes."*

> **TAURUS**: The conquering Ruler comes, the sublime vanquisher, to execute the great judgment, he is the ruling Shepherd King.

> **AQUARIUS**: He pours out "living water" from on high, humanity drinks of the Heavenly river and the faithful live again

> **Hebrews 13:20-21**
> 20 Now may the God of peace (Yahuah), who through the blood of the eternal covenant brought back from the dead our King and great Shepherd Yahusha, 21 equip you with everything good for doing His (Yahuah's) will, and may He work in us what is pleasing to Him through the Yahushaic Covenant, to whom (Yahuah) be glory for ever and ever. HalleluYahuah!

# Chapter 8

# Introduction

After the interlude in Chapter 7, the Battle of the Ages turns in favor of the Prince of Peace waging war against the Dragon. It is the first 4 Trumpets that begin sounding on Yom Teruah (*Trumpets*) and take us to The Day of Yahuah (*Atonement Yom Kippur*) when a massive sacrifice of atonement is made on Earth.

- Yahusha opens the seventh seal and there is silence in Heaven for about a half an hour.

- Gabriel is given the seventh trumpet.

- The 24-elders offer incense and the prayers of all the saints, at the golden altar before the throne.

- After the smoke and the prayers ascend to Yahuah, the Elders fill the censer with fire, from the altar, and throws it to the Earth causing noises, thunderings, lightnings, and an Earthquake.

- The **first** angel sounded his trumpet: "And hail and fire followed, mingled with blood, and they were thrown to the Earth" burning a third of the Earth's flora, scorching all green grass.

- The **second** angel sounded his trumpet: "And something like a great mountain burning with fire was thrown in the sea, and a third of the sea became blood" killing a third of everything in the ocean.

- The **third** angel sounded and waters and rivers and springs were poisoned by the great star, named Wormwood falling from Heaven.

- The **fourth** angel sounded: The Sun, the moon and stars are struck, so that a third of their light diminished to the point of complete darkness for a third of a day, even during the night.

- Another angel appears to declare three "Woes" for the next three trumpet blasts.

In this chapter, Yahusha breaks the seventh seal over The Heavenly Scroll revealing the full Plan of Salvation written in the stars at creation. This prompts a moment of silence of about half an hour. This silence follows a time of jubilation in Heaven we see in Revelation Chapter 7. Then there is a sudden and dramatic silence as the Judge enters the courtroom and sits on His Throne. We see this event in Daniel:

### Daniel 7

1 In the first year of Baalshazzar king of Babylon, Daniyl had a dream, and visions in his mind (as he studied The Heavenly Scroll of Enoch) as he lay on his bed (looking up at the stars and constellations). Then he wrote down his dream (*H2493*. A revelation from Yahuah, he was not asleep, he was wide awake writing down his visions), beginning the account of these matters: 2 Daniyl spoke, and said; I saw (The Heavenly Scroll) in my vision by night (by night - because he was observing the stars, not sleeping), and behold (in The Heavenly Scroll), ... 9 I beheld (the Enoch Zodiac) until the 4 thrones were set in place (the 4 living creatures on the outer rim of the Enoch Zodiac that move it about until they had moved The Heavenly Scroll in position), and the Ancient of days (Yahuah) did sit (on the judgement seat), Whose vesture was white as snow, and the hair of His head like the pure wool; His throne was like the fiery flame, and His wheels as burning fire (the judgment seat/rainbow thrown sits on wheels of fire).

10 A fiery stream issued (from His mouth) and came forth from before Him (His words are like an all-consuming fire Jeremiah 23:29 and Hebrews 12:29); thousand upon thousands (of stars in the Heavens) ministered to Him, and ten thousand times ten thousand (of stars) stood before Him (stars are symbolic of angels); the judgment was set (or rather the Judge Yahuah, had taken His seat, the battle is about to begin between the Son of Man and the Son of Perdition), and the books (of The Heavenly Scroll, there are 3 books as I revealed in Creation Cries Out!) were opened (to see who had fulfilled it).

Much like in our courts of law today when the Judge enters the room and all stand in silence. Now all of Creation can see the plan laid out from the foundation of the world and Yahuah's Righteousness to judge the wicked and destroy evil is on full display! Job comes to mind:

**Job 40:4**
"I am unworthy--how can I reply to you? I put my hand over my mouth.

With The Heavenly Scroll laid open and the coming judgments on full display, all Creation "puts their hand over their mouth" in total silence, not even a breath is heard as The Plan of Salvation is brought to its conclusion by The Creator. The 7 Angels are handed their 7 Trumpets to blow to introduce the bowl judgments. This Earth is about to enter The Day of Yahuah and pay for its sin, the worst period of human history is about to begin (*Mark 13:19-20*). This prompts a moment of total silence and complete stillness with awesome expectation.

**Zechariah 2:13**
Be silent, all flesh before Yahuah, for he has roused himself from his holy dwelling

**Zephaniah 1:7**
Be silent before the Sovereign Creator, for the day of Yahuah is near

**Habakkuk 2:20**
Yahuah is in his holy temple; let all the Earth be silent before him"

In this chapter we see the fulfillment of Isaiah and The Great and Terrible Day of Yahuah where Yahuah offers the remaining people of Earth to atone for sin.

**Isaiah 9**
See, the day of Yahuah is coming —a cruel day, with wrath and fierce anger— to make the land desolate and destroy the sinners within it. 10 The stars of Heaven and their constellations will not show their light. The rising Sun will be darkened and the moon will not give its light. 11 I will punish the world for its evil, the wicked for their sins.

**Isaiah 24**
4 The Earth mourns and withers; the world languishes and fades; the exalted of the Earth waste away. 5 The Earth is defiled by its people; they have transgressed the laws; they have overstepped the decrees and broken the everlasting covenant of the Sabbath. 6 Therefore a curse has consumed the Earth, and its inhabitants must bear the guilt; the Earth's dwellers have been burned, and only a few survive....

# Revelation 8 Restored

## *The Seventh Seal - Completion*

1 - When the Lamb opened the seventh seal (over The Heavenly Scroll), there was silence in the Heavens for about half an hour. 2 - And I saw the seventh messenger (the one) who stands before Yahuah (who is Gabriel see Luke 1:19), and Gabriel was given the seventh trumpet.

3 - Then other messengers (called Elders - Revelation 5:8), who had a golden censer came and stood at the (golden) alter. They were given much incense, representing the prayers of all the saints, to offer on the golden alter before the Throne in Heaven. 4 - And the smoke of the incense, together with the prayers of the saints, rose up before Yahuah from the hand of Gabriel.

> **Revelation 5:8**
> 8 And when he had taken the Scroll, the four living creatures and the twenty-four elders fell down before the Lamb, each holding a harp, and golden bowls full of incense, which are the prayers of the saints. 9 And they sang a new song…

5 - Then Gabriel took the (golden) censer, filled it with fire (judgment, Yahusha is the Great Judge, TAURUS, Matthew 25) from the (golden) alter, and hurled it to the Earth; and (as the King returned) there were peals of thunder, thundering, flashes of lightening and an Earthquake (Revelation 6:12, Revelation 16:18, Psalm 18).

> **Psalm 18**
> 6 In my distress I called to Yahuah; I cried to my God for help. From his temple he heard my voice; my cry came before him, into his ears. 7 *The Earth trembled and quaked*, and the foundations of the mountains shook; they trembled because he was angry. 8 Smoke rose from his nostrils; consuming fire came from his mouth, burning coals blazed out of it. 9 He parted the Heavens and came down; dark clouds were under his feet. 10 He mounted the cherubim and flew; he soared on the wings of the wind. 11 He made darkness his covering, his canopy around him — the dark rain clouds of the sky. 12 *Out of the brightness of his presence clouds advanced, with hailstones and bolts of lightning*.
> 13 *Yahuah thundered from Heaven*, the voice of the Most High resounded. 14 He shot his arrows and scattered the enemy, *with great bolts of lightning* he routed them. 15 The valleys of the sea were exposed, and the foundations of the Earth laid bare at your rebuke, Yahuah, at the blast of breath from your nostrils

## *The First Four Trumpets*
## *The Coming of the King and the Day of Yahuah*

6 - And the seven angels with the seven trumpets prepared to sound them (on The Feast of Trumpets).

7 - Then the first angel sounded his trumpet, and hail rained down upon the Earth. A third of the Earth was burned up, along with a third of the trees and all the green grass.

8 - Then the second angel sounded his trumpet, and something resembling a great mountain burning with fire was thrown into the sea (Jeremiah 51:25). A third of the sea turned to blood.

> **Jeremiah 51:25**
> *"I am against you, you 'destroying mountain', you who destroy the whole Earth,"* declares Yahuah. *"I will stretch out my hand against you, roll you off the cliffs, and make you a burned-out mountain"*

9 - A third of the living creatures in the sea died, and a third of the ships were destroyed.

10 The third angel sounded his trumpet, and a great morning star (Lucifer defeated by Michael was cast down - Isaiah 14:12, Daniel 12:1, Revelation 12), blazing like a torch, fell from the sky on a third of the rivers and on the springs of water.

> **Isaiah 14:12**
> 12 How you have fallen from Heaven, morning star, son of the dawn! You have been cast down to the Earth, you who once laid low the nations!

> **Revelation 12:12**
> Therefore rejoice, you Heavens and you who dwell in them! But woe to the Earth and the sea, because the devil has been cast down (by Michael) to you! He is filled with fury, because he knows that his time is short."

> **Daniel 12:1**
> 1"At that time Michael, the great prince who stands watch over your people, will rise up (and ascend to Heaven to battle the Dragon – Revelation 12). There will be a time of distress, the likes of which will not have occurred from the beginning of nations until that time. But at that time your people—everyone whose name is found written in the book—will be delivered.

**Revelation 12:7-9**

7 Then war broke out in Heaven. Michael and his angels fought against the dragon, and the dragon and his angels fought back. 8 But he was not strong enough, and they lost their place in Heaven. 9 The great dragon was hurled down—that ancient serpent called the devil, or Satan, who leads the whole world astray. He was hurled to the Earth, and his angels with him.

11 the morning star was a poisonous curse (Wormwood means a poisonous curse). A third of the waters turned bitter, and many people died from the waters that had become bitter.

12 - Then the fourth angel sounded his trumpet and a third of the Sun and moon and stars were struck. A third of the stars were darkened a third of the day was without light and a third of the night as well (the Day of Yahuah is coming with the next 3 trumpets come see Isaiah 13:9-11).

13 - And as I observed, I heard an eagle (AQUILLA Decan) flying overhead (John continues revealing the contents of The Heavenly Scroll's contents),

*Aquilla Decan – The Flying Eagle*

calling in a loud voice of "Woe! Woe! Woe! to those who dwell on the Earth, because of the 3 trumpet blasts about to be sounded by the remaining 3 messengers".

145

# Chapter 9

# Introduction

The 5th and 6th Trumpets occur concurrently with the prior 4 Trumpets. Trumpets 1-6 are blown during the 10-days of Tribulation rehearsed each year during the 10 Days of Awe between Yom Teruah and Yom Kippur. The Son of Man wages all-out war on Earth and overcomes the Dragon and those who follow her.

- The **fifth** angel sounds his trumpet signaling the First woe.

- A star falls from Heaven to the Earth and is given the key to the bottomless pit.

- The pit is opened, and smoke rises causing the Earth to fall into darkness.

- *Locusts* come out of the smoke coming out of the bottomless pit, and Abaddon commands them to torment any man who does not have the seal of Yahuah on his forehead. This lasts for five months.

- The **sixth** angel sounds his trumpet for announcing the Second woe.

- The *four angels* bound at the great river Euphrates are released.

- A massive 200-million-man army raised by the four angels cross the Euphrates River invading the Middle East from the Far East. A third of mankind dies.

# The 5 Months of Darkness

### Revelation 9:5, 10

5 They were allowed to torment them for **five months**, but not to kill them, and their torment was like the torment of a scorpion when it stings someone... 10 They have tails and stings like scorpions, and their power to hurt people for **five months** is in their tails.

Each year there is what is called The Annual Day and the Annual Night at Earth's North Pole. It is a time when the Sun shines at the North Pole continuously for 7 months (*March 4 – October 6*).

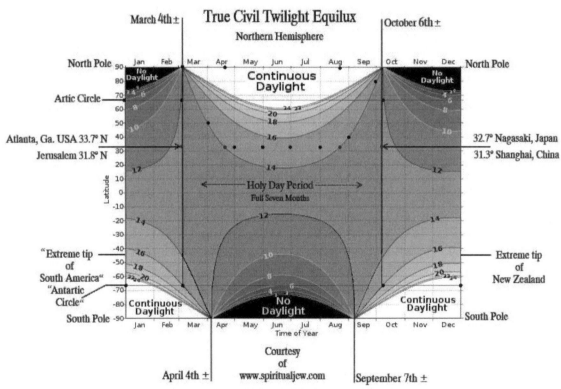

The Beginning of Months and all Holy Days should fall within the seven months "Holy Day Period" shown in chart in pink.

The Annual Day is when Yahuah's Feasts are celebrated. This is when all of the Northern Hemisphere is in sync with Jerusalem. Yahuah's people are called *"children of the day"* as we keep the Creator's holy days during the Annual Day.

The Annual Night runs from October thru the end of February (*5 months*). This 5 months of physical darkness is also a time of Spiritual Darkness when the false religion, *children of the night*, celebrate the Babylonian Festivals of Halloween, Christmas, New Year Eve, etc. This 5 months of darkness we call Winter is when the Sun shines less and there is more darkness than light and the foliage dies and turns brown. In this physical shadow we find a Spiritual Parallel between the battle of "the Sun" and "darkness" as the Earth is furthest from the Sun and its healing wings.

In The Plan of Salvation celebrated each year in The Feast Cycle, these 5 months of "darkness" runs from the end of Sukkot to the Passover. This is ESPECIALLY important. It is when Yahusha "spreads his tabernacles over us" and we are "taken to the wilderness" and protected from the wrath of Yahuah. Yahusha return on the Feast of Tabernacles, followed by the 10 days of awe (*tribulation*),

> ### Revelation 2:10
> Do not be afraid of what you are about to suffer. I tell you, the devil will put some of you in prison to test you, and you will suffer tribulation (persecution) for ten days. Be faithful, even to the point of death, and I will give you life as your victor's crown.

then The Day of Yahuah on Yom Kippur. We are taken "to the wilderness on the wings of an Eagle" and protected (*Sukkot*) and then Earth enters the 5 months of "darkness" leading up to a "new year" and a "new day" on Passover. This represents the beginning of the 1,000-year reign.

# Scorpion Sting Metaphor

As we witnessed in Chapter 7, the four angels hold back the four "winds" and Yahuah's Grace, Mercy, and Ruach, are withheld from the inhabitants of the Earth. There is no more forgiveness or mercy for sin. The time has come to pay up and with that come the "sting of a scorpion".

The "sting of a scorpion" is a metaphor used to illustrate the effects of sin on the heart and mind. In this period, salvation is closed and there is no forgiveness or reprieve from sin. It just compiles from one sin to the next and love "grows cold" and the heart hardens leading to panic and terror outside the Love of Yahuah. The symptom of a scorpion sting is the same effects of a "panic attack". The reality of events and compounding effects of sin cause the hearts of man to fail with sure panic. Below are the common symptoms of both a "scorpion sting" and a "panic attack":

- Difficulty breathing

- Drooling, sweating, nausea and vomiting

- Restlessness or excitability or insoluble crying

- Muscle twitching or thrashing

- High blood pressure (Hypertension)

- Accelerated heart rate (Tachycardia)

- Unusual head, neck and eye movements

We see the effect of the curse found in violation of The Torah prophesied in Isaiah 24:

### Isaiah 24
4 The Earth mourns and withers; the world languishes and fades; the exalted of the Earth waste away. 5 The Earth is defiled by its people; they have transgressed the laws; they have overstepped the decrees and broken the everlasting covenant of the Sabbath. 6 Therefore a curse has consumed the Earth, and its inhabitants must bear the guilt; the Earth's dwellers have been burned, and only a few survive....

Love has grown cold and humanity has failed in keeping the most basic aspect of Yahuah's Righteousness… to "honor your father and mother" and "love your neighbor as yourself".

### Matthew 24:12
Because lawlessness is increased, the love of most people will grow cold.

As love grows cold so does the heart, and with that comes the sting of a scorpion.

# Revelation 9 Restored

## *The Fifth Trumpet*

1 - Then the 5th angel sounded his trumpet and I saw a star (Satan) that has fallen from (the Throne in) Heaven (Luke 10:18) to the Earth and she (Satan) was given a key to the abyss (Sheol/Hades). 2 - The (morning) star (Satan) opened the pit of the abyss and smoke (lies/false doctrines John 8:44) rose out of it resembling the smoke of a great furnace and the (light of the) Sun and the air (Spiritual inspiration) were darkened (the Dragon's lies blots out the Sun and moon Acts 2:20, Joel 2:31, Revelation 6:12 meaning obscure the meaning of The Heavenly Scroll) by the smoke (false doctrines) from the pit (of hell such as incarnation the Spirit of the False Messiah).

3 - And out of the smoke (lies); locusts (the rest of Lucifer's angelic army Revelation 12:9)

> ### Revelation 12:9
> 9 The great dragon was hurled down—that ancient serpent called the devil, or Satan, who leads the whole world astray. He was hurled to the Earth, and his angels with him.

descended on the Earth and were given power **resembling** the sting of scorpions of the Earth (cause panic and anxiety).

> **NOTE**: This is the time frame Yahusha spoke about in Luke:

> ### Luke 21
> 25 There will be signs in the Sun and moon and stars (Revelation 12), and on the Earth will cause dismay among the nations, bewildered by the roaring of the sea and the surging of the waves (global unrest). 26 Men will faint from **fear and anxiety** over what is coming upon the Earth (Lucifer and her angels with her are cast to Earth Revelation 12), for the powers of the Heavens will be shaken (by the war in Heaven). 27 At that time they will see the (Sign of the) Son of Man coming in a cloud with power and great glory (will understand the meaning of The Heavenly Scroll and realize it is TRUE; - Matthew 24:30) ....

> ***Scorpion sting***: Some common symptoms of a scorpion sting are a tingling or burning at the sting site, numbness, difficulty swallowing, difficulty breathing, blurry vision, or seizures.

*__Panic/Anxiety Attack:__* Some common symptoms of a panic attack are numbness, tingling, feel like you are choking (difficulty swallowing), shortness of breath (trouble breathing), dizziness (blurry vision), shaking and trembling (seizure)

4 - They were told not to harm the grass of the Earth or any plant or tree (fruit of the Earth metaphorically speaking of mankind) only those who do not have the Seal of Yahuah (YHVH – He alone is God) on their foreheads (metaphor for "what you believe"). 5 – And for 5 months, the locusts (fallen angels) were given power to kill them (those not sealed) and their torment (for the rest of humanity) **resembles** the stinging of a scorpion (causes panic and anxiety).

6 - In those days men will seek death (as severe depression befalls mankind from panic and anxiety) and they will not to find it (the Dragon has the key to the abyss and her goal is to torment not kill); they will long to die but death will escape them.

7 - And the locusts (fallen angels) looked like horses prepared for battle with something resembling crowns of gold on their heads (mankind worships these fallen angels) and faces resembling the faces of men (they are worshipped in the form of demi-gods i.e., Jesus the False Messiah). 8 - They had hair resembling that of a woman, and teeth resembling those of lions.  9 - they had breastplates like breastplates of iron, and the noise of their wings was like the noise of many chariots with horses rushing into battle. 10 They have tails and stings like scorpions, and their power to hurt people for five months is in their tails. 11 They have as king over them, the angel (with the keys to the) abyss. His name in Hebrew is Abaddon (Job 26:6), and in Greek he is called Apollyon (Destroyer - 1 Peter 5:8).

12 - The first woe has passed. Behold two woes are still to follow.

## The Sixth Trumpet

13 Then the sixth angel blew his trumpet, and I heard a voice (of the Son of Man coming) from the four horns (g2768: symbol of power) of the golden altar before Yahuah, 14 saying to the sixth angel who had the trumpet, "Release the four angels (Revelation 7:1) who are bound at the great river Euphrates (Revelation 16:12)."

### Revelation 16:12

12 The sixth angel poured out his bowl on the great river Euphrates and its water was dried up, to prepare the way for the kings from the east.

15 So the four angels, who had been prepared for the hour, the day, the month, and the year, were released to kill a third of mankind.

16 The number of mounted troops was twice ten thousand times ten thousand; I heard their number.

17 And this is how I saw the horses in my vision and those who rode them: they wore breastplates the color of fire and of Hyacinthus (a flower with blue blooms) and of sulfur (yellow), and the heads of the horses were like lions' heads, and fire and smoke and sulfur came out of their mouths. 18 By these three plagues a third of mankind was killed, by the fire and smoke and sulfur coming out of their mouths. 19 For the power of the horses is in their mouths and in their tails, for their tails are like serpents with heads, and by means of them they wound.

20 The rest of mankind, who were not killed by these plagues, did not repent of the works of their hands nor give up worshiping demons and idols of gold and silver and bronze and stone and wood, which cannot see or hear or walk, 21 nor did they repent of their murders or their sorceries or their sexual immorality or their thefts (because the love of their hearts had grown cold).

# Chapter 10

# Introduction

The 7th Trumpet sounds on Yom Kippur. After Yahusha makes atonement, the 7th Trumpet is sounded by Gabriel to announce Yahusha as the fulfillment of The Heavenly Scroll. This is the same event Daniel witnessed in Daniel chapter 7 as The Son of Man is judged alongside The Dragon (*False Messiah*). Yahuah anoints the Son of Man the King over The Kingdom and fulfillment of The Heavenly Scroll.

- The mighty King (messenger/malak means 'king' in Hebrew) appears standing with one foot on the sea and the other on land, holding The Heavenly Scroll to reach it as he descends from The Throne in Heaven.

- The King cries out the Mystery of the Ages written in The Heavenly Scroll sounds like seven (perfect) thunderings.

- The apostle John is commanded to seal up what the thunders say about The Heavenly Scroll, and not reveal its contents.

- The King declares that the Mystery of God found in The Heavenly Scroll to redeem a family from the grave would be revealed on the sounding of the seventh trumpet.

- John, like many Prophets before him, is instructed to take The Heavenly Scroll and to eat it.

What is it that the King read out of The Heavenly Scroll that John was told to seal up and not write down? It is called *The Mystery of the Ages*. The secrets contained in the stars that mankind has striven to learn since creation!

### Enoch 9:6,7
6 Thou seest what Azazel hath done, who hath taught all unrighteousness on Earth and revealed (twisted) the eternal secrets which were (preserved) in The Heavenly Scroll, which 7 men were striving to learn.

Let us discern this Mystery from context of the Scriptures and finally reveal at the "end" what the 7 Thunders proclaimed written in the stars since creation.

# Do not to write down The Mystery of the Ages

**Revelation 10**

4 I was about to write (what was revealed in The Heavenly Scroll), but I heard a voice from Heaven saying, "Seal up what the seven thunders have said, and do not write it down." ... 7 but that in the days of the trumpet call to be sounded by the seventh angel, the Mystery of God (proclaimed in The Heavenly Scroll) would be fulfilled (Revelation 11:15-19),

The Mystery of Yahuah, hidden from the foundation of the Universe in The Heavenly Scroll, is that Yahuah's predestined plan was to procreate a family of "godlike ones" called Elohim in His Image to rule His Creation given them as an inheritance. Humanity has sought the answer in the stars to the question "why are we here" since creation. Each one of these family members, like the first born-again son, were known before the foundation of the world.

**Romans 8**

28 And we know that Yahuah works all things (after the Divine Council written in the stars Daniel 4:35)

**Daniel 4:35**

"All the inhabitants of the Earth are accounted as nothing, but He does according to His will written in the host of Heaven (The Zodiac which hosts constellations. Constellations "host stars")

together for the good of those who love Him, who are called according to His purpose (to beget a family of Gods Psalm 82:6).

**Psalm 82:6**

"I said, 'You are "gods"; you are all sons of the Most High.'

29 For those Yahuah knew before the foundation of the world (Ephesians 1:4),

**Ephesians 1:4**

For Yahuah chose us in covenant with Yahusha before the creation of the world to be holy and blameless in his sight. In love

He also predestined to be conformed to the image of His (firstborn of the dead) son, so that Yahusha would be the firstborn among many brothers (born of the resurrection, he is our elder brother not our God). 30 And those Yahuah predestined (as children), He also called; those He called, He also justified; those He justified, He also glorified....

This family is likened unto a "body" which will be the Spiritual Temple of Yahuah in and through which Yahuah dwells. The head of this body is the first-born son Yahusha, and the body is the assembly of Chosen Sons of Yahuah known as Remnant Israel. It is through this family of "godlike ones" or elohim that the Universe will be governed in righteousness for eternity by the Kingdom of Yahuah. This body is His Temple the risen sons of Yahuah.

Below are the scriptures to support this revelation with my commentary in parenthesis. We see Sha'ul in Hebrews explain that we and the Messiah are "brothers and sisters" all sons and daughters of Yahuah.

### Hebrews 2:10-18

10 In bringing many sons and daughters to glory, it was fitting that Yahuah, for whom and through whom everything exists; (Yahuah) should make the pioneer of their salvation (Yahusha) perfect through what he suffered (a life and death on Earth). 11 Both the one who makes people holy (Yahuah) and those who are made holy (Yahusha and all his brother/sisters) are of the same family (we are literally "elohim" and offspring of Yahuah). So Yahusha is not ashamed to call them (Remnant Israel) brothers and sisters (Yahusha is our elder brother, not our Elohim). 12 He says, "I (Yahusha) will declare Your Name (Yahusha declares the Shema or "Seal" of the Kingdom of Yahuah) to my brothers and sisters; in the assembly I will sing Your praises (we don't sing praises to "Jesus" we worship Yahuah alone)." 13 And again, "I (Yahusha) will put my trust in Him (Yahuah)." And again he says, "Here am I, and the (rest of the) children Yahuah has given me (to shepherd and rule)." 14 Since the (future) children have flesh and blood (are trained by a life on Earth), he (Yahusha) too shared in their humanity (as a human trained by a life on Earth) so that by his death (Yahusha's NOT Yahuah's) he, Yahusha, might break the power of him who holds the power of death that is, the devil (the blood of Yahusha covers the decrees in the Law overcoming the Law of Sin and Death. With the decrees in the Law covered; the Law then becomes the Law of the Spirit of Life)— 15 and free those who all their lives were held in slavery by their fear of death (Yahusha freed us from the Law of Sin and Death by covering the decrees in the Law that demand our death. We are not held in slavery to the Law but fear of death for disobeying it). 16 For surely it is not angels Yahusha helps, but Abraham's descendants (the bloodline of the sons of Yahuah remains defined by the Abrahamic Covenant). 17 For this reason he (Yahusha) had to be made like them (he was made human not a demi-god), fully human in every way (can't get any clearer than that, incarnation is a LIE) in order that he might become a merciful and faithful high priest (NOT "God in the flesh" but a Wonderful Counselor Isaiah 9:6) in service to Yahuah (he is Yahuah's High Priest, not Yahuah in the flesh), and that he might make atonement for the sins of the people (because the Law that governs sacrifices and atonement has been transposed to Heaven to serve Melchizedek). 18 Because he

himself suffered when he was tempted, he is able to help those (brothers and sisters in the Family of Yahuah) who are being tempted (as our High Priest).

Next, Sha'ul continues describing this amazing Mystery of the Family of Yahuah. This "family" is known as "Elohim" which means "gods". We are human all came according to the flesh. Yahuah is not human He is "Elohim". Upon resurrection or the transposition of our bodies from physical to Spiritual we too will be "elohim", begotten in Yahuah's full image as sons. We see that pro-creating a family of "gods" was the very "purpose of Yahuah" in creation.

### Ephesians 1

1 Sha'ul, an apostle of Messiah Yahusha by the will of Yahuah, to the saints which are at Ephesus, and to the faithful in (covenant with) Messiah Yahusha: 2 Grace be to you, and peace, from Yahuah our Father (of Elohim), and from the King Messiah Yahusha. 3 Blessed be the Elohim (Sha'ul declares the Shema or "Seal" of the Kingdom of Yahuah) and Father of our King Messiah Yahusha (Yahusha is NOT Yahuah in the flesh), who (Yahuah) hath blessed us (His sons, Elohim) with all spiritual blessings in Heavenly places (The Heavenly Scroll) in (covenant with) Yahusha (we are co-heirs): 4 According (to Yahuah's purpose) as He (Yahuah) hath chosen (predestined) us in covenant with Yahusha (we are in covenant with Yahuah through the Yahushaic Covenant which is a marriage covenant where "the two shall become one". It is in that way that Yahusha and all his brothers/sisters are ONE with Yahuah) before the foundation of the world (it was Yahuah's purpose from the beginning before creation to pro-create a family and govern in with His King written in The Heavenly Scroll), that we should be holy and without blame before Him (Yahuah) in love (through a marriage covenant with the firstborn from the dead son Colossians 1:18): 5 Having predestinated us unto the adoption of children-in-law (through marriage covenant called The Yahushaic Covenant whereby Yahuah becomes our Father by Law) by (the life sacrifice of) Messiah Yahusha to Himself (Yahuah as a sin offering Romans 8:3, Hebrews 9:11-14, 1 Peter 1:18-19, Hebrews 7:27), according to the good pleasure of his (Yahuah's) will (to pro-create a family... His Purpose),

6 To the praise of the glory of His (Yahuah's) grace, wherein Yahuah hath made us (through Yahusha whose blood covers the decrees) accepted in the beloved (family of Elohim). 7 In whom (Messiah Yahusha) we have redemption (from the Law of Sin and Death) through his blood (Yahusha is the Passover Lamb), (we have) the forgiveness of sins (decrees in the Law for violating His Commands are covered by the blood), according to the riches of His (Yahuah's) grace (it is Yahuah who forgives sin and accepts Yahusha's sacrifice to satisfy the decrees that demand our death for breaking His Law, that is the definition of Grace);

8 Wherein (covenant with Yahusha) He (Yahuah) hath abounded toward us (unlimited Grace) in all wisdom and prudence; 9 Having made known unto us (elohim) **the mystery of His will**

(to beget a family), according to His (Yahuah's) good pleasure which He hath purposed (predestined to create) in (the full image of) Himself (He is the Father of the family of Yahuah called elohim, Yahuah is the One True Living Elohim): 10 That in the dispensation of the fullness of times (proclaimed in The Heavenly Scroll... the end of the Age of ARIES when the "lamb dies") He (Yahuah) might gather together (again) in one (family through the covenant of marriage, the two shall become one) all things in (covenant with Yahusha the) Messiah, both that which is written in The Heavenly Scroll, and which written on Earth (the Prophets); even in Him(self, Yahuah will reconcile creation through the sacrifice of His Son): 11 In whom (the first born Son, Messiah Yahusha) also we (too) have obtained an inheritance (as sons of Yahuah, we inherit the Universe), being predestinated according to **the purpose of Yahuah** who worketh all things after the Divine Council of His own will (which is written in the stars, which Yahusha brought with him to fulfill "on Earth as it is written in The Heavenly Scroll" - Matthew 6:10):

# ◀ 305. anabainó

## Strong's Concordance

anabainó: to go up, ascend

Original Word: ἀναβαίνω

Short Definition: I go up, mount, ascend

Definition: I go up, mount, ascend; of things: I rise, spring up, come up.

## Thayer's Greek Lexicon

## STRONGS NT 305: ἀναβαίνω

ἀναβαίνω; (imperfect ἀνέβαινον Acts 3:1; future ἀναβήσομαι Romans 10:6, after Deuteronomy 30:12); perfect ἀναβέβηκα; 2 aorist ἀνέβην, participle ἀναβάς, imperative ἀνάβα Revelation 4:1 (ἀνάβηθι Lachmann), plural ἀνάβατε (for R G ἀνάβητε) Revelation 11:12 L T Tr (WH, cf. WHs Appendix, p. 168{b}); Winers Grammar, § 14, 1 h.; (Buttmann, 54 (47); from Homer down); the Sept. for עָלָה;

a. to go up, move to a higher place, ascend: a tree (ἐπί), Luke 19:4; upon the roof of a house (ἐπί), Luke 5:19; into a ship (εἰς), Mark 6:51; (Matthew 15:39 G Tr text; Acts 21:6 Tdf.); εἰς τό ὄρος, Matthew 5:1; Luke 9:28; Mark 3:13; εἰς τό ὑπερῷον, Acts 1:13; εἰς τόν οὐρανόν, Romans 10:6; Revelation 11:12 εἰς τόν οὐρανόν is omitted, but to be supplied, in John 1:51 (); , and in the phrase, ἀναβέβηκα πρός τόν πατέρα, John 20:17. (It is commonly maintained that those persons are figuratively said ἀναβεβηκέναι εἰς τόν οὐρανόν who have penetrated the heavenly mysteries John 3:13, cf Deuteronomy 30:12; Proverbs 24:27 (), Baruch 3:29. But in these latter passages also the expression is to be understood literally. And as respects John 3:13, it must be remembered that Christ brought his knowledge of the divine counsels with him from heaven.

12 That we (sons of Yahuah) should be to the praise of His glory, who first trusted in Messiah Yahusha (and express our faith in the Passover Lamb not the Easter Pig of Ishtar).

13 In whom (Yahusha) you also trusted (was the Messiah proclaimed in the stars), after that you heard the word of truth (preserved in The Heavenly Scroll Psalms 119:89, Psalm 89:2), which is the gospel of your salvation: in whom (Yahusha) also after that you believed, you were sealed with that holy Spirit of promise (the Spirit of Yahuah is the "blood of the family of Yahuah" a Spiritual Parallel of a human bloodline or family).

14 Which is the earnest (guarantee) of our (future) inheritance (as sons of Yahuah) until the redemption (transposition of our bodies from the Physical Realm to the Spiritual Realm) of the purchased possession unto the praise of His glory.

....

17 That **the** Elohim (Sha'ul again declares the Shema) of our King Messiah Yahusha (Yahuah is Yahusha's Elohim too), the Father of glory, may give unto you the spirit of wisdom and revelation in the knowledge of Him(self): 18 The eyes of your understanding being enlightened (to His Purpose to procreate a Family); that you may know what is the hope of His (Yahuah) calling (you as a son), and what the riches of the glory of His inheritance in the saints (we inherit the Universe created by Yahuah to give to His children),

19 And what is the exceeding greatness of Yahuah's power toward us (as sons) who believe, according to the working of His (Yahuah's) mighty power, 20 Which He (Yahuah) demonstrated in the Messiah, when Yahuah raised Yahusha from the dead (confirming Yahusha's sonship), and Yahuah set Yahusha at Yahuah's own right hand (of the throne of Creation. Yahusha is Yahuah's proxy King who sits on the Throne that governs Creation) in the Kingdom of Yahuah, 21 Far above all principality, and power, and might, and dominion, and every name that is named, not only in this world, but also in that which is to come:

22 And (Yahuah) hath put all things under his (Yahusha's) feet, and Yahuah gave Yahusha (the first born Son) to be the head (of His Family) over all things to the assembly (of His sons), 23 Which is His (Yahuah's Temple or) body, the fullness of Him (Yahuah) that fills all in all.

Sha'ul is describing the Mystery of the Ages, which is the revelation of the eternal family of Yahuah predestined and purchased through the blood of the Lamb. That Yahuah's family is His Glory. The head of the body (*Yahuah's Spiritual Temple*) is the Messiah, the first-born Son, and the rest of His sons are the body. This body of sons of Yahuah (*head and all*) will liberate creation and rule over it within a divine system of government.

This "mystery" is written in The Heavenly Scroll:

**Daniel 4:35**
"All the inhabitants of the Earth are accounted as nothing, but He does according to His will written in the host of Heaven (The Zodiac which hosts constellations. Constellations "host stars")

**Psalm 119:89**
Your Word (LOGOS/DABAR), Yahuah, is eternal; it stands firm written in The Heavenly Scroll.

**Psalm 19:1-6**
1The Heavenly Scroll (Shamayim - stars, Sun, and constellations) are telling of the Glory of Elohim (John 1:14); And their expanse is (The Divine Council) declaring the Work of His Hands (Enoch 35:3, John 1:3). 2 Day to day The Heavenly Scroll pours forth speech, And night to night the Sun/stars/constellations reveal knowledge. 3 There is no speech, nor are there words; Their voice is not heard.

**Psalm 89:2**
I will declare that Your Love stands firm forever, that you have established your faithful Promise (LOGOS) of Salvation in The Heavenly Scroll itself.

**Jubilee Chapter 6:16-18** – The Rainbow the sign of Shav'uot
16 He set His bow in the cloud for a sign of the Eternal Covenant (*Heavenly Wedding*) that there 17 should not again be a flood on the Earth to destroy it all the days of the Earth. For this reason, it is ordained and WRITTEN IN THE HEAVENLY SCROLL, that they should celebrate the Feast of Weeks in this 18 month once a year, to renew the Wedding Vows of the covenant every year.

**Psalm 68:32-34**
32 "Sing to Elohim, O Kingdoms of the Earth, Sing Praises to Yahuah, Selah." 33 To him (ORION the Bearer of the Light of Life) who rides upon the highest (clouds of) Heaven**, which Yahuah declared from ancient times to Enoch** (in The Heavenly Scroll the Ancient Paths Jeremiah 6:16, Enoch 35:3) "Behold The Heavenly Scroll", Yahuah Speaks forth with His Voice, a Mighty Voice (as His Creation Cries Out! The stars/constellation proclaim the Plan of Salvation 'day after day, night after night to all mankind' - Psalm 19). 34 The (meaning of the) Constellations ascribe strength to Elohim; His Glory is proclaimed over (the course of the year as the Sun travels through them) and His strength is revealed in The Heavenly Scroll (Sun/stars/constellations Shamayim as SIGNS of the Zodiac - Enoch 35:3, Psalm 19, Genesis 1:14)...."

### Enoch 35:3

When I beheld them (the stars and constellations), I blessed the Creator; every time in which they appeared, I blessed the King of Glory (Yahuah, the stars tell of His Glory Psalm 19), Who had made those great and splendid signs (constellations), that they might display the magnificence of this works to Angels and to the souls of men; and that these might glorify all His Works and Operations; might see the effect of His Power; might glorify the great labour of His Hands; and bless Him forever.

### Hebrews 10:7

Then I said, 'Here I am--it is written about me in The Heavenly Scroll-- I have come to do Your Will, my Elohim! (Matthew 6:10)

### Matthew 6:10

Your Kingdom (declared in Heaven Matthew 4:17) come, Your Will be done, on Earth as it is written in The Heavenly Scroll (Psalm 19, 119:89, 89:2, Daniel 4:35).

### Matthew 4:17

17 From that time on Yahusha began to proclaim, "Repent and be Mikveh'd, for the kingdom proclaimed in The Heavenly Scroll is near (to being fulfilled)."

**Note:** I realize I keep posting these verses, but I cannot stress this enough. The Earthly Scrolls (OT and NT) are literally based on what is written in the stars no matter what organized religion which is **The Beast** tells you.

# Revelation 10 Restored

## *Yahusha fulfills The Heavenly Scroll*

1 Then I saw another, a mighty King (King foretold in the stars *malak* h4397)

## 4397. malak

### Strong's Concordance

**malak: a messenger**

Original Word: מַלְאַךְ
Part of Speech: Noun Masculine
Transliteration: malak
Phonetic Spelling: (mal-awk')
Definition: a messenger

### Strong's Exhaustive Concordance

ambassador, angel, king, messenger

From an unused root meaning to despatch as a deputy; a messenger; specifically, of God, i.e. An angel (also a prophet, priest or teacher) -- ambassador, angel, king, messenger.

coming down from (what was written in) The Heavenly Scroll (ORION), wrapped in a cloud (riding the clouds of heave/Milky Way Galaxy), with a rainbow over his head (Ezekiel 1:26-28),

> ### Ezekiel 1:26-28 –Ezekiel reads The Heavenly Scroll
> 26... high above on The Throne in Heaven was a figure like that of a man. 27 I saw that from what appeared to be his waist up he looked like glowing metal, as if full of fire, and that from there down he looked like fire; and brilliant light (like the Sun) surrounded him. 28 Like the appearance of a rainbow in the clouds on a rainy day, so was the radiance around him (Revelation 10:1).

and his face was like the Sun (the Sun is a metaphor of the coming King Psalm 19), and his legs like pillars of fire. 2 He had a little Scroll open in his hand (as he revealed the contents of The Heavenly Scroll and demonstrated he had fulfilled it). And he set his right foot on the sea, and his left foot on the land (conquered the

Earth - LEO), 3 and called out with a loud voice, like a lion (LEO) roaring. When he called out, the seven thunders sounded (Joel 3:16). 4 And when the seven thunders had sounded (The Heavenly Scroll was fulfilled Revelation 11:15 and the Kingdom of Earth became the Kingdoms of Yahuah and Yahusha), I was about to write (what was revealed in The Heavenly Scroll), but I heard a voice from Heaven saying, "Seal up what the seven thunders have said (the Mystery of God to beget a family), and do not write it down." 5 And the Malak (King) whom I saw standing on the sea and on the land <u>raised his right hand to Heaven</u> (Daniel 12:7) 6 and swore by him who lives forever and ever (Yahuah The Creator), who created Heaven and what is in it, the Earth and what is in it, and the sea and what is in it (Isaiah 44:24),

> **Isaiah 44:24**
> "This is what Yahuah says-- your Redeemer, who formed you in the womb: I am Yahuah, the Maker of all things, Who stretches out the Heavens, Who spreads out the Earth (I created it all) **by myself**,

> **Daniel 12:7**
> 7 And I heard the man clothed in linen, which was upon the waters of the river, when he held up his right hand and his left hand unto Heaven, and swear by Him that lives forever that it shall be for a time, times, and an half; and when he shall have accomplished to scatter the power of the holy people, all these things shall be finished.

that there would be no more delay, 7 but that in the days of the trumpet call to be sounded by the seventh angel, the *Mystery of God* (proclaimed in The Heavenly Scroll) would be fulfilled (Revelation 11:15-19),

> **Revelation 11 – The 7th Angel Sounded; The Heavenly Scroll Fulfilled**
> 15 The seventh angel sounded his trumpet, and there were loud voices in Heaven, which said: *"The kingdom of the world has become the kingdom of our God and of his Messiah, and he (the Messiah) will reign for ever and ever. (fulfillment of LEO)"* 16 And the twenty-four elders, who were seated on their thrones before Yahusha, fell on their faces and worshiped Yahuah, 17 saying: *"We give thanks to you, Yahuah God Almighty, the One who is and who was, because you have taken your great power and have begun to reign. 18 The nations were angry, and your wrath has come. The time has come for judging the dead, and for rewarding your servants the prophets and your people who revere your name, both great and small—and for destroying those who destroy the Earth."* 19 Then Yahuah's temple in Heaven was opened, and within His temple was seen the ark of His Covenant. And there came flashes of lightning, rumblings, peals of thunder, an Earthquake and a severe hailstorm.

164

**Hebrews 10:7**
Then I said, 'Here I am--it is written about me in The Heavenly Scroll-- I have come to do Your Will, my Elohim! (Matthew 6:10)

**Matthew 6:10**
Your Kingdom (declared in Heaven Matthew 4:17) come, Your Will be done, on Earth as it is written in The Heavenly Scroll (Psalm 19).

**Matthew 4:17**
17 From that time on Yahusha began to proclaim, "Repent and be Mikveh'd, for the kingdom proclaimed in The Heavenly Scroll is near (to being fulfilled)."

just as he announced to his servants the prophets (Yahuah showed all His Prophets The Plan of Salvation by showing them The Heavenly Scroll - Amos 3:7).

**Ezekiel 2:9-10**
Then I looked (into the Heavens), and behold, a hand was extended to me; and lo, a Scroll was in it.

**Zechariah 5:2-3**
And he said to me, "What do you see (as you look into the Heavens)?" And I answered, "I see a flying Scroll!"

8 Then the voice (of Yahuah) that I had heard from Heaven (that sounded like a loud shofar blast - Revelation 1:10, Daniel 7:11, Exodus 19:16-191, Thessalonians 4:16, Hebrews 12:19), spoke to me again, saying, "Go, take The Heavenly Scroll that is open in the hand of the Malak (King) who is standing on the sea and on the land." 9 So I went to the King and asked him to give me the little Scroll. And he said to me, "Take and eat it (digest the meaning of it); it will make your stomach bitter, but in your mouth, it will be sweet as honey." 10 And I took the little Scroll from the hand of the angel and digested it (Jeremiah 15:16, Ezekiel 3:2-3).

**Ezekiel 3**
2 So I opened my mouth, and He fed me The (Heavenly) Scroll. 3 "Son of man," He said to me, "eat and fill your stomach with this Scroll I am giving you." So I ate, and it was as sweet as honey in my mouth. 4 Then He said to me, "Son of man, go now to the house of Israel and speak My words to them....

It was sweet as honey in my mouth, but when I had eaten it my stomach was made bitter (it was coming back up because he was to go out and prophecy the meaning of it). 11 And I was told, "You must (regurgitate it) again prophesy about many peoples and nations and languages and kings (just like Ezekiel, Zechariah, Jeremiah, Yahusha, Sha'ul)."

# Chapter 11

# Introduction

This chapter takes a deeper look at the period just prior to the 7th Trumpet during the announcement of woes.

- John measures the temple of Yahuah, the altar, and those who worship in it with a measuring rod he is given.

- John is told that the nations will tread under foot, the holy city of the temple, for forty-two months *(1,260 days)*.

- During which time the two witnesses, dressed in sackcloth, will prophesy and torment the nations then the time of the Gentiles will end.

- The Beast "Christianity" will overcome these two witnesses (*abolish The Law and the Prophets*) and kill them (*metaphorically*).

- There is celebration on Earth for three and a half days at the death of the two witnesses who have tormented the inhabitants of Earth for 42 months (*3.5 prophetic years*).

- The two witnesses are resurrected from the dead (*Yahuah re-establishes His Law and Prophets, turns the hearts of his children back to their Father Luke 1:16-18*)

    **Luke 1:16-18**
    16 Many of the sons of Israel he will turn back to Yahuah their God. 17 And he will go on before Yahuah in "the spirit and power of Elijah", to turn the hearts of the fathers to their children and the disobedient to the wisdom of the righteous— to make ready a people prepared for Yahuah (in covenant with Yahusha).

- This resurrection of The Law and the Prophets strikes fear on everyone witnessing this revival (*because they have violated His Laws and His Everlasting Covenant of the Sabbath Isaiah 24*), and the two witnesses ascend to Heaven or rather confirm The Heavenly Scroll.

- In the next hour, a great Earthquake occurs and kills seven thousand people, destroying a tenth of the city.

- The "Third woe" is signaled by the sound of the seventh trumpet.

- Loud voices in Heaven proclaim Yahusha as ruler over the "Kingdom of Yahuah".

- Creation gives thanks to Yahuah, the Almighty and praise for the wrath that came, the dead who were judged, and the bondservants rewarded.

> **TAURUS**
> The conquering Ruler comes, the sublime vanquisher, to execute the great judgment, he is the ruling Shepherd King.
>
> NOTE: Below Yahusha reads The Heavenly Scroll declaring he is the fulfillment of ORION the Son of Man coming in the clouds of Heaven to fulfill TAURUS:
>
> **Matthew 25:31-46** – *Fulfillment of TAURUS – The Ruling Shepherd and Great Judge*
> 31 "When the Son of Man comes in his glory and all his angels are with him, he will sit on his glorious throne (fulfillment of LEO). 32 The people of every nation will be gathered in front of him. He will separate them as a shepherd separates the sheep from the goats (The Great Shepherd TAURUS). 33 He will put the sheep on his right but the goats on his left. 34 "Then the king will say to those on his right, 'Come, my Father has blessed you! Inherit the kingdom prepared for you from the creation of the world (reference to The Heavenly Scroll). ... 41 "Then the king will say to those on his left, 'Get away from me! God has cursed you! Go into everlasting fire that was prepared for the devil and his angels! ... 46 "These people will go away into eternal punishment, but those with God's approval will go into eternal life."

- The temple of Yahuah in Heaven opens, and the Ark of the covenant appears in His temple.

- Lightning and the peals of thunder occur followed by an Earthquake and a great hailstorm.

Now before we continue with Chapter 11, we need to lay some more foundation from which to build our understanding "line upon line, precept upon precept".

# 42 Months – The Battle of the Ages

The Heavenly Scroll called The Word of His Testimony proclaims the life of a chosen man who would grow to become the King of Yahuah's Kingdom that will govern His Creation. This man would be a "double natured seed" meaning he would also be the Eternal High Priest. He would be given the name/title Melchi Zadok meaning Royal High Priest from the House of David and the House of Zadok.

> **SAGITTARIUS**: The double-natured seed (*King and High Priest*) triumphs as a warrior and pleases the Heavens, builds fires of punishment, casts down the dragon.

This man is referred to in The Heavenly Scroll as the Branch (*VIRGO*) and the Son of Man (*ORION*). There is a battle that rages on the pages of this Heavenly Scroll between the Son of Man and the Dragon. It is the central theme of the Book of Revelation and many other books of Prophecy (*Isaiah, Ezekiel, Daniel, Zechariah, Enoch*). This battle is recorded in all the prophets and in detail in the Book of Daniel. In Revelation we see the finale battle between them. The symbol of the Dragon/Beast is χξϛ (*the 3-letter symbol Chi, Xi, and Sigma, the mark of Jesus Christ erroneously translated 666*).

*All paintings in Antiquity of "Jesus" contain the symbol χξϛ see my book The Antichrist Revealed!*

# 6 x 7 = 42 the symbolic number of The Battle of the Ages

The Battle of the Ages between 6 (*the Dragon*) and 7 (*the Son of Man*) is symbolically represented by the number 42 months, 1290 days, and 3.5 years in Scripture. We see the number 42 recorded in the books of Daniel and Revelation. Below are passages of Scripture where the number 42 is found:

- When added together, all the flowers, knobs, and branches of the Golden Menorah in the physical Temple equals 42. Exodus 25:31-40.

- Balaam used 7 altars with 2 sacrificial animals on each one to make his sacrifices. For a total of 14 animals. He made 3 sacrifices of 14 animals = 42 animals slaughtered to the pagan deity. Numbers 23:2, 14, 29

- There were forty-two stages of the Israelites' exodus from Sinai to the Plains of Moab – a journey to end their rebellion against Yahuah and accept their future. Numbers 33:1-49.

- When Elijah was "taken up" there were forty-two men who mocked Yahuah's choice of Elisha. 2 Kings 2:23-24.

- In the Book of Revelation, the number forty-two symbolically represents the conflict of the Dragon/Beast the offspring of the Woman, "the final battle of the seed of the serpent and the seed of Adam". Genesis 3:15, Revelation 11:2; 13:5.

- The Tribe of Levi's inheritance in the land included 48 cities; 6 of which were set aside as a refuge for sinners. Leaving (*48-6*) 42 cities.

Keeping in mind the Books of Revelation and Daniel where 42 months, 1260/1290 days, and 3.5 years all referencing the same things in VISIONS. They are not literal but symbolic. Instead of attempting to understand 42 months in literal time we should be using our Spiritual Minds to interpret Spiritual Things.

### 1 Corinthians 2:10-16
13 These things we also speak, not in words which man's wisdom teaches but which the Spirit

of Holiness teaches, <u>comparing spiritual things with spiritual</u>. 14 But the natural man does not receive the things of the Spirit of Yahuah, for (he is filled with the Spirit of Error) they (Spiritual Visions) are foolishness to him; nor can he know them, because they are spiritually discerned.

Let us not make the same mistakes over and over as every other teacher has before us! The number 42 is not referring to a literal timeframe, but rather <u>The Battle of the Ages</u>. This battle rages for 6 prophetic days from Adam until The Son of Man (*Yahusha*) defeats the Dragon at the end of the Age of PISCES *(which is the focus of the Book of Revelation)* and the beginning of the 7<sup>th</sup> Millennium…. 6 prophetic days (*Ages TAURUS thru PISCES*) plus a 7th (*prophetic day, half of the Age of AQUARIUS*) we celebrate this as The Sabbath Covenant. The Sabbath is a weekly celebration every 7<sup>th</sup> day of The Plan of Salvation written in the stars.

Yahuah does not go from figurative to literal and back in the same context. In other words, if 42 months is literal then so should be the Dragon. We should see a literal Dragon chasing us around for 42 months. The Dragon is figurative and therefore so is the number 42 months. Everything in the visions of Daniel and John (in Revelation) is figurative… everything. Therefore, so should our understanding be, or we will, as man has for 2,000 years, misunderstand the meaning of these prophetic books.

Sources:

- <u>The Handbook of Biblical Chronology</u>, Jack Finegan; Hendrickson Publishers
- <u>Numbers in Scripture</u>: *Its Supernatural Design and Spiritual Significance*, E.W. Bullinger; Kregel Publications.
- <u>The Stromata</u>, Clement of Alexandria; Ante-Nicene Fathers: Volume 2; Hendrickson Publishers.

# 42-Months in History

<u>http://en.wikipedia.org/wiki/Day-year_principle</u>

*42 months using the day/year principle was fulfilled when The Papacy ascended to power as the Head of State. 1260-year period should commence with 755 AD, the actual year Pepin the Short invaded Lombard territory, resulting in the Pope's elevation from a subject of the Byzantine Empire to an independent head of state. The Donation of Pepin, which first occurred in 754 and again in 756 gave to the Pope temporal power of the Papal States.*

# Two Olive Trees

The Two Olives Trees are The House of Judah and The House of Israel. The House of Judah was called a "green olive tree, fair, and of goodly fruit" (*Jeremiah 11:16*). Those Nazarenes of The House of Israel who followed the Messiah are called "the olive tree which is wild by nature" *(Romans 11:24)*. The Re-Unification of Israel, the Bride, will be led by those few among both houses who proclaim <u>The Two Witnesses</u> who call the Elect out of the Nations and reunite Remnant Israel (*two sticks/branches of Ezekiel 37:15-28*).

**<u>Jeremiah 11:16</u>**
16 Yahuah called you a thriving olive tree with fruit beautiful in form. But with the roar of a mighty storm he will set it on fire, and its branches will be broken (into a second "wild Olive Tree" Romans 11:24).

**<u>Romans 11:24</u>**
24 After all, if you were cut out of an olive tree that is wild by nature, and contrary to nature were grafted into a cultivated olive tree, how much more readily will these, the natural branches, be grafted into their own olive tree!

**<u>Ezekiel 37:15-28</u>**
15 The word of Yahuah came to me: 16 Mortal, take a stick (Olive branch) and write on it, 'For Judah, and the House of Judah associated with it'; then take another stick (Olive branch) and write on it, 'For Joseph (the stick of Ephraim) and all the House of Israel associated with it'; 17 and join them together into one stick (Olive branch), so that they may become one (remnant) in your hand. 18 And when your people say to you, 'Will you not show us what you mean by these?' 19 say to them, Thus says Yahuah your God: I am about to take the stick of Joseph (which is in the hand of Ephraim) and the tribes of Israel associated with it; and I will put the stick of Judah upon it, and make them one stick, in order that they may be one in my hand. 20 When the sticks on which you write are in your hand before their eyes, 21 then say to them, Thus says Yahuah your God: I will take the people of Israel from the nations among which they have gone, and will gather them from every quarter, and bring them to their own land. 22 I will make them one nation in the land, on the mountains of Israel; and one king shall be king over them all.

**Zechariah 4:11-14**
11 Then I asked the angel, "What are these two olive trees on the right and the left of the lampstand?" 12 Again I asked him, "What are these two olive branches beside the two gold pipes that pour out golden oil?" 13 He replied, "Do you not know what these are?" "No, my lord," I said. 14 So he said, "These are the two (Olive branches) anointed (of Abraham) to serve Yahuah (to shed light) over all the Earth."

# Two Witnesses

Together, The Heavenly Scroll and the Earthly Scroll are the two witnesses, the two lampstands proclaimed by the Two Olive Trees (*Remnant Israel*) to give light (*witnesses*) to the world Matthew 5:14-16. We are to "let our light shine" by proclaiming these two witnesses: **The Heavenly and Earthly Scrolls of Yahuah.**

**Matthew 5:14-16**
14"You are the light of the world. A city set on a hill cannot be hidden; 15 nor does anyone light a lamp and put it under a basket, but on the lampstand, and it gives light to all who are in the house. 16"Let your light (witness) shine before men in such a way that they may see your good works, and glorify your Father who is (revealed) in Heaven (The Heavenly Scroll).

**John 12:36**
While you have the Light, believe in the Light, so that you may become sons of light." After Yahusha had spoken these things, He went away and was hidden from them.

Two Witnesses and the associated signs are key to end events in scripture. I'm sure as time progresses it will become ever clearer who or what exactly The Two Witness really are. Yahuah literally has established two personal witness to mankind:

- **The Heavenly Scroll** – The Divine Council or Word of His Testimony that Yahusha is the Messiah (anointed King). The stars witness to all mankind.

- **The Earthly Scroll** – The Law and the Prophets. These two spoke the words of Yahuah directly to mankind. Elijah represents the Prophets of Yahuah and Moses who represents "The Law". Moses and Elijah are simply physical to Spiritual parallels of The Law and The Prophets, respectively.

We see the Two Witnesses spoken of in scripture in multiple locations. Let us first look in Revelation where they are spoken of:

### Revelation 11

I was given a reed like a measuring rod and was told, "Go and measure the temple of God and the altar, with its worshipers. 2 But exclude the outer court; do not measure it, because it has been given to the Gentiles. They will trample on the holy city for 42 months. 3 And I will appoint my two witnesses, and they will prophesy for 1,260 days, clothed in sackcloth." 4 They are "the two olive trees" and the two lampstands, and "they stand before Yahuah of the Earth." 5 If anyone tries to harm them, fire comes from their mouths and devours their enemies. This is how anyone who wants to harm them must die. 6 They have power to shut up the Heavens so that it will not rain during the time they are prophesying; and they have power to turn the waters into blood and to strike the Earth with every kind of plague as often as they want.

7 Now when they have finished their testimony, the beast that comes up from the Abyss will attack them and overpower and kill them. 8 Their bodies will lie in the public square of the great city—which is figuratively called Sodom and Egypt—where also their Lord was crucified. 9 For three and a half days some from every people, tribe, language, and nation will gaze on their bodies and refuse them burial. 10 The inhabitants of the Earth will gloat over them and will celebrate by sending each other gifts, because these two prophets had tormented those who live on the Earth.

In my understanding, Revelation 11:10's two witnesses are The Heavenly Scroll and The Earthly Scroll (*The Law* and *The Prophets)* as foretold in Malachi 4:5. Below is how the *Book of Yahweh* translated Revelation 11:10 (*NOTE: The Prophets proclaimed the original prophecy, Gospel to all mankind written in the stars called The Heavenly Scroll*):

### Revelation 11:10

because these two prophets; the Law and the Prophets proclaimed every word of Yahuah to those residing throughout the Earth

One difference between me and most others is the translation we use. I have long since abandoned the traditional translations in favor of the ***Book of Yahweh*** (*at www.yahweh.com*) which is a much more true and accurate translation to the original Hebrew. Below is how Malachi 4:5 reads:

### Malakyah 4:5

Behold, I will send Yliyah: The Law and The Prophets, which is The Strength of Yahuah, before the coming of the great and dreadful day of Yahuah.

It has the following footnote:

### 1. Verse 4:5
Because of the way in which this Scripture was written, many people down through the centuries have erroneously believed that Malakyah was speaking about Yahuah's servant and prophet, who's name was Yliyah. The word Yliyah means "*The Strength of Yahuah*". Yahuah's Laws and the Prophets are the righteous strength of Yahuah.

### Romans 1:6
"for I am not ashamed of the message, for it is The Strength of Yahuah unto everlasting life"

### Psalms 10:29
"The Way of Yahuah is STRENGTH to the righteous."

Yahuah's Laws show His righteousness and ruling authority; and all of His Prophets proclaimed His Laws. Yahusha Messiah proclaimed the Law and the Prophets *(two Witnesses)* to be Yliyah (*The Strength of Yahuah*) which was to come, as He said in Matthew 11:13-14.

The Prophet Malachi was inspired to write that just before the great Day of Yahuah would come, Yahuah would establish a work to bring on last warning to this world. This Work of Yahuah is to proclaim Yahuah's Laws and Yahuah's Prophets, thereby turning the remnant sons and fathers to Yahuah before the end comes (*Matthew 24:14 and Mark13:10*).

I believe the Two Witness are:

1.  The Earthly Scrolls (*The Law and The Prophets*) who proclaimed…The Heavenly Scroll

2.  The Heavenly Scroll (*The Word of His Testimony, Divine Council*) witnesses to all mankind Psalm 19.

The Heavenly and Earthly Scrolls ARE the Strength of Yahuah known as Elijah. They are once again being proclaimed by His anointed at this time. This is not speaking of a man who is reincarnated (*the Prophet Elijah*) but a SPIRIT…

### Luke 1:17
And he will go on before Yahusha, in the <u>spirit and power of Elijah</u>, to turn the hearts of the parents to their children and the disobedient to the wisdom of the righteous--to make ready a people prepared to receive Yahusha."

The entire world is in rebellion against them as they witness to the entire Truth of Yahuah (*declared by His Two Witness*) and the world turns away from them and in effect KILLED them rendering them null/void/abolished... OLD (*i.e., the OT*). The Earth has fallen under the curse found in the Torah... and is in torment as a result; Revelation calls this torment like "the sting of a scorpion".

Please consider the meaning of the word Elijah in prophetic terms. Is it referring to the literal second coming of the physical prophet Elijah? Or was Elijah so named by Yahuah given the physical prophets role to stand up for Yahuah's Word and His Laws... which are *The Strength of Yahuah* and the literal interpretation of the name Elijah? Below is Malachi (*also quoted in Hebrews*):

### Malachi 4:1-6

1 For, behold, the day comes that will burn like an oven; and all the proud, yes, and all who do wickedly, will be stubble--the day that comes will burn them up (for breaking The Law and the Sabbaths Isaiah 24), says Yahuah of hosts; and it will leave them neither root nor branch.
2 But for you who revere My Name (Yahuah), the light of righteousness (reference to the fulfillment of The Heavenly Scroll) will arise with healing in its wings; and you will go out, leaping like calves released from the stall.
3 And you will tread down the wicked; for they will be ashes under the soles of your feet in the day that I will do this, says Yahuah of hosts.
4 Remember the LAW of Mosheh My servant, which I commanded through him in Horeb for all Israyl, with the statutes and the judgments.
5 Behold, I will send YLIYAH *1 *2 (the strength of Yahuah --the correct teaching of The Heavenly and Earthly Scrolls) before the coming of the great and dreadful day of Yahuah;
6 And His Word (written in Heaven and on Earth) will turn the hearts of the fathers (teachers) to the children (converts), and the hearts of the children (converts) to their fathers (teachers); before I come and strike the Earth with a curse; (cherem: utter destruction in The Day of Yahuah).

#### Footnotes:
*1 - [ YLIYAH] - Traditionally and erroneously represented as Elijah the Prophet. This word is composed of two parts: 'yl, (the original 'yl i.e. alef, yod, lamed) meaning: strength, power and might ["*strength, power*"
- The New Brown-Driver-Briggs-Gesenius Hebrew-English Lexicon p.43a; "*It is commonly thought that the term derived from a root yl or wl, meaning to be powerful*"
- Encyclopedia Judaica, God, names of, EL; & "#410-el from #352-'yl"
- Strong's Hebrew Dictionary; and yah, which is the first syllable and representation of the Name of Yahuah. "

177

*The strength of Yahuah* which is conveyed to His people is the correct teaching of His Word (preserved in Heaven Ps. 119:89 and on Earth) as taught by His anointed ones. [Ps. 105:4; Mic. 5:4(3); I Chr. 16:11; Prov. 24:5;Zech. 8:9; Matt. 5:17; Acts 14:24; Acts 9:22; Rev. 3:8]

*2 - *ha-nabia* Usually translated as "the prophet" but also can be applied to those whom Yahuah made known His will and has authorized to bring forth the correct interpretation of the Law and the Prophets. ["The idea of a prophet is sometimes more widely extended, and is applied to any one admitted to the familiar intercourse with [Yahuah], to whom [Yahuah] made known his will"
- Gesenius Hebrew-Chaldee Lexicon, p. 528b ; "*nabia - spokesman, speaker, prophet*"
- The New Brown-Driver-Briggs-Gesenius Hebrew-English Lexicon p611b; root "*nub: Action of speaking by inspiration; producing exteriorly the spirit with which one is filled.*"
- Hebraic Tongue Restored, p. 396 , Fabre D'Olivet; See Zecharyah 4:12-14].]

In prophetic language was the future Elijah to be a literal man? or the return of The Strength of Yahuah "Elijah" being the proper teaching and proclamation of His Word (*proclaimed in The Heavenly and Earthly Scrolls*) by those so anointed at the time of the end? Remember, Yahusha claimed John the Baptist was "Elijah" and John taught The fulfillment of The Heavenly Scroll (***"Repent and be Mikveh'd for the Kingdom proclaimed in The Heavenly Scroll has been fulfilled!"*** *Matthew 3:1-2*)... And Yahusha correctly identified The Strength of Yahuah or rather "Elijah" to be the" Law and the Prophets" which was to come in

### Matthew 11:13-14
13 For all the prophets (who prophesied The Heavenly Scroll) and the law prophesied until John. 14 And if you are willing to receive it, he is Elijah who is to come. 15 He who has ears to hear, let him hear (this is a Spiritual metaphor)!

Malachi was inspired to write that just before the Great and Terrible Day of Yahuah comes, Elijah (*The Strength of Yahuah*) or more specifically Yahuah's Name, His Laws, and His Prophets would once again be proclaimed by His anointed as they prophecy one last warning to the World (*reference Matthew 24:14 and Mark 13:10...*) This "Gospel" that would be preached once again is the Truth of Yahuah found in His Heavenly and Earthly Scrolls and the fulfillment found in the Messiah.

Let's look at a few terms in prophetic language; what does the word "rain" mean and what does it imply? And in that prophetic language, what do "water" mean and what does it imply? It would be a grave mistake to take what was a prophetic language spoken by His prophets and apply this language literally not acknowledging the proper meaning and implication of this language in His Word. "Elijah", "Rain", "Waters of Earth", etc. were all used by His prophets speaking in a specific prophetic language ordained by Yahuah meaning:

- Elijah - The "Strength of Yahuah" being His Heavenly and Earthly Scrolls proclaimed by His Witnesses or Lamps bringing forth light to a lost world in "darkness" or disobedience to Yahuah.

- Rain, Dew, Living Water, etc. - the graces and doctrines of the Spirit of Truth poured out on the Earth by Yahuah.

- Drought - Spiritual barrenness.

- Seas - nations of people.

- Waters - nations of people.

- Light - Spiritual enlightenment.

- Darkness - Evil, unrighteousness, disobedience.

- Winds - The Spirit of Yahuah.

- Scorpion Sting - panic attach.

- Turning to blood – war.

In proper context, the lack of "rain" prophesied by "Elijah" is the lack of Spiritual knowledge of mankind in rebellion as Yahuah's Words proclaimed in The Heaven Scroll and the Earthly Scroll are once again proclaimed on this Earth and the "waters" or nations are turned to blood meaning WAR ...

All too often we take what was written in prophetic language and incorrectly apply literal meaning to what was symbolic leading to a misunderstanding of end events. As humanity has committed the Transgression of Desolation (*breaking His Law and Sabbaths Isaiah 24*) and is in idolatry against Yahuah by the worship of pagan doctrines.

The story of Elijah in the Old Testament and the 3.5-year famine/drought was a physical metaphor of a greater Spiritual event to later occur during the end of the 6th prophetic day and beginning of the 7th... Yahuah established Spiritual truths using physical events in history as metaphors to teach us Spiritual Truths concerning Himself, His Messiah (*Passover Lamb*), and His timeline. Please see the following for more on the prophetic language used by Yahuah to speak through His prophets... http://www.isaacnewton.ca/daniel_apocalypse/pt1ch02.html

So, I ask you... in the prophetic sense...who is Elijah? Who are the Two Witnesses? Has there been a lack of "rain" and has the "waters" turned to blood and what about plagues in the prophetic language? As I write this book, the four winds have been held back, His Spirit restrained, there is no "rain" in prophetic terms. The waters (nations) have been turned into blood as war has erupted across this Earth. Love has waxed cold and this Earth is reeling from the effects of sin.

I submit to you that with the proper understanding of physical metaphors to Spiritual truth and the correct application of prophetic language to historical/current events; there will be no two human "witnesses" at the end, they have been proclaiming His Word written in the stars and on Earth for 6,000 years.

# Two Lampstands

What are the Two Lampstands in The Heavenly Scroll? His Word is the light unto our path which is proclaimed in The Heavenly and Earthly Scrolls by the "*light*" of the Sun/Stars:

### Psalm 119:105
Your word (Heavenly and Earthly Scrolls) is a lamp for my feet, a light on my path.

### Psalm 119:89
Your word, Yahuah, is eternal; it stands firm written in The Heavenly Scroll.

### Daniel 4:35
"All the inhabitants of the Earth are accounted as nothing, but He does according to His will

written in the host of Heaven (The Zodiac which hosts constellations. Constellations "host stars")

## Psalm 89:2
I will declare that your love stands firm forever, that you have established your faithfulness in The Heavenly Scroll itself.

## Psalm 19
1 The Heavens (The Heavenly Scroll) declare the glory of God; the skies proclaim the work of his hands. 2 Day after day they pour forth speech; night after night they reveal knowledge. 3 They have no speech, they use no words; no sound is heard from them. 4 Yet their voice goes out into all the Earth, their words (bear witness) to the ends of the world.

## Enoch 35:3
3 I Blessed Yahuah Author of Glory (The Heavenly Scroll Psalm 19:1), Who had made those Great and Splendid Signs (of the Zodiac), that they might display (to all mankind Deut. 4:19) the Magnificence of the Works of His Hands (The Plan of Salvation Psalm 19) to Angels and to the souls of men (His Divine Council); and that these (Splendid Signs in The Heavenly Scroll) might Glorify all His Works and Operations (The Plan of Salvation); that we might see the effect of His Power (as Creator to Write His Plan into the fabric of Creation on Day 4 and control the flow of history and fulfill His Promise); and The Heavenly Scroll might Glorify the Great Labor of His Hands (and we might come to know Him Romans 1, John 8:19 and His Son Psalm 19); and Bless Him Forever.

## Jubilee 6:16-18
16 He set His bow in the cloud for a sign of the Eternal Covenant (Heavenly Wedding) that there 17 should not again be a flood on the Earth to destroy it all the days of the Earth. For this reason, it is ordained and WRITTEN IN THE HEAVENLY SCROLL, that they should celebrate the Feast of Weeks in this 18 month once a year, to renew the Wedding Vows of the covenant every year.

# The Sun is a physical to Spiritual Parallel of Yahusha who is The Light of the world.

### John 8:12
When Yahusha spoke again to the people, he said, "I am the light of the world. Whoever follows me will never walk in darkness, but will have the light of life."

### John 9:5
While I am in the world, I am the light of the world."

78 because of the tender mercy of our God, by which the Dawn of the Sun will visit us from on high (The Heavenly Scroll), 79 to shine on those who live in darkness and in the shadow of death, to guide our feet into the path of peace."

# A "Man with a measuring rod"

Yahuah gave the Prophet Zechariah a vision of John where in the Book of Revelation he is given a measuring rod to measure the Holy City that is given over to the Gentiles.

**Zechariah 2:1–3:10** - *A Vision of a John with a Measuring Line*
1 And I lifted my eyes (to see a vision) and saw (with my Spiritual Eyes), and behold, a man (the Prophet John) with a measuring rod in his hand! (see Revelation 11)

### Revelation 11
1 - Then I was given a measuring rod (Zechariah 2:1-3) resembling a (shepherd's) staff. and was told, "Go and measure the temple of Yahuah"

2 Then I said, "Where are you going John?" And John said to me, "To measure Jerusalem, to see what is its width and what is its length." 3 And behold, the messenger who talked with me came forward, and another messenger came forward to meet him 4 and said to the first messenger, *"Run, say to that young man John, 'Jerusalem shall be inhabited as villages without walls, because of the multitude of people and livestock in it. 5 And I will be to her a wall of fire all around, declares Yahuah, and I will be the glory in her midst.' "*

6 *Up! Up! Flee from the land of the north, declares Yahuah* (The Greater Exodus).
*For I have spread you abroad as the four winds of the Heavens, declares Yahuah* (His Elect are living among the nations where they were dispersed). 7 *Up! Escape to Zion, you who dwell with the daughters of Babylon* (the nations).

Isaiah 48:20
Leave Babylon, flee from the Babylonians! Announce this with shouts of joy and proclaim it. Send it out to the ends of the Earth; say, "*Yahuah has redeemed his servant Jacob.*"

8 For thus said Yahuah of hosts, after His glory sent me to the nations who plundered you, for he who touches you touches the apple of Yahuah's eye: 9 *"Behold, I will shake My Hand over them* (who have come against Jerusalem), *and they shall become plunder for those who served*

*them* (Revelation 17 and 18). *Then you will know that Yahuah of hosts has sent me. 10 Sing and rejoice, O daughter of Zion* (Revelation 7), *for behold, I come and I will dwell in your midst, declares Yahuah. 11 And many nations shall join themselves to Yahuah in that day, and shall be my people.*

> ### Zechariah 8:22
> And many peoples and powerful nations will come to Jerusalem to seek Yahuah Almighty and to entreat him."

> ### Isaiah 2:2
> In the last days the mountain of the house of Yahuah will be established as the chief of the mountains; it will be raised above the hills, and all nations will stream to it.

*And I will dwell in your midst, and you shall know that Yahuah of hosts has sent me to you* (Revelation 20). *12 And Yahuah will inherit Judah as his portion in the holy land and will again choose Jerusalem* (Revelation 21)." 3 Be silent, all flesh, before Yahuah, for he has roused himself from his holy dwelling (Revelation 7).

# Let us review...
# the message in the stars

At this point, let me refresh the memory of the reader because that written in the stars is literally being fulfilled on the pages of Revelation:

### Story Told through major constellations

*VIRGO*: A young maiden will give a virgin birth (*the Branch will open her womb and be the firstborn and heir*) to a beautiful glorious and righteous branch. The seed of the woman will be a man of humiliation to rise to be the desire of nations and will become exalted first as shepherd (*High Priest/Spring Feasts*) then as harvester (*Conquering King/Fall Feasts*). *LIBRA*: The scales demand a price to be paid of this seed (*he must pay the dowry with his life*), the wood of the sacrifice to carry; the victim will be slain and purchase a crown. *SCORPIO*: There is a conflict between the seed and the serpent leading to a struggle with the enemy; the enemy is vanquished. *SAGITTARIUS*: The double-natured seed (*King and High Priest*) triumphs as a warrior and pleases the Heavens, builds fires of punishment, casts down the dragon. *CAPRICORNUS*: Eternal life comes from his death, he's the Arrow of Yahuah, he is pierced, yet springs up again in abundant life. *AQUARIUS*: He pours out "living water" from on high, humanity drinks of the Heavenly river and the faithful live again, he is the deliverer of the good news (*Gospel*), Carrying the wood of the sacrifice over the Earth. *PISCES*: The Redeemer's people multiplied, supported and led by the Lamb, The Bride is exposed on Earth, the Bridegroom is exalted. *ARIES*: The Lamb is found worthy, the Bride is made ready, Satan is bound, the strong man triumphs. *TAURUS*: The conquering Ruler comes, the sublime vanquisher, to execute the great judgment, he is the ruling Shepherd King. *GEMINI*: The Marriage of the Lamb, the enemy is trodden down, the Prince comes in great Glory. *CANCER*: The great Bride, the two Houses of Judah and Israel are united, they are brought safely into the kingdom. *LEO*: The Lion King is aroused for rending,

184

the Serpent flees, the Bowl of Wrath is upon him, his Carcass is devoured. The Lion of the tribe of Judah rules as King.

### Story Told through minor constellations called Decans

A *virgin* Maiden is the mother of an Infant Prince who is half mortal and half god (*Centaur*) and who will grow up to be the Good Shepherd (*Herdsman*). He is the Redeemer who will pay the price of sin (*Balance*) through his suffering (*Cross*) as a sacrifice (*Beast*) in order to win the Crown. He will be the great Healer who will crush sickness and death (*Scorpion*). He is the Savior (*Archer, Hercules*) who slays the Dragon, resulting in great rejoicing (*Harp*). He is also the Goat (*Sea Goat*) sacrificed on the Altar, but then resurrecting (*Dolphin*). He is the messenger of his Father (*Eagle and Arrow*). He is the Master Teacher (*Waterman*), who pours out knowledge and blessings on his church (*Southern Fish*), carrying it upward (*Flying Horse*) to someday be glorified (*Swan*). He is the Ram who breaks the Bands of Death, and the Hero who looses the chains of hell which bind and shackle both the House of Israel and House of Judah (*Fishes*) to the awful Sea Monster. The Hero is also the Bridegroom who then marries his Bride (*Princess*). He is enthroned as the King and the glorified Bride becomes his Queen. At the beginning of the Millennium, Yahusha reigns as King and King of the Kingdom of Yahuah (*Bull*). As the royal Hunter he destroys the harlot (*Hare*) who has perverted religions and governments worldwide, and he executes judgment on the wicked (*River*). He is both the High Priest and King (*Twins*). He who comes in power to destroy the great harlot (*Hare*) at the Second Coming (*Big Dog*) is also he who came in meekness and allowed himself to be slain by her at the First Coming (*Little Dog*). He is the Deliverer (*Crab*) who leads the dead up out of hell (*Ship*) and delivers his flocks (*Big and Little Bears*). As the millennial King (*Lion*), he permanently overcomes the fleeing *Water Serpent*, who suffers the *Cup of the wrath* of God, and whose corpse is eaten by birds of prey (*Raven*).

With that foundation, let us now reveal the meaning of Chapter 11 in context.

# Revelation 11 Restored

*Time of the Gentiles*
*The Battle of the Ages*

1 - Then I was given a measuring rod (Zechariah 2:1-3) resembling a (shepherd's) staff. and was told, "*Go and measure the temple of Yahuah* (the body of His Elect 1 Corinthians 3:16) and *the* (golden) *alter* (the hearts and minds of His Elect Hebrews 13:10) *and count the number of worshipers there* (this is measuring The Temple. The Temple is made up of the sum total of His Children, it is Spiritual not physical).

### Revelation 21
15 The malak who spoke with me had a golden measuring rod to measure the city and its gates and walls.

### Zechariah 2:1–3:10 - *A Vision of a John with a Measuring Line*
1 And I lifted my eyes (to see a vision) and saw (with my Spiritual Eyes), and behold, a man (the Prophet John) with a measuring rod in his hand! 2 Then I said, *"Where are you going John?"* And John said to me, *"To measure Jerusalem, to see what is its width and what is its length."*

2 *but do not measure the court outside the temple; leave that out, for it is given over to the nations, and they will trample the holy city for forty-two months* (Luke 21:24).

### Luke 21
22 For this is the time of punishment in fulfillment of all that has been written. 23 How dreadful it will be in those days for pregnant women and nursing mothers! There will be great distress in the land and wrath against this people. 24 They will fall by the sword and will be taken as prisoners to all the nations. Jerusalem will be trampled on by the Gentiles until the times of the Gentiles are fulfilled.

## *Climax of The Battle of the Ages*
## *The Two Witnesses*

3 - *And I will empower my two witnesses* (The Heavenly and Earthly Scrolls are His Two Witnesses to mankind) *and they will prophesy for 1260 days* (their prophecies will be) *clothed in sackcloth*" (come with great mourning against Babylon Revelation 19:19)."

### Revelation 18
19 they will throw dust on their heads as they weep and mourn and cry out: "Woe, woe to the great city, where all who had ships on the sea were enriched by her wealth! For in a single hour she has been destroyed (the destruction of Babylon is the subject of the Prophets in the OT)."

4 And these are *"the two olive trees* (House of Israel and House of Judah... the Bride) *and the two lampstands"* (light) that stand before the King (to give light) over the Earth (Zechariah 4:11-14).

### Zechariah 4:11-14
11 Then I asked the angel, "What are these two olive trees on the right and the left of the lampstand?" 12 Again I asked him, "What are these two olive branches beside the two gold pipes that pour out golden oil?" 13 He replied, "Do you not know what these are?" "No, my King," I said. 14 So he said, "These are the two anointed to serve Yahuah (to shed light) over all the Earth."

5 And if anyone would harm them, fire (judgment – Yahuah's word is all consuming fire Jeremiah 23:29)

### Jeremiah 23:29
"Is not My word like fire," declares Yahuah.

pours from their mouth and consumes their foes (Jeremiah 5:14).

### Jeremiah 5:14
Therefore, thus says Yahuah, the God of hosts, "Because you have spoken this word, Behold, I am making My words in your mouth fire And this people wood, and it will consume them.

## *Fulfillment of LEO and the Bowl of Wrath*

---

**LEO:** The Lion King is aroused for rending, the Serpent flees, <u>the Bowl of Wrath is upon him</u>, his Carcass is devoured. The Lion of the tribe of Judah rules as King.

---

If anyone would harm them (does not keep His Testimony proclaimed in His Two Witnesses; The Heavenly and Earthly Scrolls), this is how he is doomed to be killed (consumed by His Judgment). 6 They have the power to shut the sky, that no rain (Spiritual Inspiration) may fall during the days of their prophesying (4th bowl judgment), and they have power over the waters to turn them into blood (2nd and 3rd bowl judgment) and to strike the Earth with every kind of plague (1st bowl judgment), as often as they desire (as Yahusha brings his people out of the nations like Moses led Israel out of Egypt).

---

**NOTE**: Keep in mind, this is a Spiritual Vision of events that occur in the Spiritual Realm during the last days. This is NOT literal... There is not a literal "beast" that comes rising out of the Earth from a bottomless pit. There are no literal "dead bodies" that lay in the streets etc. This is symbolism, metaphors, figures of speech, Spiritual Mysteries.

---

7 And when they have finished their testimony, the beast that rises from the bottomless pit (The Dragon rising from the horizon seen as the bottomless pit in The Heavenly Scroll to battle - **ORION**) will make war on them and conquer them (Revelation 13) and kill them, 8 and their dead bodies will lie in the street of the great city that symbolically is called Sodom and Egypt, where their King was crucified. 9 For three and a half periods of time (Greek word for "day" is hemera Strong's 2250 which also means "period of time" or "years" - Daniel uses the same wording in Hebrew as "times, time, and half of time" Daniel 12:7 denoting an unspecified period of time)

# 2250. hémera

## Strong's Concordance

**hémera: day**
Original Word: ἡμέρα, ας, ἡ
Part of Speech: Noun, Feminine
Transliteration: hémera
Phonetic Spelling: (hay-mer'-ah)
Definition: day

*NASB Translation*

always* (1), court (1), daily* (10), day (207), day's (1), day...another (1), daybreak (1), days (148), daytime (2), midday* (1), time (12), years (4).

some from the peoples and tribes and languages and nations will gaze at their dead bodies and refuse to let them be placed in a tomb, 10 and those who dwell on the Earth will rejoice over them and make merry and exchange presents, because these two prophets had been a torment to those who dwell on the Earth (Matthew 24:37-39).

## *First 6 Trumpets and the First Resurrection*
## *The Two Witnesses*

11 But after the three and a half periods of time the breath of life from Yahuah entered them (first resurrection of the two Olives Trees who proclaim the Two Witnesses, unification of Ezekiel's two branches), and they stood up on their feet, and great fear fell on those who saw them. 12 Then they heard a loud voice from Heaven saying to them, *"Come up here!"* And they went up to Heaven in a cloud, and their enemies watched them. 13 And at that hour there was a great Earthquake, and a tenth of the city fell. Seven thousand people were killed in the Earthquake, and the rest were terrified and gave glory to Yahuah revealed in The Heavenly Scroll. 14 The second woe has passed; behold, the third woe is soon to come.

## The Seventh Trumpet
## The Battle of the Ages is over

15 Then the seventh angel blew his trumpet, and there were loud voices in Heaven, saying, *"The kingdom of the world has become the kingdom of our Creator and of his King, and He* (Yahuah through Yahusha) *shall reign forever and ever."* 16 And the twenty-four elders who sit on their thrones before Yahusha fell on their faces bowing in respect to Yahusha their King (who has fulfilled The Heavenly Scroll), 17 saying, *"We give thanks to you, Yahusha the (proxy of the) Almighty (Ruler –* **SAGITTARIUS/LEO**), *who is and who was (**CAPRICORNUS**), for you have taken your great power and begun to reign (over the Kingdom that will govern Yahuah's Creation -* **LEO**). 18 The nations raged, but your wrath came (and defeated the Dragon - **SCORPIO**), and the time for the dead to be judged (**TAURUS**), and for rewarding your servants (**PISCES /AQUARIUS**), the prophets and saints, and those who show reverence to (the covenant that bears) your name (Isaiah 42:6), both small and great, and for destroying the destroyers of the Earth (**LEO**)."

## The King takes His Thrown in Heaven

19 Then Yahuah's temple in Heaven was opened, and the ark of his covenant was seen within his temple. There were flashes of lightning, rumblings,4 peals of thunder, an Earthquake, and heavy hail.

# *Chapter 12*

# Introduction

The duration of the Battle of the Ages begins with the birth of the Messiah (*sign of the birth of the son of man*), then Satan is thrown down to Earth and wages war on those who follow the Messiah. Those faithful who keep The Word of His Testimony written in the stars "love their lives not, even unto death". The remnant "woman/Bride" is given renewed strength (*wings of an eagle*) and are brought through the "wilderness" (*Sukkot*) and into the Kingdom.

We see in antiquity, paintings showing the Prophet John on the Island of Patmos looking up to The Heavenly Scroll writing down its contents where he is given a vision of the woman (*Virgo*) and the Dragon (*DRACO*):

*Landscape with St John the Evangelist at Patmos by Tobias Verhaecht, 1598. The woman and the dragon are shown in the sky.*

# War in Heaven

What happens in the Spiritual Realm is reflected in the Physical Realm. We see this in "the last days" (*which is The Age of PISCES which is two prophetic 1,000-year days 2 Peter 3:8, Psalm 90:4*). During this last Age we see the culmination of "The Battle of the Age".

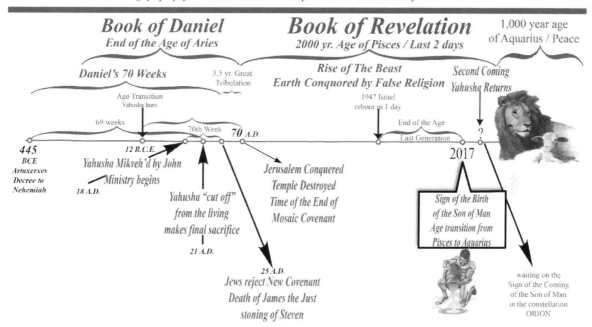

# Battle of the Ages
*The "last days" of the Age of Pisces*

*Image property of The Sabbath Covenant Ministry www.sabbathcovenant.com by Rav Sha'ul*

193

# The Identity of "The Dragon"

In this chapter we are introduced to The Dragon. We need to know who this mysterious figure represents in our world in physical terms. We know who the Son of Man is represented by ORION, OPHIUCHUS, PERSIUS, etc. It is Yahusha the Messiah who fulfilled The Heavenly Scroll during his life on Earth. The next allegory (*pictograph*) in The Heavenly Scroll we must identify is The Dragon whose spirit does battle with the Son of Man in The Battle of the Ages.

> **Revelation 12:9**
> And the great dragon was cast out, that old serpent (***DRACO***), called the Devil, and Satan, who deceives the whole world. He was cast out into the Earth, and his angels were cast out with him.

The full description of the "battle" that is waged over the course of this Age (*of PISCES*), is laid out in Revelation Chapter 13 in great detail and in the graphic novel in the "sky" called The Heavenly Scroll. The players involved are not named specifically in either Scroll, the Earthly or Heavenly, but instead are represented in the Mystery Language of prophecy, using metaphors, pictographs, and allegories.

In Revelation 13 we see a Dragon, a "beast coming out of the sea", a first beast, a second beast, a False Prophet, a False Messiah, a False Mark, and so forth. The mystery is what and who do these metaphors/images speak of over the course of the last 2000 years (*since this Book of Revelation was written*)? We are at the end of the Age now, and they have been fulfilled!

John was shown The Heavenly Scroll in the Book of Revelation and given the meaning of the pictograms and The Battle of the Ages. The Book of Revelation could be more aptly titled "Revelation of The Heavenly Scroll".

> **Revelation 5:1 -** The Opening of the Scroll of the Mazzaroth.
> Then I saw in the right hand of the one who was seated on the Throne a Scroll written on the front and back (3D Scroll of Heavenly pictographs) and sealed with seven seals.

As I have been pointing out, all the Prophets of Yahuah based their prophetic understanding on The Heavenly Scroll called The Mazzaroth (*Zodiac*). When breaking the seals over the Book of Revelation, we must search all the Prophets of Yahuah, because Scripture interprets Scripture. ALL the Prophets of Yahuah used The Heavenly Scroll as a guide, as the constellations and stars are literal signs (*and pictographs*) that layout in "Heaven" what must take place on Earth. We see the Prophet Zachariah was shown The Heavenly Scroll (*as was all the Prophets*) and based his prophecies upon that which was written within this "Scroll flying about in Heaven".

We see Zachariah speak of two women, the two witnesses, two lampstands, and a standard of measurement (*ephah*) which is a metaphor of the standard of perfection of Yahuah's two literal witnesses; The Heavenly and Earthly (*Law and Prophets*) Scrolls. The point below is, again, The Heavenly Scroll is the "source" of understanding! Notice also, the mention of a "Babylonish" land in the end, and the description of the false religious temples. This is a key to understanding The Dragon. Below I put Zachariah back into 'context' using parenthesis (). When this is done, we see Scripture agree with no contradictions and come alive!

### Zachariah 5:1-9

[1] Then again I raised my eyes (up) and looked (at the stars and constellations), and behold (in Heaven), a flying Scroll! [2] He said to me: What do you see (when you look up at the stars)? And I answered: I see a flying Scroll; its length is twenty cubits; about 30 feet, and its width is ten cubits; about 15 feet. [3] Then he said to me: This is the curse that goes out over the face of the whole Earth (to all who deny The Heavenly Scroll and commit the two evils *Jeremiah 2:13*) Everyone who steals will be cut off (from the Book of Life *Revelation 13:8*) according to what is written on this side of the (Earthly) Scroll (The Torah); and every one who vows falsely will be cut off (from the Book of Life *Revelation 13:8*), according to what is written on the other side of the (Earthly) Scroll (The Torah). [4] I will send the curse out (*Isaiah 24:5*), says Yahuah (Creator) of (the starry) hosts (constellations which 'host stars' *Isaiah 45:12*): and the curse will enter into the house (worship centers) of the thief, and into the house of him who vows an oath with My Name for the sake of falsehood (saying Yahuah came to Earth as a man and died *Romans 1*); and the curse will remain in the midst of his house, and will consume it together with the sacred (Ashtaroth) poles and the stones (of its temples) measured off for desolation. [5] Then the Malak who was speaking with me came forward, and said to me: Lift up your eyes now (and read the stars), and understand that which is sent by commandment ('Your Word, oh Yahuah, is eternal, it stands firm in The Heavenly Scroll' *Psalm 119:89*). [6] And I asked: What is it (that I am beholding in The Heavenly Scroll)? And he answered: This is the ephah (standard of measurement); The Standard of Perfection, which is sent by Yahuah's command. Then he added: The Heavenly Scroll is honor, knowledge, and understanding throughout the whole Earth (*Psalm 19*). [7] And behold (The Dragon fighting against The Son of Man), the sum total of the heaviest cover (over the minds of the people); of deception and delusion, was taken away from their eyes. And there was the First Woman; The First Era of The House of Yahuah, established in the midst of the ephah; [8] And this is the wickedness: And Satan (The Dragon) overthrew The House of Yahuah within the midst of the ephah (with the Temples with Ashtaroth Poles); by casting the same weight of lead (over the minds of the people); cover of deception, against her mouth; successfully suppressing the Word of Yahuah (corrupted The Heavenly Scroll). [9] Then I lifted up my eyes and looked, and behold: Two

women (remnant Bride take from The House of Israel and the House of Judah); The Spirit of Yahuah (denial of incarnation) came to overspread them (the Elect); and they were protected by the covering of (mark of the) saints (The Shema - Yahuah is ONE, not a trinity or bi-entity). And they (their minds being sealed with the Mark of God) exalted, magnified, and extolled the ephah; The Standard of Perfection sent by Yahuah's Laws, separating the way of the world (Easter Pig/Wide Gate) from The Way of Yahuah (Passover/The Narrow Gate). 10 Then I said to the Malak who was speaking with me: Where are they (who being filled with the Spirit of Elijah, who teach); The Two Witnesses (The Heavenly and Earthly Scrolls), going with the ephah? 11 And he said to me: To build The House of Yahuah in a Babylonish land which does not yet exist (The USA). And it will be established at that time; when (those with the Spirit of Elijah who teach) The Two Witnesses (The Heavenly and Earthly Scrolls) are called out to their work (restore the hearts of the children back to Yahuah their Father *Malachi 4:6*)

With that clear understanding of what The Heavenly Scroll proclaimed to Zachariah, I will begin to shed light on The Dragon so that we will be equipped at the end of the Age to witness the fulfillment of The Fall Feasts.

- The Temples with Ashtaroth Poles that spread the Spirit of the Dragon.

- We are going to trace back the Spirit of the Dragon which spread across the Earth after the Tower of Babel and was/is identified by Obelisks (Ashtaroth Poles). Zachariah 5:1-11 gave us several clues:

  o The Spirit of the Dragon is known by Ashtaroth Poles

  o The Dragon's temples are built with stones with Ashtaroth Poles as a signature mark!

  o The land of this great deception will be Babylonish and not discovered at that time!

You see, in the religion born in Babylon, the Ashtaroth Poles or "Poles of Ishtar" were a symbol of fertility. They represented Nimrod's private parts, which were never found after Nimrod was cut into pieces and spread all over the Babylonian Empire. Both the Religion of Babylon, and the "Babylonish land" at the end will be clearly marked with these poles! They are known in history as Obelisks and Steeples.

These poles adorn EVERY religion of The Dragon in history, to clearly mark this deception throughout every Age (if we simply open our eyes).

*From Babylon to Rome to the USA... The Spirit of The Dragon is obvious. Notice the Obelisk at the Vatican in the middle of the corrupted Zodiac circle. Notice the steeple on the Christian Church with the cross of Tammuz on top, All symbols of Sun Worship.*

To identify the Dragon (*the Spirit behind the First and Second Beast that gives the beast its throne and power*) we must begin our search by going back to Babylon. It was in Babylon that the corrupted version of The Heavenly Scroll (*Sun worship*) was formulated into a formal Mystery Religion. To know how things end, we must first know where they began. So, let's take a journey back to Babylon where this religious lie was created that today has the entire world in deception (*Revelation 18:23, 17:5, and 18:23*).

197

> The Spirit of The Dragon is a religious spirit formulated in Babylon of Sun Worship known by beliefs and rituals of Sunday, Easter, Christmas, Incarnation, and the Trinity.

# Incarnation: The Spirit of the False Messiah

Every pagan "God in the flesh" is based on the corrupted version of The Heavenly Scroll (*Sun worship*). These abominations (*incarnated godmen*) are identified by the rebirth of the Sun on December 25th as their birthdays. Every culture tried to fulfill the message in the stars by creating demi-gods to worship to fulfill the false corrupted version of the Zodiac... all "God the Son" or God came to Earth as a man.

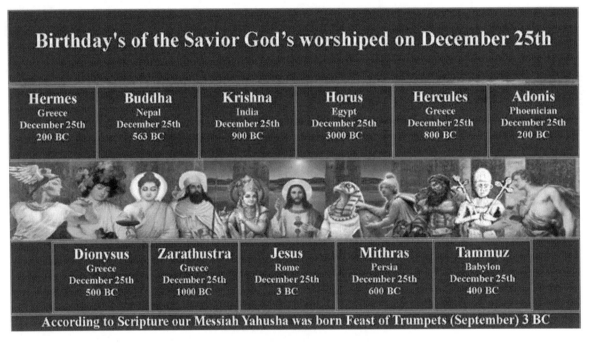

**Birthday's of the Savior God's worshiped on December 25th**

| Hermes | Buddha | Krishna | Horus | Hercules | Adonis |
|--------|--------|---------|-------|----------|--------|
| Greece | Nepal | India | Egypt | Greece | Phoenician |
| December 25th | December 25th | December 25th | December 25th | December 25th | December 25th |
| 200 BC | 563 BC | 900 BC | 3000 BC | 800 BC | 200 BC |

| Dionysus | Zarathustra | Jesus | Mithras | Tammuz |
|----------|-------------|-------|---------|--------|
| Greece | Greece | Rome | Persia | Babylon |
| December 25th | December 25th | December 25th | December 25th | December 25th |
| 500 BC | 1000 BC | 3 BC | 600 BC | 400 BC |

According to Scripture our Messiah Yahusha was born Feast of Trumpets (September) 3 BC

*Every pagan god-man is based on The Spirit of the False Messiah or Spirit of The Dragon... the doctrine of Incarnation*

# The Dragon in The Heavenly Scroll

The identity of the Dragon is, as we all know, Satan. That is clearly defined in the Book of Revelation:

### Revelation 12:9

And the great dragon was cast out, that old serpent, called the Devil, and Satan, who deceives the whole world. He was cast out into the Earth, and his angels were cast out with him.

First let us "look up and behold The Heavenly Scroll!" as all the Prophets of Yahuah openly declare in all their writings. What was it in The Heavenly Scroll that they saw written in the stars as pictographs they called The Dragon? When speaking of The Dragon, it is mainly the constellation DRACO. "DRACO" is Latin for "Dragon". In the Book of Job (*where many constellations are named by name, and Yahuah openly declares that it is He who authored the Zodiac*), we see a reference to the constellation DRACO. When describing Yahuah's majesty in the Heavens, Job declares:

### Job 26:13

"By His breath the Heavens (The Heavenly Scroll) are garnished (with pictographs/constellations); His hand has pierced the crooked serpent (*DRACO*).

The "crooked serpent" is the constellation DRACO, which stretches out across a third of the "Heavens".

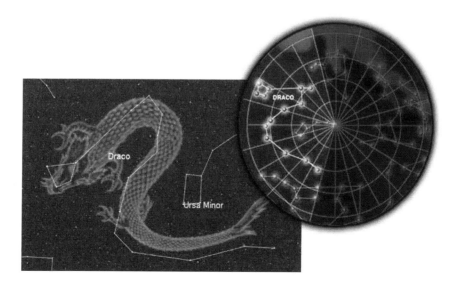

### Revelation 12:3-4

[3] And there appeared another wonder in Heaven: And behold, a great red dragon (DRACO), having seven heads and ten horns, and seven crowns upon her heads. [4] And her tail drew the third part of the stars of Heaven

In The Heavenly Scroll we see several constellations represent the Son of Man and the Dragon that depict different scenes in The Battle of the Ages. The pictograph of OPHIUCHUS is the Son of Man battling the Serpent while crushing the head of the scorpion (*the enemy SCORPIO*) who is striking his heel.

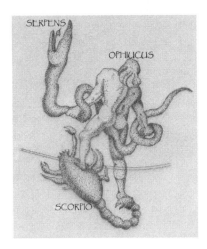

This battle was first announced in the very first pages of the Bible:

### Genesis 3:15

And I will put enmity between you and the woman, and between your offspring and hers; he (the Son of Man) will crush your head (SCORPIO), and you will strike his heel."

The battle continues in The Heavenly Scroll as described by John below:

### Revelation 12:7-9

[7] And there was war in Heaven; Michael and the Angels fought against the dragon; and the dragon fought with the Angels, [8] But did not prevail, nor was their place found any more in Heaven. [9] And the great dragon was cast out, that old serpent, called the Devil, and Satan, who deceives the whole world.

The Heavenly Scroll reveals the battle between the Son of Man and the Dragon in multiple pictographs formations (*constellations*). Let's look at "who" The Dragon really is, and how its spirit has "deceived the whole world" exactly as prophesied as it is The Wide Gate. The Dragon is the religions of the gentiles called The Way of the Gentiles.

# The Dragon in History - the "Spirit" behind all false religions

We read in Revelation Chapter 13 that a "beast" comes out of the sea (*sea monster*)

### Revelation 13:1-4

[1] And I stood upon the sand of the sea, and saw a beast rise up out of the sea... and the dragon gave him his power, and his throne, and great authority... [4] And they worshiped the dragon which gave power to the beast; and they worshiped the beast, saying: Who is like the beast? Who is able to make war with him?

We read that The Dragon gives this "beast out of the sea" a throne, great power and authority.

### Revelation 13:2

And the dragon gave the beast his power and throne and great authority.

### Revelation 13:4

People worshiped the dragon because he had given authority to the beast

To understand clearly where this "beast out of the sea or sea monster" originated, we need to take a journey back to Babylon. We are going to clearly define what this "Dragon" was, and the spirit behind it. To do this, I am going to quote from my book ***Christianity and the Great Deception***.

# FROM DAGON TO THE DRAGON THE "SPIRIT" BEHIND CHRISTIANITY...

*Excerpt from Christianity and the Great Deception by Rav Sha'ul*

The word "dragon" comes from the word "Dagon" one of, if not the, oldest pagan gods dating back to Nimrod in Babylon and to the Sumerian culture before that. Dagon evolved over time and cultures into the dragon:

### DAGON

Dagon (fish god)= Neptune= Posiedon (who carries the Trident) = 5atan = Leviathan = Taneen = dragon = seraph

man creates everything in his own image

*Dagon is where the word dragon came from. When a nation conquered another nation, they would take their gods and incorporate them into their belief system eventually remaking everything in our own image.*

Semaramis (*queen of Babylon*) became Isis, who became Ishtar/Easter, who became Venus, who became Aphrodite, and finally the Catholic version of the Virgin Mary. In the same way Nimrod (*King of Babylon*) became Dagon then became the sea serpent, then the dragon, then Neptune, then Poseidon, and then Zeus, and finally Satan.

The reason Neptune carried the trident, is the same reason you see Satan with the pitchfork. The trident was the article from the Jewish Tabernacle for turning the sacrifice. The Taneem (*great sea monster Genesis 1:21*) was created on the 5th day when God created the fishes and the birds. The association to the goat is also in Scripture as well as in satanic worship. The goat fish Capricorn was also a direct association to Satan as well as DRACO the Dragon, Hydra the Septa (the sea Monster), and Serpens the serpent.

As I demonstrated my book **Mystery Babylon: The Religion of the Beast**, Nimrod was the first false messiah ruling over the first attempt at a world government. Beginning with Nimrod in Babylon, mankind began to worship leviathan (*sea serpent*) they called Dagon, later known as The Dragon:

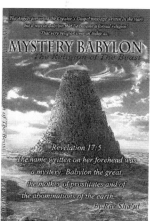

- Job 41:1 Can you draw out leviathan with a hook? or his tongue with a cord which you let down?

- Isaiah 27:1 In that day Yahuah with his great and strong sword shall punish leviathan the piercing serpent, even leviathan that crooked serpent (DRACO and SERPENS); and he shall slay the dragon (or Taneem in Hebrew) that is in the sea.

- Job 41:7 Can you fill his skin with barbed irons? or his head with fish spears?

This Dragon in the Sea, or DAGON the Fish God, called leviathan the sea monster in Scripture, was worshipped by those in ancient Babylon and associated with Nimrod the first high priest of Dagon. Worship of Dagon was passed down after Yahuah confused the languages and scattered humanity across the Earth at The Tower of Babel. It was this religion originating in Babylon around the corrupted Zodiac that was prevalent throughout the pages of Scripture and continued at the time Rome destroyed Jerusalem.

The Israelites on several occasions fell to this deception and worshiped Dagon, erected Ashtaroth Poles, and worshiped Semaramis as "The Queen of Heaven". They even worshiped Tammuz and to this day that remains the name of one of the Jewish Months of the year to prove it to their utter shame!

It was this religion of Dagon that permeated the high priestly ranks of paganism and was the foundation of The Christian Church which even today continues to wear the priestly garments of Dagon.

# Where did Satan come from?

The etymology of the name "Satan" is directly connected to Leviathan. Sa-TAN and Levia-TAN

both are derived from the word TANeem (*sea creature*) which is plural. The singular of Taneem is TAN. Sa-TAN and Levia-TAN are simply later versions of the Taneem god Dagon later known as The Dragon as the word Dagon evolved over time. It is Dagon the Dragon that is the spiritual source behind the Christian Church the Religion of Babylon (Rome formally transferred the religion of Babylon to Rome). Any Sunday/Christmas/Easter/Trinity/Jesus church is the Religion of Babylon founded on The Spirit of the Dragon. The Pope and priesthood of the Catholic Church is the high priest and priests of Dagon the Dragon in disguise (*not a very good disguise actually*).

204

The Priests of Dagon even to this day wear the "fish hat" called a Mitre Hat. They have dictated Christian theology world-wide including Protestant Theology from the City of Rome for 1500 years. Every fundamental doctrine of the Christian Church such as Sunday worship, Christmas, Easter, The Trinity, abolishment of The Law, pagan holidays, etc. were all Papal Edicts not found in Scripture. They violate clear explicit commands in Scripture, so we are taught "Jesus did away with the Law" to sell this lie.

# Rome = Babylon

Rome is called "Babylon" in The Bible because it embodied the same Mystery Religion of Babylon.

### 1 Peter 5:13
The church that is at Babylon (speaking of the church in Rome), elected together with you, saluteth you; and so does Marcus my son

Cybele, the Phrygian goddess, known to her followers as "the mother of god", was closely related to the worship of Mithra. Just as Mithraism was a man's religion, the worship of Cybele was practiced by women. The priests of Mithra were known as "Fathers" and the Priestesses of Cybele as "Mothers". After baptism into the Mysteries of Mithra, the initiate was marked on the forehead with an X. The sign of the cross formed by the elliptic and the celestial equator was one of the signs of Mithra. Sunday (*Deis Solis*), the day of the Sun, was considered by Mithraist a sacred day of rest. December 25th (*the birthday of Mithra*) was celebrated as the birth of the Sun, given birth by the "Queen of Heaven" – "Mother of god." The Mithraists celebrated a mithraic love feast. This feast consisted of loaves of bread decorated with crosses with wine, over which the priest pronounced a mystic formula. Mithra was considered mediator between god and man (*another "Demi-God" or "God in the Flesh"*). All of which, originated in Babylon as a religion based on the corrupted Zodiac.

This is the true origin of Christianity! Once we fully understand what "Christianity" actually is, what it is based on, and where it came from, then we can begin to understand why Christianity abolished the Law of Yahuah, abolished His Sabbath Day, and changed the sacrifice of the Passover Lamb to the Easter Pig. Every one of the above moves (*not commanded by Yahuah*) were made by the Pope of Rome… The High Priest of Dagon… The Dragon.

# The Mitre Hat

The priests of Dagon were known by their "Mitre Hat" which resembled an open mouth of a fish. The same hat worn even today by The Pope as well as Cardinals and Bishops. All "priests of Dagon" and the religion that surrounds them, even to this day, is identical to that born in Babylon.

As the pagan religion of Babylon was forced upon humanity by the Roman Emperor Constantine, the pagan aspects of worshipping Dagon, the fish god, was toned down. This was to make assimilation of other religions easier as to not offend other religions. All pagan religions were assimilated into The Universal Church of Rome through the process of syncretism. Syncretism is the blending of pagan religion with the worship of Yahuah. It is an abomination to Yahuah.

Not only are the ancient Priests of Dagon (*Fish Worship*) found wearing the Mitre hat, but also the Pope and Bishops of Rome are frequently found wearing this Mitre Hat.

This "clergy" system forms a pagan priest class NOT defined in The Word of Yahuah, but rather clearly defined in Ancient Babylon transferred to Rome becoming the official religion of Rome. And it is from this false class of "priests" we get every doctrine of the Christian Church.

We see the Priest of Dagon on the ancient wall drawing in every culture, even as far back as the Sumerians, when The High Priest of Dagon then served the Nephilim rulers (*see center figure in image below*):

The "beast coming out of the sea" that John saw in Revelation Chapter 13 is a direct reference back to Babylon and the god Nimrod worshipped.

"Oannes" or "Dagon"

DAGON or OANNES - "He would go back into the sea to spend the night, because he was amphibious. He had the head of a man; covered by the head of a fish and had the legs and feet of a man and the torso of a man but was covered by the scales and tail of a fish. " **Berossus; from ancient fragments (Isaac Preston Cory)**

Christianity (*or shall I say the Dragon behind it*) has done a very masterful job at concealing its true identity. However, that mask is coming off as knowledge increases at exponential rates mainly due to the internet. We are no longer bound by the mental chains of the Christian Church who has made it a top priority to keep the masses in total ignorance for 1500 years.

We can now actually research its origins and test the historical accuracy of its claims. Many over the centuries have questioned its rituals and practices simply because they cannot be found in the Bible. But now, we can fully unmask this false religion and expose it for what it is… paganism dating back to Babylon.

**Babylon and Nineveh, p. 343**
"The great apostate church of the Gospel Age, true to its Babylonish origin, has actually adopted this fish god in its ritual; for the pope on certain occasions manifests by his head gear that he is the direct representative of Dagon.

As it was an indispensable rule in all idolatrous religions that the high priest should wear the insignia of the god that he worshipped, so the sculptures discovered by Layard show that the priests of Dagon were arrayed in clothing resembling fish. This is probably the "strange apparel" referred to in Zeph. 1:8. Berosus tells us that in the image of Dagon the head of the man appeared under the head of the fish, while Layard points out that in the case of the priests "the head of the fish formed a mitre above that of the man, while its scaly, fan-like tail fell as a cloak behind, leaving the human limbs and feet exposed."

Originally the High Priest of Dagon literally wore a gutted fish over their head with the body of the fish draped down like a cape behind them. That "dress" evolved over time...The Dagon priests in Babylon wore hats that represented the open mouth of the fish, as if it were placed upon their heads - and the fish's body was seen extending from that head and mouth, down the priest's back to form a "robe". These exact priestly garments adorn the ranks of the Christian Clergy.

"The two-horned mitre, which the Pope wears, when he sits on the high altar at Rome and receives the adoration of the Cardinals, is the very mitre worn by the priests of Dagon, the fish-god of the Philistines and Babylonians.". - *The Two Babylons; Alexander Hislop; p. 215*

Not only does the Pope wear this "Mitre" hat, but so do the Cardinals on certain occasions when they are dressed in their royal regalia... a far cry from the suffering servant Yahusha the Messiah and what he taught.

These "priests" of Dagon today known as The Pope, Cardinals, and Bishops have elevated their station literally to Royalty among men.

There is nothing in The Word of Yahuah or the historical record indicating that The Messiah Yahusha ever wore such a hat or created such a priestly High Class of Royalty.

# Nimrod was "god incarnate" Dagon in the flesh

"...there are strong evidences that Dagon was Nimrod.... All scholars agree that the name and worship of Dagon were imported from Babylonia." - *The Two Babylons, Hislop, p. 215*

"In their veneration and worship of Dagon, the high priest of paganism would actually put on a garment that had been created from a huge fish! The head of the fish formed a mitre above that of the old man, while its scaly, fan-like tail fell as a cloak behind, leaving the human limbs and feet exposed." - *Babylon and Nineveh, Austen Henry Layard, p. 343*

"The most prominent form of worship in Babylon was dedicated to Dagon, later known as Ichthys, or the fish. In Chaldean times, the head of the church was the representative of Dagon, he was considered to be infallible, and was addressed as 'Your Holiness'. Nations subdued by Babylon had to kiss the ring and slipper of the Babylonian god-king. The same powers and the same titles are claimed to this day by the Dalai Lama of Buddhism, and the Pope. Moreover, the vestments of paganism, the fish mitre and robes of the priests of Dagon are worn by the Catholic bishops, cardinals and popes - *The Wine of Babylon; Pg. 9*

## *ICHTHYS - Symbol of "The Fish"*

Dagon (*fish worship*) is the source of the Christian symbol of the fish. Actually, ICHTHYS can be traced back to fish worship of Dagon and the Zodiac Sign of PISCES. We are "told" it is because some of the Disciples were "fisherman" or that Yahusha would make us "fishers of men" among other excuses. The truth is that it is nowhere defined in Scripture, but yet… the real source of the Christian fish symbol is that of Dagon fish worship. Just like the Mitre Hat.

**Smith's Bible Dictionary Dagon Fish Worship - from "Ancient Pagan and Modern Christian Symbolism"**
It was said that a fish ate one of these chunks and became transformed. Later, Isis [Semaramis] was fishing along the river bank when she fished up a half-man, half-fish. This sea creature was Dagon, the reincarnated Nimrod. And Dagon is the representation of Nimrod (of ancient Babylon) resurrecting out of the ocean depths as a half-man, half-fish

**Manners and Customs of the Bible; by James Freeman**
"Dagon is the diminutive of dag, and signifies… fish… The Babylonians believed that a being, part man and part fish, emerged from the Erythraean Sea, and appeared in Babylonia in the early days of its history… Representations of this fish-god have been found among the sculptures of Nineveh. The Philistine Dagon was of a similar character."

This also explains the symbol for Christianity, the fish – the "Ichthys" which is Dagon:

**Oxford English Dictionary (C. E.)**
Definition – "Ichthyic" – "of, pertaining to, or characteristic of fishes; the fish world in all its orders."

The worship of Dagon also affected people's eating habits. Now the mystery of why the Catholics abstain from eating fish on all days except Fridays comes into focus. This restriction of eating fish is not found in Scripture. Whether they realize it or not, they are practicing the ancient pagan rite of worshipping Dagon. The Catholic Encyclopedia even admits such abominations of the "so-called Church":

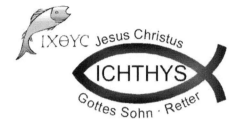

**The Catholic Encyclopedia, 1913, Encyclopedia Press**
*"As to the ritual of his worship... we only know from ancient writers that, for religious reasons, most of the Syrian peoples abstained from eating fish, a practice that one is naturally inclined to connect with the worship of a fish-god."*

The pagan Christian Church twisted the Nazarenes use of the Age of PISCES symbol.

# Conclusion

The Dragon in the Book of Revelation is the constellations DRACO, SERPENS, SCORPIO, and others which are shown in The Heavenly Scroll as being in a cosmic 'war' with ORION, OPHIUCHUS, PERSIUS, and others. The Dragon is traced back to Babylon where the false religion originated. It was the worship of Dagon, the fish god, that was the spirit behind the religion in Babylon then Rome then Christianity. That religion was based on the corrupted version of the Babylonian Zodiac known as Sun worship. It was formally introduced (*as Sun worship*) when Nimrod, the High Priest of Dagon, died and 'became the Sun'. He was then known as Ba'al. The religion in Babylon was known for:

- Ba'al (*Sun Worship*) was known as The LORD which is a title for Ba'al!

- Ashtaroth Poles called obelisks and now steeples.

- The Godhead was a "trinity" in the images of Nimrod, his wife Semaramis, and their son Tammuz.

- Tammuz was the second member of the Trinity, who was considered the "son of the Sun" and "God in the flesh" as his mother Semaramis was believed to be impregnated by the "rays of the Sun" or rather the Spirit of The LORD in a virgin birth.

- The "sacrifice" of that religion was a pig on what they called Ishtar Day. In English… Easter.

- They hunted Ishtar Eggs as Ishtar was believed to come to Earth in a giant egg!

- Tammuz was said to be born on December 25th, the rebirth of the Sun each year.

The Priests of Dagon (*even to this day*) wear the "fish hat" and dictate Christian theology world-wide including Protestant Theology from the City of Rome (*modern Babylon*). Every fundamental doctrine of the Christian Church (such as Incarnation, Sunday worship, Christmas, Easter, The Trinity, abolishment of The Law, pagan holidays, etc.) were all Papal Edicts coming down from The Dragon High Priest… not found in Scripture. They violate clear explicit commands in Scripture.

Rome is called "Babylon" in The Bible because it embodied the same Mystery Religion of Babylon that was formally transferred to Rome when Rome conquered Babylon.

> **1 Peter 5:13**
> The church that is at Babylon (speaking of the church in Rome), elected together with you, saluteth you; and so does Marcus my son

Once we fully understand what "Christianity" actually is, what it is based on, and where it came from, then we can begin to understand why Christianity abolished the Law of Yahuah, abolished His Sabbath Day, and changed the sacrifice of the Passover Lamb to the Easter Pig. Every one of the above moves (not commanded by Yahuah) were made by the Pope of Rome… The High Priest of Dagon… The Dragon. Because it is The Dragon that gives this pagan High Priest his thrown and power today just as it did in the days of Babylon. The Pope is the High Priest of Dagon the Dragon and literally sits on a throne!

*The High Priest of Dagon, The Dragon and the throne of the Devil.*

This is what the Bible calls Mystery Babylon the Whore because it prostitutes out the worship of the ONE True God to a plurality of gods (the Trinity, Saints, Jesus, Holy Spirit, etc.)

### Revelation 17:4

The woman was dressed in purple and scarlet, and was glittering with gold, precious stones and pearls. She held a golden cup in her hand, filled with abominable things and the filth of her adulteries.

Beginning to sound familiar? I explain in my book **Mystery Babylon the Religion of the Beast** exactly what they believed. Then I compare that religion to Christianity in my book **Christianity the Great Deception**. They are identical!

*End of Excerpt*

# The "Wilderness"?
## *A Divine Rehearsal*

In Revelation 12:13-17 we see that the Woman is led into the "wilderness" on the "wings of an eagle". Before we restore Chapter 12, we must understand this prophetic symbolism. This event in Revelation 12 is celebrated annually in the Feast of Sukkot.  Below is an excerpt from my book **The Fall Feasts: An invitation to the wedding**.

*Excerpt from The Fall Feasts: An invitation to the wedding by Rav Sha'ul*

Sukkot is a Divine Rehearsal of a future event! In the religious circles today, we are only taught to look back to Israel wandering in the wilderness living in Sukkot after crossing The Red Sea.

The first Exodus was a Divine teaching tool for us to study to understand the Greater Spiritual Truth that at the end of the Age of PISCES, per The Heavenly Scroll, the children of Yahuah would exodus the nations of Earth. They would be sealed on their foreheads, pass through the wilderness, shed their physical bodies (*temporary dwellings*) and enter The Promised Land (*Kingdom of Yahuah*) on The Last Great Day.

## A Thousand years is a day, a day is a thousand years, so the Last Great Day represents The Kingdom Reign (*1,000-year reign*) during the Age of ***AQUARIUS***!

We also see Yahusha fulfill the Spiritual Truth when he was Mikveh'd by John then fled into "the wilderness" where he was tempted, tested, and perfected. This event occurred as part of Yahusha being consecrated High Priest...

### Hebrews 4:14-15
[14] Therefore, since we have such a great High Priest who has passed through the Heavens (fulfilled The Heavenly Scroll), Yahusha the Son of Yahuah (by adoption at his Mikveh), let us hold firmly to what we profess. [15] For we do not have a High Priest who is unable to sympathize with our weaknesses, but we have one who was tempted (in the wilderness) in every way that we are yet was without sin (AFTER being consecrated High Priest).

### Matthew 4:1
<u>Then Yahusha was led</u> (did not plan on going, this was NOT a fast) **by the Spirit** into the wilderness to be tempted (and tested not to fast).

### Hebrews 5:8-9
[8] though he was (an adopted) Son (of Yahuah), yet he learned obedience (to Yahuah) by the things which he suffered. [9] And having been perfected, he became the author of eternal salvation to all who obey him (and walk The Way of Mikveh, Circumcision, and Offering),

Then our Groom has "gone and prepared a place for us to live with him in his Father's estate" John 14:3 and returns for us on Trumpets, enter into a marriage covenant with us on Yom Kippur, then we too enter that same "wilderness" for a period of time at the end of The Age of PISCES.

### John 14:2-4
[2] "In my Father's house are many dwelling places; if it were not so, I would have told you; for I go to prepare a place for you (in my Father's Estate). [3] "If I go and prepare a place for you (my Bride), I will come again and receive you to myself (as my Bride), that where I am, there you may be also (to live in covenant of Marriage together). [4] "And you know the Way (Mikveh, Circumcision, Offering) where I am going."

# Revelation and The Greater Exodus

We see in the Exodus out of Egypt, a Divine example of the Spiritual Truths concerning the Plan of Salvation for Remnant (Spiritual) Israel at the end of the Age of PISCES, all laid out in The Heavenly Scroll.

- PISCES/Trumpets - Physical Israel taken out of bondage in Egypt – Remnant Israel called out of every nation.

- AQUARIUS/Shav'uot - Physical Israel Mikveh'd in the Red Sea – Spiritual Israel Mikveh'd by The Water Bearer Yahusha.

- AQUARIUS/Shav'uot – Physical Israel circumcised (sealed) at the foot of Mt. Sinai to obey the letter of the Law – Spiritual Israel circumcised of heart to obey the Intent of the Law.

- TAURUS/Days of Awe - Physical Israel commanded to purge the Promised Land of all lawbreakers (pagan inhabitants) – Yahusha sends his Angels to remove all Law breakers from Earth. Wedding invite goes out to Elect.

- GEMINI/Yom Kippur – The Bride and Groom are married at the Altar in Heaven the Yahushaic Covenant fulfilled.

- CANCER/Sukkot – Physical Israel led through the wilderness to purge Israel of the pagan practices it had adopted before entering The Promised Land – Spiritual Israel led through a Spiritual Wilderness to purge them of pagan beliefs before entering The Kingdom.

- LEO/Last Great Day – Physical Israel defeating the Kingdom of Jericho as the wall came tumbling down – Yahusha defeats every Kingdom and turns all kingdoms of Earth over to his Father.

# Do we "flee to the mountains" in fear of The Dragon?

Very little of the Book of Revelation is literal. John was reading and interpreting the contents of The Heavenly Scroll.

Many today are preparing to flee to the mountains and claim Revelation 12 as their justification. Is this wise? Or is Revelation speaking of the Greater Exodus out of the nations and a "Spiritual wilderness".

On Sukkot, the training aid for Spiritual Children was to look back at Israel being taken out of bondage in Egypt and traveling through the wilderness (*where they lived in temporary dwellings*) to get to The Promised Land. That training aid was to develop Spiritually Mature sons/daughters teaching us through physical to Spiritual parallels that we too are taken out of bondage to the nations, we too, travel through a Spiritual Wilderness in temporary dwellings whereby we are purged from all the false doctrines, pagan beliefs, and human traditions before entering The Kingdom.

We see this in Revelation Chapter 12 where the "woman" or Spiritual Israel is taken on wings of an Eagle into a wilderness where she is sealed, disciplined, and protected from deception. We are taught this is literal when nothing in Revelation Chapter 12 is literal, it is John reading The Heavenly Scroll! We are being told by our teachers today to prepare to "escape" into the mountains when we are already in the "wilderness".

In Revelation 12, the Woman (*we*) are pursued by the False Religion (*the Dragon*) because of our beliefs and rejection of The False Messiah. Like in the physical shadow of Israel coming out of Egypt and pursued by the Egyptian Army and the Red Sea parted; We are pursued by the Dragon (*False Religion*) who spews out water to overtake us. We are delivered out of water again as the Earth swallow up the waters just like the Red Sea.

The question is, what are these things that John is seeing (*waters, Eagle, wings, wilderness, etc.*)?

### Revelation 12:13-17

[13] When the dragon saw that he had been hurled to the Earth, he pursued the woman who had given birth to the male child. [14] The woman was given the two wings of a great eagle, so that she might fly to the place prepared for her (to be perfected) in the wilderness, where she would be taken care of for a time, times and half a time, out of the serpent's reach. [15] Then from his mouth the serpent spewed water like a river, to overtake the woman and sweep her away with the torrent. [16] But the Earth helped the woman by opening its mouth and swallowing the river that the dragon had spewed out of his mouth. [17] Then the dragon was enraged at the woman and went off to wage war against the rest of her offspring—those who keep Yahuah's Commands and hold fast their testimony about Yahusha (that he fulfilled The Heavenly Scroll).

First, the entire chapter of Revelation 12 is John reading The Heavenly Scroll and is not literal; it is figurative. It is speaking of Spiritual things using physical terminology. We, the "wheat", are not literally wheat nor are we a woman, we do not sprout "wings" and therefore the "wilderness" is not literal either. To switch from figurative to literal requires a clear context change. Everything between clear context changes is either figurative or literal, it doesn't switch back and forth in the same context.

# The Woman and the Wheat

The "woman" is VIRGO. We are called "wheat" because VIRGO (*the woman*) holds Remnant Israel (*the wheat*) in her left hand (*a stalk of wheat*), and a Palm Branch (*representing victory over the Dragon and eternal life*). The woman has sprouted "wings of an eagle":

Yahusha is The Branch or Seed because he is represented among "the wheat" by the star Spica, the brightest star in VIRGO. In Hebrew, Spica means "seed/branch" which is in the stalk of wheat in VIRGO's hand.

# The Flood flowing forth from The Father of Lies

What we have in Revelation is John seeing what is called The Greater Exodus. It is the Greater Exodus that we are supposed to be celebrating on Sukkot! The Greater Exodus at the end of the Age of PISCES when we are taken out of the bondage of the nations through "the wilderness" where we are purged and perfected (*this life*). We live in temporary dwellings (fleshly bodies), and we are brought safely into the promised land (*The Kingdom*).

It is a greater event Spiritually likened to the parting of the Red Sea. Where Moses led Israel through the Red Sea which parted, in this case we have the reverse, the Dragon attempts to sweep us away with a flood of water and again "the Earth swallows it up".

## Revelation 12:15-16

[15] So the serpent spewed water out of his mouth like a flood after the woman, that he might cause her to be carried away by the flood. [16] But the Earth helped the woman, and the Earth opened its mouth and swallowed up the flood which the dragon had spewed out of his mouth.

We see in Revelation above, the Dragon spews forth waters which tries to overtake the woman like a flood. This "flood" is a "flood of lies and false doctrines" which lead us astray (see Jeremiah 8:8,16:19). Jeremiah describes the Greater Exodus of the Gentiles coming out of the nation fleeing the Dragon (who is called "the Father of lies" John 8:44):

> ### Jeremiah 8:8
> "How can you say, 'We are wise, and the word of Yahuah is with us'? But behold, the lying pen of the scribes has made it into a lie.

> ### Jeremiah 16:19
> O Yahuah, my strength, and my fortress, and my refuge in the day of affliction, the Gentiles shall come unto thee from the ends of the Earth, and shall say, Surely our fathers have inherited lies, vanity, and things wherein there is no profit

We see that "flood of water" is associated with lies and false doctrines below:

### Isaiah 28:15-17

15 We have made a covenant with death, and with hell we are in agreement. The overflowing scourge (Heb. : combination of two words "rod" and "flood") shall not come to us when it passes through, for we have made lies our refuge and under falsehood we have hid ourselves . . . 17 then the hail shall sweep away the refuge of lies and the waters shall overflow the hiding place.

The Spiritual Understanding of Revelation is found in The Mystery Language and The Heavenly Scroll and then confirmed throughout the Scriptures.

# Wings of an Eagle

Now, let's look at the wings of an Eagle! The "wings" the woman spouts to carry her (*Remnant Israel*) into a place of "wilderness". We must spend an allotted time in this wilderness to be prepared to enter The Promised Land (*the Kingdom*).

As I stated earlier, VIRGO is "the woman" and she is depicted with "wings of an Eagle" in The Heavenly Scroll. She carries the "wheat" in her left hand. The "wings of an Eagle" are defined clearly in Scripture as well... Again, John is describing The Greater Exodus and drawing comparisons (*like the flood and the Red Sea*) and he is using the events in Exodus as a guide.

### Exodus 19:4

You have seen what I did to the Egyptians, and how I bore you on eagles' wings and brought you to Myself

So again, we know Israel was not flown by an Eagle into the promised land, they were led through the wilderness! "Wings of an Eagle" is an idiom for STRENGTH ...

### Isaiah 40:31

But those who wait on Yahuah shall renew their strength; They shall mount up with wings like eagles, they shall run and not be weary, They shall walk and not faint.

So, we do not go to some place in the wilderness, we do not flee to the hill in fear, we are given STRENGTH not to run from our persecution and not grow weary during this Great Exodus out of the Nations. We are purged from our pagan practices we have inherited just as Physical Israel had to be purged coming out of Egypt (*after building the Golden Calf*).

# The Seal of Protection from the flood of lies and deception

We, the Chosen, then receive a seal of protection over our minds from this flood of lies and deceit to protect as we go through "the wilderness". The Shema is a seal over the frontal lobe of our brain which, the frontal, protects us from deception, lies, and false doctrines spewed out by The Dragon (*Christianity*).

> ### Revelation 3:12
> Him who overcomes (the flood of lies spewed out by The Dragon *Revelation 12:15*) I will make a pillar in the temple of my God. Never again will He (Yahuah) leave it (that Spiritual Temple). I will write on him (who overcomes) the name of my God (YHVH)

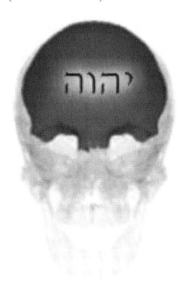

The frontal bone in our cranium is a physical parallel of the Seal on our forehead. We see below, in verse 8, this Seal is "as the frontal bone between your eyes"

### Deuteronomy 6:4-9

[4] "Hear, O Israel: Yahuah our God, Yahuah is One! [5] You shall love Yahuah your God with all your heart, with all your soul, and with all your strength. [6] "And these words which I command you today shall be in your heart. [7] You shall teach them diligently to your children, and shall talk of them when you sit in your house, when you walk by the way, when you lie down, and when you rise up. [8] You shall bind them as a sign on your hand, and they shall be as frontlets between your eyes. [9] You shall write them on the doorposts of your house and on your gates.

This physical to Spiritual parallel employed by Yahuah in Deuteronomy can only now be understood in the context it was meant. Science has defined the "purpose" of the Frontal Lobe of the human brain and we can see why that lobe MUST be sealed by Yahuah. The Frontal Lobe has been identified and described as follows, according to **Dr. Donald Stuss of The Rotman Research Institute**:

> *The frontal lobe is a critical center and it controls the "essence" of our humanity. The frontal lobes, which are also called the cerebral cortex, are the seat of emotions and judgments related to sympathy, which is the ability to feel sorrow for someone else's suffering, and empathy, which the ability to understand another's feelings and problems. They are also the seat of understanding humor, including subtle witticisms and word plays. The frontal lobes also recognizes sarcasm and irony. And they are where recognition of deception occurs guiding our judgment between right and wrong. The cerebral cortex, or frontal lobes, is indeed the seat of our essence and nature.*

We need to always keep in the foremost of our mind (*literally*) that Yahuah's purpose is to govern the Universe with His Sons. The Frontal Lobe is critical in all aspects of judgment, empathy, and knowing right from wrong. Yahuah literally provides a protective shield called The Seal of Yahuah which protects that very part of our mind that enables us to have empathy toward others, recognize deceptive philosophies, and the frontal lobe literally determines our essence and nature. The very seat of Righteous Government is in our Fontal Lobe.

For a detailed look at the seal of protection over our frontal lobes in the brain which shield us from this flood of lies please read my book The Kingdom.

# Temporary Dwellings?

What is the Spiritual Intent behind staying in a Sukkot? Yahuah's temporary dwelling was the first the Tabernacle then the physical Temple, which was designed as a shadow of the Greater Truth revealed in The Yahushaic Covenant. That truth is that His final dwelling would be the resurrected bodies of His born again and adopted children. The ones He brings out of the nations who shed their own "temporary dwellings" as these temporary bodies are transposed from physical to Spiritual bodies (*resurrection*).

Yahusha was the first to shed his temporary dwelling and receive his permanent dwelling (*Spiritual Body*) and was laid as the Chief Cornerstone of the 3rd and final Temple of Yahuah. We then follow him in the regeneration as we too shed our temporary dwellings and receive our inheritance (*Spiritual Bodies*).

> **Matthew 19:28**
> And Yahusha said unto them, truly I say to you, That you which have followed me, in the regeneration when (now he reads The Heavenly Scroll) *"the Son of man shall sit in the Throne of his glory"* (the center of The Enoch Zodiac, The Throne in Heaven), you also shall sit upon twelve Thrones, judging the twelve Tribes of Israel.

These bodies are the Spiritual Parallels of the temporary dwellings of Sukkot, this life is the wilderness we pass through to enter the Promised Land in fulfillment of the shadow picture of the first Exodus. This life is our journey through the wilderness. We are strangers passing through... as the Israelites migrating to the Promised Land through the wilderness.

> **1 Chronicles 29:15**
> For we are strangers before you, and sojourners, as all our fathers were (through the wilderness in Exodus): our days on the Earth are as a shadow, and there is no abiding (in these temporary dwellings/physical bodies).

> **1 Peter 2:11**
> "Beloved, I beg you as sojourners and pilgrims (like our forefathers in the wilderness), abstain from fleshly lusts (of these temporary dwellings) which war against the soul (our Spiritual Bodies)."

This natural body is a temporary dwelling (our Sukkot). We will put away these Sukkots when we too enter The Kingdom on The LAST GREAT DAY ... This temporary dwelling is at war against our Spiritual Body and must die...

### 1 Corinthians 15:43-45

[43] Our body is sown in dishonor (in the Flesh); it is raised in glory (Spiritually). It is sown in weakness; it is raised in power. [44] It is sown a natural (temporary) body; it is raised an eternal Spiritual body. If there is a natural body, there is also a Spiritual body. [45] So it is written: "The first man Adam became a living being;" the last Adam a life-giving Spirit (through regeneration)....

Just like the physical Temple was a shadow/temporary dwelling pointing to the totality of the resurrected Spiritual Children of Yahuah, Yahusha the chief cornerstone.

So Yahuah lived in a temporary dwelling too for a time, until such time as The Yahushaic Covenant was consummated, then the old shadow was permanently and for all time destroyed, not one stone left on another like our physical bodies. There will NEVER be another physical temple built in Jerusalem as we are taught by these blind guides in their unspiritual minds.

### John 2:19-21

[19] Yahusha answered and said unto them, Destroy this temple, and in three days I will raise it up. [20] Then said the Jews, Forty and six years was this temple in building, and wilt thou rear it up in three days? [21] But he spake of the Temple of his body.

### I Corinthians 6:19

Do you not know that your body is a Temple of the Spirit of Yahuah Who is in you, whom you have from Yahuah?

### II Corinthians 6:16

What agreement has The Temple of Yahuah with idols? For we are the Temple of the living God; just as Yahuah said, "I will dwell in them and walk among them; and I will be their God, and they shall be My people."

### Ephesians 2:19-22

[19] So then you are no longer strangers and aliens, but you are fellow citizens with the saints, and are of Yahuah's household, [20] having been built upon the foundation of the Apostles and Prophets, the Messiah Yahusha himself being the corner stone (of The Temple of Yahuah), [21] in whom the whole building, being fitted together is growing into a Holy Temple of Yahuah; [22] in whom you also are being built together into a dwelling of Yahuah in the Spirit (The Kingdom of Yahuah).

### I Peter 2:5

You also, as living stones, are being built up as a Spiritual house (*Temple*)...

We see this Spiritual Truth clearly in Revelation as the physical Temple was not seen in the City of Jerusalem, but rather that Temple is now Spiritual:

### Revelation 21:22
I did not see a Temple in the city, because Yahuah Almighty and the Lamb are its Temple. If we had true Spiritually inspired teachers like Sha'ul and Yahusha, we would be taught the transposition of all physical things into the Spiritual Yahushaic Covenant! Including the Spiritual Intent of the physical sukkots! Instead, we are surrounded by self-appointed teachers who are but children in maturity still teaching the letter of the Law not the Spiritual Intent..

### Colossians 2:16-18
...[16] Therefore (speaking of the letter of the Law) let no one judge you by (physical adherence as to) what you eat or drink, or with regard to (how you keep) a Feast, a New Month Celebration, or a Sabbath. [17] These (physical letters of the Law) are <u>a shadow of the greater Spiritual things to come</u>, but the body that casts it belongs to The Yahushaic Covenant (Yahusha fulfilled The Heavenly Scroll where the Feasts are defined). [18] Do not let anyone who delights in false humility (fasting from food or outward displays of Righteousness) and the worship of angels disqualify you with speculation about what he has seen (it is speculation because you cannot see or judge Intent of the heart which is what Yahuah judges). <u>Such a man is puffed up without basis by his</u> **unspiritual mind** (following the physical letter not the Spiritual Intent)

Interesting to note, the temporary dwelling of Yahuah (*the physical temple in Jerusalem*) was destroyed; when? During the Fall Feasts around the 9th of Aviv or August. If we had more data, probably during Sukkot! That is why over a million Jews were slaughtered, Sukkot is one of the 3 annual pilgrimages when all of Israel were to be in Jerusalem... For more information on the transposition of all things from their physical shadow to Spiritual.

*The Kingdom by Rav Sha'ul. Available on all on-line bookstores.*

# The Sign of the Son of Man

In The Heavenly Scroll there are two signs that are given of "the Son of Man". There is one that proclaims the birth of the King in the constellation VIRGO; and then there is a sign in the Son of Man constellation ORION that is defined as "the brightness of his coming". So, we have The Sign of the *Birth* of the Son of Man and the Sign of the *Coming* of the Son of Man.

## The Sign of *the Birth* of Son of Man

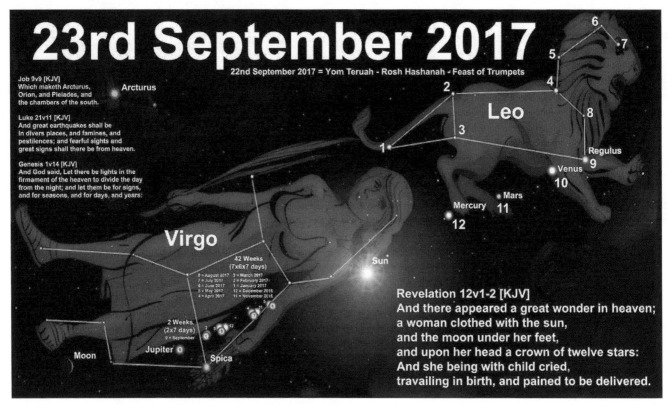

The birth of the King in The Heavenly Scroll is when both the Sun and the planet Jupiter (*which means King*) are in VIRGO (*which is the princess Bride / woman*). Jupiter is in the womb of the woman and goes into retrograde motion appearing to go back and forth inside the womb of VIRGO for exactly 9 months (*the time of human gestation*) then exits through the birthing canal of VIRGO. This is the sign of the woman in birthing pains giving birth to the King.

**Revelation 12:1-5**

[1] A great SIGN appeared in The Heavenly Scroll: a woman (*VIRGO*) clothed with the Sun, with the moon under her feet and a crown of twelve stars on her head. [2] She was pregnant and cried out in pain as she was about to give birth (to a King/Jupiter). [3] Then another sign appeared in Heaven: an enormous red dragon (*DRACO*) with seven heads and ten horns and seven crowns on its heads. [4] Its tail swept a third of the stars out of the sky and flung them to the Earth. The dragon stood in front of the woman (*VIRGO*) who was about to give birth (to the King/Jupiter), so that it might devour her child the moment he was born. [5] She gave birth to a son, a male child, who "will rule all the Nations (as King) with an iron scepter (*LEO*)"

The Sun and Jupiter in VIRGO with Jupiter in retrograde motion for 9 months is so unique it is proven to have only appeared in the sky 3 times prior in human history. 2,000 years ago, at the time of the Messiah's birth, 4,000 years ago at the time of Abraham's birth, and 6,000 years ago with the birth of Adam as the Scriptures record. While the basic sign of the Sun and Jupiter in VIRGO has happened a few times in the past, there was a sign with more detail that was uniquely fulfilled on September 23, 2017.

This sign appeared in The Heavenly Scroll on the Feast of Shofars in 2017 exactly 1 generation (*70 years*) from when Israel was reborn as a nation in 1 day as prophesied. Right on time to transition from the Age of PISCES to the Age of AQUARIUS.

This sign in the image on the previous page has never appeared in this much perfect detail in history going back 10,000 years and will never appear again in the future. It was unique in history.

# The Sign of *the Coming of* The Son of Man

The sign of the Coming of the Son of Man on the clouds of Heaven is another sign in The Heavenly Scroll that appears in the constellation ORION (*the Son of Man, Conquering King*). As I stated in this book, ORION rides the clouds of Heaven (*the Milky Way Galaxy*) each year beginning in the Fall Feasts. This event is celebrated as Yom Teruah with the blowing of Shofars as we rehearse the events prophesied in Scripture:

**Zachariah 9:14**

Then (the proxy of) Yahuah (who is Yahusha who 'comes in Yahuah's Glory' *Matthew 16:27*) will appear over them (in The Heavenly Scroll as *ORION* the Light Bearer), and his arrow (*H2671*: figurative of the Messiah's weapons or sword, the sword of *ORION*) will go forth like lightning (*H130*: flash like lightning (1), flashing (1), gleaming (2), glittering point). The (the Angel of) Yahuah our Elohim will sound the shofar and advance (of the return of the King on Yom Teruah) in the tempest of the south.

ORION is known as "the Light Bearer" and Yahusha time and again confirmed he was the fulfillment of the one who bears the light. Below is the meaning of the pictograph of ORION in The Heavenly Scroll:

### ORION the Bearer of The Light of Life
"**The** coming **Prince of Peace**, the Light (of the World), the one who holds the double-edged sword in his hand (the Word of Yahuah), he is the coming of *The Branch*, the one wounded by the serpent, the foot that crushes the head of the serpent."

# Yahusha is known as the Bearer of the Light of Life

### Isaiah 42:5-6
5 Thus says Yahuah in The Heavenly Scroll, Who created The Heavenly Scroll and stretched out the stars and constellation (in order) to proclaim His Plan of Salvation (*Isaiah 48:13*), Who spread out the Earth and its offspring, Who gives Breath to the people on it and revive the Spirit of those who walk in *The Way* of Mikveh (*AQUARIUS*), 6 "I Am Yahuah, I have called Yahusha in **The Path of Righteousness** (to show My People how they can fulfill The Law and be found Righteous in My Sight through Mikveh with Living Water *Ezekiel 36:25*), I will also hold Yahusha by the hand and watch over him to walk *The Way* by example (*John 13:5*), And I will appoint Yahusha as a Covenant to the People (Called The Yahushaic Covenant), As a Spiritual Light Bearer (*ORION*) to the Nations

### Isaiah 60:1
Arise (*ORION* and ride the clouds of Heaven), shine; for your Light (*ORION*) has come (been fulfilled in Yahusha), And the Glory of Yahuah (proclaimed by The Sun/stars/constellations *Psalm 19* and *Enoch 35:3*) has risen upon you.

### Luke 2:32
a Light (Bearer) for revelation to the Gentiles (*ORION* coming in the clouds of Heaven), and the Glory (the Sun/stars/constellations tell of the Glory of Yahuah *Psalm 19* and *Enoch 35:3*) of Your People Israel.

### John 8:12
When Yahusha spoke again to the people, he said, I am the (Spiritual) Light (Bearer) of the world (*ORION* The Son of Man/Light Bearer and fulfillment of the Physical light of the Sun *Psalm 19*). Whoever follows me

(in walking The Way) will never walk in darkness but will have (**ORION**) the (Bearer of the) Light of Life (to show them The Way of Salvation **AQUARIUS**).

### Matthew 4:16-17

16 the people living in darkness (following The Way of the Gentiles, the corrupted Zodiac **Romans 1**) have seen a great Light (as 'the Sun has come to us from The Heavenly Scroll' to show us The Way/Doctrine of Righteousness of Mikveh, Circumcision, and Offering **Luke 1:77-78**, **Malachi 4:2**); on those living in the land of (the Gentiles who live in) the shadow of death (of the corrupted Babylonian Zodiac **Romans 1**. 'I will make you a covenant to the Nations, I will also give you for a Light, fulfillment of The Light of the Sun, to the Gentiles' **Isaiah 42:7-9**), a Light has dawned (been fulfilled on Earth in the flesh **John 1:1-4, Luke 1:77-79**). 17 From that time on Yahusha began to teach **_The Way_** of *Mikveh, Circumcision, and Offering* saying, Repent (Circumcision of Heart) and be Mikveh'd (washed clean of your sin **Jeremiah 31** and **Ezekiel 36**), for The Kingdom proclaimed in The Heavenly Scroll (Shamayim – 'the stars') is within your reach (he has come to fulfill it).

---

## What will it be like when the Messiah returns bearing "the Light"? Will there be a physical parallel to the Spiritual Truth at that time, a great light in the Heavens in the constellation *ORION*???

---

# The brightness of his coming

There is a specific sign in ORION that occurs only 1 time in history (*just like the Sign of the Birth of the Son of Man Rev. 12 occurs only once in human history*). It is a sign identified by its overwhelming brightness that "all the world" can see at once. This occurs in the "Heavens" and is so bright it competes with the Sun and Moon both day and night to herald the return of the King.

### Matthew 24:30-31

30 At that time (3.5 years AFTER the Sign of the Birth of the son of Man see **Revelation12**) the sign of the Son of Man will appear in (the) Heaven(ly Scroll), and all the tribes of the Earth will mourn. They will see (Spiritually perceive see with the mind **G3708**. horaó) the Son of Man coming on the clouds of Heaven (**ORION**) with power and great glory (**GEMINI**). 31 And He will send out His Angels with a loud shofar call (to announce that the Groom has arrived for his Bride and the Marriage Supper of the Lamb is at hand)

**GEMINI**: The Marriage of the Lamb, the enemy is trodden down, the Prince comes in great Glory (*Matthew 24:30*)

### Revelation 1:7

Look (up in The Heavenly Scroll)! He (the Son of Man) comes with the clouds of Heaven (**ORION** who rides the clouds of Heaven/milky way). **And everyone will see (**Spiritually perceive see with the mind **G3708**. Horaó**)_ him**— even those who pierced him. And all the Nations of the world will mourn for him.

### 2 Thessalonians 2:8

And then shall that Wicked be revealed, whom the King shall consume with the Spirit of his mouth (Word of His Testimony), and shall destroy with the **brightness of his coming**"

Above the Messiah is giving us the sign that will appear on Yom Teruah, the blowing of the Shofars to announce the immediate return of the King with a very obvious sign of brightness in the constellation ORION. We see that ORION will have a flashing, gleaming, glittering POINT on this occasion as the Shofar heralds his return. We see further information on what occurs on this Yom Teruah when the Sign of the Son of Man is gleaming forth from ORION.

### 1 Corinthians 15:52

in an instant, in the twinkling of an eye (the light from the supernova of Betelgeuse will appear to twinkle in the sky), at the last shofar. For the shofar will sound (on Yom Teruah), the dead will be raised imperishable, and we will be changed.

### 1 Thessalonians 4:16

For The King himself will descend from Heaven with a loud command, with the voice of an Archangel, and with the shofar of Yahuah (on Yom Teruah), and the dead in covenant with Yahusha will be the first to rise (from the dead).

### Revelation 11:15

Then the seventh Angel sounded his shofar (on Yom Teruah), and loud voices called out in Heaven: "*The kingdom of the world has become the Kingdom of our God Yahuah and of His Anointed King Yahusha, and he (*Yahusha*) will reign forever and ever* (constellation **LEO**)."

The Groom comes for his Bride as the Bride is prepared and received on this day.

### Isaiah 49:18

Lift up your eyes (to The Heavenly Scroll) and behold (Spiritually Perceive); all Your Children gather and come to you. As surely as I live," declares Yahuah, "you will wear them (the constellations) all as ornaments; you will put them (the stars) on, **like a Bride**.

We see a period where there is a battle (*called Armageddon*) where the armies of man are destroyed, and all lawlessness removed from Earth.

This is called the Days of Awe which are the 10 days from Yom Teruah until Yom Kippur.

**Revelation 2:10**
Do not be afraid of what you are about to suffer. I tell you; the devil will put some of you in prison to test you, and **you will suffer persecution for ten days**. Be faithful, even to the point of death, and I will give you life as your victor's crown.

**Matthew 13:41**
The Son of man shall send forth his Angels, and they shall gather out of his Kingdom all things that offend, and them which do iniquity;

**Revelation 19:15**
And from his mouth proceeds a sharp sword (the sword of **ORION**) with which to strike down the Nations, and he will rule them (**LEO**) with an iron scepter (**Revelation 12**). He treads the winepress of the fury of the wrath (or weapon/sword) of Yahuah, the Almighty.

# The Star Betelgeuse and the Sign in ORION

Is there just such an event identified in the constellation ORION that is expected to occur eminently? One that would fulfill these requirements in Scripture. Yes. The largest star in the constellation ORION is Betelgeuse and it is overdue to go supernova (*explode and die*)! This will create an event in the constellation ORION that would be brighter than our moon, seen even during the day competing with our Sun.

This bright flash will travel across Heaven as ORION (*the Son of Man*) rides the clouds of Heaven (*Milky Way*) for every eye to see the Brightness of His Coming on the clouds of Heaven. ORION runs his course every year beginning in the fall around Yom Teruah.

It was reported in the Science section of the Atlantic Periodical on January 20, 2020 that it is eminent and could occur "any day". The star Betelgeuse has been acting erratically of late indicating it could be about to go supernova… right on time 3 years from when the Sign of the Birth of the King appeared in The Heavenly Scroll on September 23, 2017 leading up to The Sign of the Coming of the Son of Man.

https://amp.theatlantic.com/amp/article/60525
1/?fbclid=IwAR3rbEqopi8gGJCxTrH7UUyRJYkKt
kB37Hqkl_4PRy-2dJm51MHjfl3LUZE

Sometime this week, you might walk outside in broad daylight, look up at the sky, and see a luminous orb as bright as a full moon. Only it wouldn't be the moon. It would be something far more explosive: the dazzling aftermath of a cataclysm hundreds of light-years away.

You'd be seeing the light from a supernova—the final, powerful flash of a dying star.

Or ... you might see the regular old sky. Supernovas are nearly impossible to predict. But astronomers have recently started discussing the rare possibility with a bit more enthusiasm than usual, thanks to some odd behavior elsewhere in the Milky Way. If the supernova did show up tomorrow, it would be the celestial event of the year, perhaps even the century, leaving a cosmic imprint in the sky for all to see.

In the night sky, the constellation ORION is most well-known for his belt, a row of three luminous stars. For the last few months, though, astronomers around the world have been particularly interested in his right shoulder, the home of a star called Betelgeuse, one of the brightest stars in the sky. Betelgeuse—which, yes, is pronounced like Beetlejuice—has been dimming more than it ever had before. Astronomers have long known that Betelgeuse is aging and, like many old stars, is bound to explode sooner or later. Could this mystery dimming mean that a supernova might be imminent?

The view would be mind-boggling, day or night. The ORION constellation can be seen from nearly everywhere on Earth, which means nearly everyone could see the exploding star. It would easily cut through the artificial-light pollution that prevents 80 percent of the world—and a staggering 99 percent of the United States and Europe—from experiencing a clear view of the night sky. "At the predicted brightness of a Betelgeuse supernova, you could be standing in the center of the biggest city in the world, and you would certainly see it," says John Barentine, an astronomer and the director of public policy at the International Dark-Sky Association, a nonprofit that works to mitigate light pollution. "You couldn't miss it."

Even more spectacular, the display would stick around. The gleaming orb would remain visible for more than a year, perhaps even longer. How strange it would be to witness day in and day out, to understand, for the most part, that the blaze is simply a natural wonder of the universe, but still feel, on a deeper, more primitive level, that the sky looks very wrong.

So how might people react? Judging by what happened in New York about a year ago, there would be confusion, even panic. One night in December, an aquamarine glow appeared over Queens, prompting 3,200 calls to 911 in half an hour. Residents shared videos and photos of the ghostly spectacle on social media, along with guesses for the source. Was this a bomb? Was it the climax of a ground-shaking battle between superheroes? A similar scenario would likely play out online in the case of a surprise supernova, with NASA and other science institutions leading the awareness campaign. "The way the world is on edge about a number of things right now, whether it's climate change or international relations, it would be interesting how people would interpret it, if some people would think that it was some kind of sign," Barentine says.

An interesting point to make here, when reading Yahusha's prophecy of this event notice it is associated with a meteor shower as "the stars fall from the sky".

### Matthew 24:29-31

[29] "But immediately after the tribulation of those days THE SUN WILL BE DARKENED, AND THE MOON WILL NOT GIVE ITS LIGHT, AND <u>THE STARS WILL FALL FROM THE HEAVENS</u>, and the powers of the Heavens will be shaken. [30] "And then the sign of the Son of Man will appear in the sky, and then all the tribes of the Earth will mourn, and they will see the SON OF MAN COMING ON THE CLOUDS OF HEAVEN with power and great glory. [31] "And He will send forth His Angels with A GREAT TRUMPET and THEY WILL GATHER TOGETHER His Elect from the four winds, from one end of the sky to the other.

So, we have The Sign of the Coming of the Son of Man, a bright light occurring in ORION the Light Bearer in association with a meteor shower occurring during the Fall Feasts in October/November. Each year in late October ORION puts on an annual show of "stars falling from the sky" called The Orionid Meteor Shower. This is the largest meteor shower visible from Earth each year:

https://en.wikipedia.org/wiki/ORIONids

The Orionid meteor shower, usually shortened to the Orionids, is the most prolific meteor shower associated with Halley's Comet. The Orionids are so-called because the point they appear to come from, called the radiant, lies in the constellation ORION, but they can be seen over a large area of the sky. Orionids are an annual meteor shower which last approximately one week in late October. In some years, meteors may occur at rates of 50–70 per hour.

# Keep watch!

I am keeping watch in the stars for this "sign" in ORION. The Groom will return for his Bride on Yom Teruah after this sign is displayed. Since this could be imminent and we are beyond the Revelation 12 sign of the Birth of the King, all eyes should be looking up because our salvation is drawing closer by the day.

### Luke 21:27-28

[27] At that time (of the end of the Age of *PISCES* 3.5 years from the Sign of the Birth of the King in *Revelation 12*) they will see (Spiritually perceive with their minds) the Son of Man coming in a cloud with power and great glory. [28] When these things begin to happen, stand up and lift up your heads (to look for the Sign of the Son of Man in the constellation *ORION*), because your redemption is drawing near."

*End of Excerpt from The Fall Feasts: An invitation to the wedding by Rav Sha'ul*

# Revelation 12 Restored

## *The Sign of the Birth of the Messiah*

1 And a great sign appeared in The Heavenly Scroll: a woman (*VIRGO*) clothed (Palms 104:2) with the Sun, with the moon under her feet, and on her head a crown of twelve stars (*LEO* plus 3 wondering stars). 2 She was pregnant and was crying out in birth pains and the agony of giving birth (to The King planet *Jupiter*).

### Micah 4:10 10

Writhe in agony, Daughter Zion, like a woman in labor, for now you must leave the city to camp in the open field. You will go to Babylon; there you will be rescued. There Yahuah will redeem you out of the hand of your enemies.

### Isaiah 66:7

7 Before she was in labor, she gave birth; before she was in pain, she delivered a boy. 8 Who has heard of such as this? Who has seen such things? Can a country be born in a day or a nation be delivered in an instant? Yet as soon as Zion was in labor, she gave birth to her children....

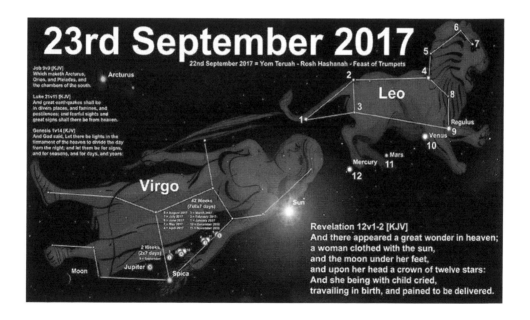

## *The Battle of the Ages – Age of PISCES*

3 And another sign appeared in Heaven: behold, a great red dragon (**DRACO**), with seven heads (head of **DRACO** made up of 7 stars) and ten horns (10 stars that make up DRACOS's tail- constellation **SERPENS'** 7 stars).

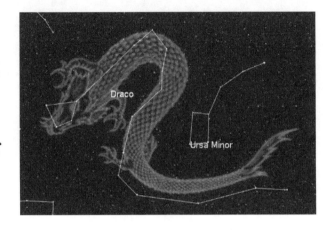

4 Her tail swept down a third of the stars of Heaven and cast them to the Earth (Constellation **DRACO**'s tail sweeps across 1/3 of the sky).

> **Daniel 8:10**
> It grew until it reached the constellations (hosts – constellations "host" stars) of the Heavens, and it threw some of the starry host (constellations) down to the Earth and trampled on them (constellations near the horizon were seen as being trampled on the ground).

And the dragon stood before the woman who was about to give birth, so that when she bore her child, she (the Dragon) might devour it (the Child).

> **Matthew 2:16**
> When Herod realized that he had been outwitted by the Magi, he was furious, and he gave orders to kill all the boys in Bethlehem and its vicinity who were two years old and under, in accordance with the time he had learned from the Magi.

5 She gave birth to a male child (Yahusha), one who is to rule all the nations with a rod of iron, but her child was caught up to Yahuah (raised from the dead **CAPRICORNUS**) and to (serve as High Priest before) His throne (in Heaven), 6 and the woman (Bride/VIRGO/Remnant Israel) fled into the wilderness, where she has a place prepared by Yahusha (John 14:3), in which she is to be nourished for 1,260 days (42 months - Revelation 11:2, 13:5).

## *Satan Thrown Down to Earth*

7 Now (Michael was removed from Earth Daniel 12:1 and waged) war in Heaven, Michael and his angels fighting against the dragon. And the dragon and her angels

fought back, 8 but they were defeated, and there was no longer any place for them in Heaven

### Daniel 12:1
"At that time (of the end) Michael, the great prince who protects your people, will arise (to wage war with The Dragon in Heaven – Revelation 12). There will be a time of distress such as has not happened from the beginning of nations until then. But at that time your people-- everyone whose name is found written in the book--will be delivered (into the "wilderness" to be tried and perfected – Revelation 12:6,13-14).

9 And the great dragon was thrown down,

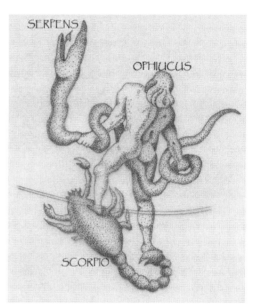

### Revelation 9 - *The Fifth Trumpet*
1 Then the fifth angel sounded his trumpet, and I saw a (morning) star that had fallen from Heaven to Earth, and it was given the key to the pit of the Abyss.

that ancient serpent, who is called the devil and Satan, the deceiver of the whole world—she was thrown down to the Earth, and her angels were thrown down with her (The Elect are now without defense as Michael was removed to Heaven to fight the Dragon who is then cast down and is unopposed on Earth leading to the "time of distress" in Daniel 1:1).

### Isaiah 27:1
1In that day Yahuah (through Yahusha/*OPHIUCIUS* ) will take His sharp, great, and mighty sword, and bring judgment on Leviathan, the fleeing serpent— Leviathan, the coiling serpent (*SERPENS*) — and He will slay the dragon of the sea (Dagon God of Babylon).

### Genesis 3:15
And I will put enmity between you (*SERENS* the serpent) and the woman (*VIRGO*), and between your offspring and hers; he (Son of Man - *OPHIUCIUS*) will crush your (*SCORPIO* "the enemy") head, and you will strike his heel."

10 And I heard a loud voice in Heaven, saying, "Now the salvation and the power and the kingdom of our God and the authority of His Anointed King have come (Revelation 7:10, 19:1), for the accuser of our brothers has been thrown down, who

accuses them day and night before our Yahuah. 11 And they have conquered her by the blood of the Lamb and by the <u>word of their testimony (faith in The Heavenly Scroll Matthew 24:14)</u>,

> ### Matthew 24
> 13 But the one who perseveres to the end will be saved. 14 And this gospel of the kingdom (proclaimed in The Heavenly Scroll) will be preached in all the world ***as a testimony to all nations***, and then the end will come....

for they loved not their lives even unto death (Revelation 2:10). 12 Therefore, rejoice, O Heavens and you who dwell in them (Revelation 18:20)! But woe to you, O Earth and sea, for the devil has come down to you in great wrath, because she knows that her time is short (Revelation 8:13)!"

## *The Remnant go through the Wilderness*
## *Sukkot*

13 And when the dragon saw that he had been thrown down to the Earth, she pursued the woman (Remnant Israel the Bride) who had given birth to the male child. 14 But the woman was given the two wings of the great eagle (we will *endure* until the end - Isaiah 40:31, Matthew 24:13)

> ### Isaiah 40:31
> But those who wait on Yahuah shall renew their strength; They shall mount up with wings like eagles, they shall run and not be weary, They shall walk (through the wilderness) and not faint (through tribulation Revelation 12:14).

> ### Matthew 24
> 13 But the one who perseveres (on wings of an eagle Isaiah 40:31) to the end (of their life) will be saved. 14 And this gospel of the kingdom (proclaimed in The Heavenly Scroll) will be preached in all the world as a testimony to all nations, and then the end will come....

so that she might fly from the serpent into the wilderness, to the place where she is to be nourished for a time, and times, and half a time (Exodus 19:4).

> ### Exodus 19:4
> You have seen what I did to the Egyptians, and how I bore you on eagles' wings and brought you (through the wilderness to be tried and tested) to Myself.

15 The serpent poured water like a river out of her mouth after the woman, to sweep her away with a flood (of lies).

**NOTE:** We see that "flood of water" is associated with lies and false doctrines below:

**Isaiah 28:15-17**
15 We have made a covenant with death, and with hell we are in agreement. The overflowing scourge (Heb.: combination of two words "rod" and "flood") shall not come to us when it passes through, for we have made lies our refuge and under falsehood we have hid ourselves . . . 17 then the hail shall sweep away the refuge of lies and the waters shall overflow the hiding place.
(See Jeremiah 8:8,16:19). Jeremiah describes the Greater Exodus of the Gentiles coming out of the nation fleeing the Dragon (who is called "the Father of lies" John 8:44):

**John 8:44**
You belong to your father, the devil, and you want to carry out your father's desires. He was a murderer from the beginning, not holding to the truth, for there is no truth in him. When he lies, he speaks his native language, for he is a liar and the father of lies.

**Jeremiah 8:8**
"How can you say, 'We are wise, and the word of Yahuah is with us'? But behold, the lying pen of the scribes has made it into a lie.

**Jeremiah 16:19**
O Yahuah, my strength, and my fortress, and my refuge in the day of affliction, the Gentiles shall come unto thee from the ends of the Earth, and shall say, Surely our fathers have inherited lies, vanity, and things wherein there is no profit

16 But the Earth came to the help of the woman (Spiritually as it did physically with Israel coming out of Egypt crossing the Red Sea), and the Earth opened its mouth and swallowed the flood (of lies) that the dragon had poured from her mouth. 17 Then the dragon became furious with the woman and went off to make war on the rest of her offspring (Revelation 11:7, 13:7), on those who keep the commandments of God and hold to the testimony of Yahusha (written in The Heavenly Scroll Matthew 24:14). *And I stood on the sand of the sea* (this line should be included in the next chapter as it goes with Revelation 13:1 – "and I saw a beast rising out of the sea").

# Chapter 13

# Introduction

In this chapter, John looks into The Heavenly Scroll and sees a beast with seven heads rise out of the sea. I will identify this "beast out of the sea" so there is no doubt about what John is revealing. As this beast comes out of the nations (*as dispersed at the Tower of Babel*), the people of Earth look in amazement at the ability of this beast to conquer nations and cause mankind to worship it (*it is a religion*).

This beast is source of the world's pagan religions and so controls the inhabitants of Earth. Over the Age of PISCES, this beast wages war not only on Yahuah's Chosen, but on all the people of Earth and is drenches in their blood.

Following the rise of the first beast, a second beast is seen as "coming from the Earth", the Earthly Beast. The most abominable "beast" in Scripture is the Pig... so in prophetic terms this is the "Earthly Pig". This Earthly Pig has a false prophet through whom it speaks like a or <u>THE</u> Dragon. This Dragon is the source of both the first and second beast. The False Prophet has two horns like a lamb and exercises its authority on behalf of the beast and is filled with The Spirit of the False Messiah.

This False Prophets speaks blasphemies against the Most High and causes all who worship the beast to get its mark (*the mark of the X or Tau*) on their forehead. Without which, no one can buy or sell in its realm which is the "known world" at that time... The Roman Empire.

In this Chapter, John is given the exact hallmarks of this "beastly system" and the one who would be called "the Lawless One" and "Antichrist". We are given multiple identification marks by which to clearly identify this False Messiah. The one whom the Earth will worship in what will become, over the Age of PISCES, the largest religion on Earth. This religion will be known by the Mystery Religion of Babylon upon which it is based.

# Physical to Spiritual Parallels

In the Book of Daniel, we see Daniel given a vision of 4 physical kingdoms that would arise in the Age of ARIES the Lamb.

> **Meyer's NT Commentary**
> Daniel portrays four worldly kingdoms succeeding one another (the Chaldean, Medan, Persian, and Greek), and that, too, in such a way that the forms of beasts which symbolize the first three kingdoms are not only like a lion, a bear, and a Leopard, but also bear within themselves other significative marks, while the fourth worldly kingdom is represented under the form of a monster, not specifically determined, as, on the one hand, by the great iron teeth, the power of this kingdom, devouring and crushing all, and on the other, however, by the ten horns, beneath which again a small horn comes forth corruptibly, it is symbolized how Antiochus Epiphanes finally rises as the blasphemous usurper of the Greek Empire ruled by the ten kings successively.

Daniel 7 tells of these world-kingdoms replaced by the Kingdom of Yahuah to be governed by The Son of Man (*Yahusha*). Four beasts come out of the sea, Yahuah sits in judgement over them, and "one like a son of man" is revealed as the fulfillment of The Heavenly Scroll and anointed King by Yahuah. These beasts are interpreted by an angel as 4 kingdoms and kings. The last kingdom will make war with the Elect but will be destroyed by the Son of Man who is given dominion and power.

Daniel was looking forward in history when he wrote the Book of Daniel and described the kingdoms to come in Daniel 7 with imagery and symbolism:

- *The lion*: Babylon. The first beast, Babylon, is transformed into a man and is given a "human mind". His wings are plucked reflecting its loss of power and authority as it is thrown down into a human state.

- *The bear*: the Medes – compare Jeremiah 51:11 on the Medes attacking Babylon.

- *The Leopard*: Persia. The four heads may reflect the four Persian kings of Daniel 11:2–7.

- The fourth beast: The Greeks and particularly the Seleucids of Syria.

In the Book of Revelation, John was looking back and described them in reverse order as he saw them in history. The beast in Revelation is a Spiritual composite of the attributes of the 3 kingdoms described by Daniel into one beast, we call the Revived Roman Empire:

### Revelation 13:2
The beast I saw resembled a Leopard but had feet like those of a bear and a mouth like that of a lion. The dragon gave the beast his power and his throne and great authority.

# Revived Roman Empire – The First Beast

We must understand that Rome followed Dagon the Dragon and the Babylonian Mystery Religion when it made this religion the State Religion of Rome.

### Revelation 13:3
One of its heads seemed to have a mortal wound (Rome conquered Babylon), but its mortal wound was healed (the Babylonian Religion conquered Rome), and the whole Earth marveled as they (Rome) followed the beast (of Babylon).

As I explain on page 57 under *The Dragon - Where did Satan come from*, it is a matter of historical fact that the Mystery Religion of Babylon was literally and FORMALLY transferred from Babylon to Rome (*when Rome conquered Babylon*) .... This Mystery Religion of Babylon became the state religion of Rome was then refashioned at The Council of Nicaea and renamed Christianity. This is the true origin of Christianity and the identity of the First Beast that came "out of the sea" who is Dagon the Babylonian Fish God.

Oannes known in Babylon as Dagon the Fish God
who "comes out of the sea" *Revelation 13:1*

Many prophecy teachers today in Christianity expect a coming world order they call the Revived Roman Empire. This physical country will fulfill the prophecy in Revelation Chapter 13. They are also expecting a physical Kingdom of God to defeat it with a flesh and blood King Yahusha to rule it. This is a fairytale, the beliefs that the last Kingdom of the Dragon and the Kingdom of God are physical kingdoms is a myth. The Kingdom of Yahuah that Yahusha governs is a Spiritual Kingdom.

> **John 18:36**
> Yahusha answered, "My Kingdom is not an Earthly kingdom. If it were, my followers would fight to keep me from being handed over to the Jewish leaders. But my Kingdom is not of this world."

So too is the beast in Revelation that opposes it. It is a Spiritual battle "in high places" taking place at the end that is the culmination of The Battle of the Ages laid out in the stars.

> **Ephesians 6:12**
> For we do not wrestle against flesh and blood, but against the rulers, against the authorities, against the cosmic powers over this present darkness, against the spiritual forces of evil in the Heavenly places.

# The Final Kingdom that Conquers the Earth and Reigns for 42-Months

When Rome fell, the title of the Emperors "Pontifus Maximus" was revived by the Catholic Church and given to the Pope. Over the Age of PISCES, the Popes ruled over what was left of the Roman Empire from the seat of the Church in Rome. It even expanded its reach through massive bloodshed and control over the people. Almost every King during this time was either coronated by the Pope or had formal diplomatic relations with the Vatican State. Those who did not had their entire population excommunicated from the faith and faced the wrath of all the armies under the control of the Papacy. The Papacy had power to literally declare any King heretical and powerless to rule called The Papal Deposition Power:

> The papal deposing power was the most powerful tool of the political authority claimed by and on behalf of the Roman Pontiff, in medieval and early modern history, amounting to the assertion of the Pope's power to declare a Christian monarch heretical and powerless to rule.

Another power of the Papacy over Kings and Kingdoms was the Interdict.

### The Interdict
While not widely imposed today (although it has been in modern times and remains an option), was a powerful disciplinary tool of the Church during the Middle Ages. It denied Church sacraments and public worship to an individual, a region or state not willing to adhere to the laws of the Church (i.e., subject to the Pope). Once imposed, the interdict remained in effect until the wrong has been corrected, which might last for only a brief period or extend out for years.

This awesome power combined with the power over the people in every country/kingdom made the Pope the most powerful ruler on Earth. The Papacy believed its Pope was "lower than God, higher than man, and the mediator between the two". We see in just this one example the power the Pope wielded as "the Father of Kings and Governor of the World".

### Pope Innocent III and the interdict
In Catholic Church history, one of the most famous controversies, and most famous crises between Church and state, between pope and king, took place in the early 13th century. The antagonists were Pope Innocent III and King John of England.

### Pope Innocent III
When Lotario di Segni, who took the name Innocent III, was elected pope in 1198, it was immediately clear that he would be dominating in his role as supreme pontiff. His intent was to effectively reign as spiritual leader over millions of Catholics and, even more vigorously, use the powers of the Church to control the ruling houses of Europe... He expanded papal supremacy to new heights and successfully interfered in the role of state governments to the extent that, during his papacy, eight European countries became vassals of the Holy See.

On the day he was installed as pope, he told those assembled, "Who am I myself or what was the house of my father that I am permitted to sit above kings, **to possess the throne of glory (*the Dragon sat himself on The Throne in Heaven (which is the Glory of God Psalm 19)*?**" He continued speaking of himself, "See therefore what kind of servant he is who commands the whole family. He is the Vicar of Jesus Christ, the successor of Peter ... he is the mediator between God and man, less than God, greater than man" ("Innocent III: Vicar of Christ or Lord of the World?" edited by James M. Powell). Until that time, all popes were considered and called the Vicar of Peter, but Innocent announced that he was the Vicar of Christ. In this capacity, he viewed his authority over the Christian world as without limit.

Innocent, schooled in law and wise beyond his 37 years, would use many means, including excommunication and the interdict (an ecclesiastical censure) to exercise Church influence over kings and kingdoms. Pope Innocent III used or threatened this disciplinary action multiple times, the most notable being against King John and the entire country of England.

History is not clear if the English populace rose up against King John. In fact, there is some evidence that many were angry with the Church. They began to question the sincerity and teachings of the Church if the sacraments could be taken away through no fault of the faithful. Without the clergy's influence, it did not take long for heresies to surface; crime and vice increased. The pope realized that neither the excommunication nor the interdict was having the effect he expected, so in 1212, Innocent deposed King John and encouraged King Phillip of France to invade England and take the throne.

Yet the most powerful tool in the arsenal of Papal Authority over the Earth is called ***Papal Disposition***.

> **https://en.wikipedia.org/wiki/Papal_deposing_power**
> The papal deposing power was the most powerful tool of the political authority claimed by and on behalf of the Roman Pontiff, in medieval and early modern thought, amounting to the assertion of the Pope's power to declare a Christian monarch heretical and powerless to rule.
>
> Pope Gregory VII's Dictatus Papae (c. 1075) claimed for the Pope "that it may be permitted to him to depose emperors" (12) and asserted the papal power to "absolve subjects from their fealty to wicked men" (27).
>
> Oaths of allegiance held together the feudal political structure of medieval Europe. The principle behind deposition was that the Pope, as the ultimate representative of God from whom all oaths draw their force, could in extreme circumstances absolve a ruler's subjects of their allegiance, thereby rendering the ruler powerless. In a medieval Europe in which all confessed the Pope as head of the visible Church, it gave concrete embodiment to the superiority of the spiritual power over the temporal—the other side, so to speak, of the role of Popes and bishops in anointing and crowning emperors and kings.

Christianity is the final "Kingdom" that is governed by the False Messiah χ$\overline{\varsigma}$ς (*Jesus Christ who it is said is "King"*) and his Prophet (*the Pope*). Prophecy teachers today miss this important distinction that the last Kingdom is a Spiritual Kingdom. The False Messiah is an imposter "King" has sat himself on the Throne in Heaven in opposition to the true King Yahusha the Messiah. The battle is for the Throne in Heaven.

**The Heveanly Scroll given to Enoch with the Messiah on rainbow throne and 4 beasts signing Holy Holy Holy**

**The Greek Zodiac signs/pictographs changed to the gods of Olympus with Zeus on throne**

**Christian Zodiac signs/pictographs changed to "Saints" with Hesus Horus Krishna on the throne**

**Satanic Zodiac origin of magic, spells, horoscopes etc....**

In the image above, we see the Dragon battle the Son of Man for control of The Throne in Heaven (*The Heavenly Scroll first picture*). First by putting the pagan demi-gods on that throne (*picture 2*). Then by elevating Hesus Horus Krishna aka Jesus H. Christ χξς on that throne (*3rd picture*). Covering both sides of the issue, the Dragon uses the corrupted Zodiac to influence creation through magic. (4th picture). They miss this obvious Truth because they have taken the Mark of the Beast (*believe in incarnation*) and committed the Abomination of Desolation (*sacrifice the Easter Pig of Ishtar on the altars of their hearts stopping the sacrifice of the Passover Lamb on their behalf destroying their body/temple*) leaving them blind, deaf, and dumb to the meaning and fulfillment of Revelation. They have denied its source, The Heavenly Scroll, and do not proclaim the "word of his testimony" to the nations. I said a lot there. For more information on this see my book The Antichrist Revealed!

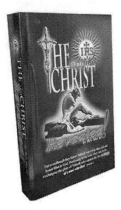

*The Antichrist Revealed! By Rav Sha'ul available on all online bookstores*

This Spiritual Kingdom, with its capital The Vatican City, is a formal country in itself with a flag and coat of arms.

It is the world's longest and most powerful international institution! Just consider for a moment the coat of arms and its meaning! Below is the meaning behind the symbols: "father of Kings, governor of the world, vicar of Christ" from the Catholic Encyclopedia:

> "I will give you the keys of the kingdom of Heaven, and whatever you bind on Earth shall be bound in Heaven, and whatever you loose on Earth shall be loosed in Heaven." Jesus to Peter in the Gospel of Matthew, 16:19

> The crossed gold and silver keys of the Holy See symbolize the keys of Simon Peter, representing the power of the papal office to loose and bind. The triple crown papal tiara symbolizes the triple power of the pope as "father of kings", "governor of the world" and "Vicar of Christ". The gold cross on a monde (globe) surmounting the tiara symbolizes the sovereignty of Jesus.

The Catholic Church exercises authority not based on physical boundaries, but Spiritual belief. It has subjects in every country on Earth. Over a billion people world-wide who pledge their loyalty to the church above the state. All worship a "man who died" above the Creator... which is blasphemy of The Holy Spirit see Romans 1.

### Romans 1
"18 The wrath of Yahuah is being revealed from (the) Heaven(ly Scroll) against all the godlessness and wickedness of people (battle between Orion the Son of Man and the Dragon), who suppress the truth (of the One and Only Elohim, Yahuah, John 17:3) by their wickedness (denying Yahuah's Immortality claiming He came to Earth and died!), 19 since what may be known about Yahuah (that He is Invisible, Col. 1:15 and John 1:18 and 1 John 4:12 and Hebrews 11:27 and 1 Timothy 6:16 and Ex. 33:20 and Job 9:11 and 1 Timothy 1:17 and Romans 1:20 and not a man, Numbers 23:19 and Hosea 11:9) is plain to them, because Yahuah has made it plain to them (through Creation, The Heavenly Scroll, and His Word). 20 For since the creation of the world (written into the stars called The Heavenly Scroll Psalm 19, 119:89, 89:2) Yahuah's Invisible qualities—his Eternal Power and Divine Nature (immortality)—have been clearly seen, being understood from what has been made (creation, the stars), so that people are without excuse (for denying the Messiah Galatians 1, he is portrayed in The Heavenly Scroll). 21 For although they knew Yahuah, they neither Glorified Him as the Invisible, Immortal Elohim nor gave thanks to Him, but their thinking became futile (believing in Incarnation) and their foolish hearts were darkened (by Yahuah so they could not "see the Truth" in Scripture). 22 Although they claimed to be wise (Hebrew Roots Teachers, Christian Pastors, Catholic Priests etc.), they became fools 23 and exchanged the Glory of the Immortal Elohim for images made to look like a mortal man who died!" (they were full of The Spirit of the False Messiah and idolized the Messiah who died, and blasphemed the Creator) ... 28 Furthermore, just as they did not think it worthwhile to retain

the Knowledge of Yahuah (that He is IMMMORTAL and INVISIBLE and SPIRIT), so Yahuah gave them over to a depraved mind (they do not understand the Scriptures), so that they do what ought not to be done (blaspheme the Holy Spirit/Ruach which declares Yahuah is an Immortal Invisible Spirit NOT a mortal man who died)."

The Catholic Church is by far the wealthiest organization on Earth. They collect no taxes, they have none of the expenses of a traditional state (*roads, armies, healthcare, etc.*) and control multitudes of billions of dollars more than many most developed nations. The Roman Catholic Church is almost certainly the wealthiest organization in the world. In the United States alone, it is estimated that the Catholic Church has an operating budget of $170 billion. By comparison, in fiscal year 2012, Apple and General Motors each had about $150 billion in revenue worldwide!

No one outside the Vatican knows for sure how much money the church has, because—unlike every other category of tax-exempt "nonprofit" organizations—religious organizations in the United States are not required to submit basic financial reporting to the IRS.

# Dripping in the blood of the Saints

The Catholic Church is the bloodiest organization or country in the history of humanity. Solely responsible for <u>hundreds of millions</u> of deaths. Many of these deaths by the most inhumane forms of torture… below are just a few quotes from historians on the brutality of this beast:

### "History of Romanism," pp. 541, 542. New York: 1871
"From the birth of Popery in 606 to the present time, it is estimated by careful and credible historians, that more than fifty millions of the human family, have been slaughtered for the crime of heresy by popish persecutors, an average of more than forty thousand religious murders for every year of the existence of popery."

### W. E. H. Lecky says:
"That the Church of Rome has shed more innocent blood than any other institution that has ever existed among mankind, will be questioned by no Protestant who has a competent knowledge of history. The memorials, indeed, of many of her persecutions are now so scanty, that it is impossible to form a complete conception of the multitude of her victims, and it is quite certain that no power of imagination can adequately realize their sufferings." -- "History

of the Rise and Influence of the Spirit of Rationalism in Europe," Vol. II, p. 32. London: Longmans, Green, and Co., 1910.

### Popery an enemy to civil liberty, 1836, pp. 104-105

In one word, the church of Rome has spent immense treasures and shed, in murder, the blood of sixty eight millions and five hundred thousand of the human race, to establish before the astonished and disgusted world, her fixed determination to annihilate every claim set up by the human family to liberty, and the right of unbounded freedom of conscience.

### The Roman Catholic Religion viewed in the light of Prophecy and History, New York, Charles K. Moore, 1843

The best writers enumerate fifty millions of Christians destroyed by fire, and the sword, and the inquisition; and fifteen millions of natives of the American continent and islands; and three millions of Moors in Europe, and one million and a half of Jews. Now, here are sixty-nine millions and five hundred thousands of human beings, murdered by "the woman of the Roman hills, who was drunk with the blood of the saints." And this horrid list does not include those of her own subjects, who fell in the crusades in Asia, and in her wars against European Christians, and in South America!

### M. D. Aletheia, The Rationalist's Manual (1897)

Let us look for a moment at the number of victims sacrificed on the altars of the Christian Moloch: -- 1,000,000 perished during the early Arian schism; 1,000,000 during the Carthaginian struggle; 7,000,000 during the Saracen slaughters. In Spain 5,000,000 perished during the eight Crusades; 2,000,000 of Saxons and Scandinavians lost their lives in opposing the introduction of the blessings of Christianity. 1,000,000 were destroyed in the Holy(?) Wars against the Netherlands, Albigenses, Waldenses, and Huguenots. 30,000,000 Mexicans and Peruvians were slaughtered ere they could be convinced of the beauties(?) of the Christian creed. 9,000,000 were burned for witchcraft. Total, 56,000,000.

# 538AD-1798AD – The Papacy Reigns for 42-Months

The beast χξς was given 42-months to reign (*1,260 days in prophetic language*). There are two options for days in prophecy, the "day = 1,000" year principle or "day for a year" principle. Using the day for a year principle we see that the sea beast of Revelation 13 χξς is given power to continue for 1260 years.

The little horn in Daniel was given power to continue for this amount of time. (*Daniel 7:25; A time, times and dividing of time is 1260 prophetic days, or 1260 literal years*). This is the exact time the Catholic Church reigned over the nations from 538AD which is the year the Roman army under Belisarius, routed the last of the tribes (*the Ostrogoths*) that opposed Roman Universal (pagan) Church.

### Thomas Hodgkin, Italy and Her Invaders, vol. 4
Driven from their place, the Ostrogoths, under Witiges, set a siege upon the city in 537, which they maintained an entire year. When a second armed force arrived against them in 538, they could hold out no longer, and in March of that year they retreated. Although two years later they attempted to regain control of Rome, they were unsuccessful. With their withdrawal from the city in 538, their power in Rome had ended. (For documentation on these events see Thomas Hodgkin, Italy and Her Invaders, vol. 4, pp. 73-113, 210-252; and Charles Diehl, "Justinian," in Cambridge Medieval History, vol. 2, p. 15.)

This reign over the nations came to an end in 1798AD when Napoleon ordered his French army into Rome to take the Pope captive and the Roman Catholic Church lost it's direct power over kings.

### Joseph Rickaby, "The Modern Papacy," the History of Religions, Vol. 3
"When, in 1797, Pope Pius VI fell grievously ill, Napoleon gave orders that in the event of his death no successor should be elected to his office, and that the Papacy should be discontinued. But the Pope recovered; the peace was soon broken; Berthier entered Rome on 10th February 1798, and proclaimed a Republic. The aged Pontiff refused to violate his oath by recognizing it, and was hurried from prison to prison into France. Broken with fatigue and sorrows, he died . . . [in] August 1799, in the French fortress of Valence, aged 82 years. No wonder that half Europe thought Napoleon's veto would be obeyed, and that with the Pope the Papacy was dead."

# The Battle is with a Spiritual Kingdom

While the false religion of Christianity has us all looking for a final world government and physical "kingdom" at the end, the Christian Church based in Rome has literally conquered the Earth for its King Hesus Horus Krishna aka Jesus H. Christ known as χξς in Revelation 13 and all paintings of this pagan god in antiquity. This symbol identifies the beast in paintings of "Jesus Christ" as it is his symbol. It was written in the upper right corner and it is the sign made by this false messiah using his left hand with the equidistant cross (the symbol of the corrupted zodiac) behind his head.

It is this beast that was seated on the "Thone in Heaven" the center of the zodiac again with the corrupted zodiac behind his head, the symbol of the beast in the upper right corner and making the hand sign χξς of the beast. The image below is blasphemy!

# The Throne in Heaven taken by force!

### Matthew 11:12
And from the days of John the Baptist until now, the kingdom of the Heavens is taken by violence and the violent seize it.

As I demonstrated earlier, the Popes (who speak for The Dragon and the Beast χξς Jesus H. Christ aka Hesus Horus Krishna) declared that THEY sit on the Throne of Glory:

### Pope Innocent III
When Lotario di Segni, who took the name Innocent III, was elected pope in 1198, it was immediately clear that he would be dominating in his role as supreme pontiff. His intent was to effectively reign as spiritual leader over millions of Catholics and, even more vigorously, use the powers of the Church to control the ruling houses of Europe… He expanded papal supremacy to new heights and successfully interfered in the role of state governments to the extent that, during his papacy, eight European countries became vassals of the Holy See.

On the day he was installed as pope, he told those assembled, "Who am I myself or what was the house of my father that I am permitted to sit above kings, **to possess the throne of glory (_the Dragon sat himself on The Throne in Heaven (which is the Glory of God Psalm 19_)**?" He continued speaking of himself, "See therefore what kind of servant he is who commands the whole family. He is the Vicar of Jesus Christ, the successor of Peter … he is the mediator between God and man, less than God, greater than man" ("Innocent III: Vicar of Christ or Lord of the World?" edited by James M. Powell). Until that time, all popes were considered and called the Vicar of Peter, but Innocent announced that he was the Vicar of Christ. In this capacity, he viewed his authority over the Christian world as without limit.

What is "the Throne of Glory" … It is The Heavenly Scroll (_Psalm 19 and Enoch 35:3_)

### Enoch 35:3
I Blessed Yahuah Author of Glory (The Heavenly Scroll Psalm 19:1), Who had made those Great and Splendid Signs (of the Zodiac), that they might display (to all mankind Deut. 4:19) the Magnificence of the Works of His Hands (The Plan of Salvation Psalm 19) to Angels and to the souls of men (His Divine Counsel); and that these (Splendid Signs in The Heavenly Scroll) might Glorify all His Works and Operations (The Plan of Salvation); that we might see the effect of His Power (as Creator to Write His Plan into the fabric of Creation on Day 4 and control the flow of history and fulfill His Promise); and The Heavenly Scroll might Glorify the Great Labor of His Hands (and we might come to know Him Romans 1, Yahuchanon/John 8:19 and His Son Psalm 19); and Bless Him Forever.

### Psalm 19

1 The Heavens declare the glory of God; the skies proclaim the work of his hands. 2 Day after day they pour forth speech; night after night they reveal knowledge.

and Yahusha sits on THAT throne <u>not the Popes</u>. It is Yahusha who is the Mediator between God and man…

### 1 Timothy 2:5

For there is One God (*Yahuah*) and one Mediator between Yahuah and mankind, *the man* (*not the God*) Yahusha the Messiah!

We do not battle against a physical kingdom and king at the end. There will be no physical world government (*beast*), no physical antichrist king over it, no physical mark to identify it! This battle we fight laid out in the stars is over the Throne in Heaven against a Spiritual Kingdom and King lead by the Dragon itself.

#### Ephesians 6:12

For we do not wrestle against flesh and blood, but against the rulers, against the authorities, against the cosmic powers over this present darkness, against the spiritual forces of evil in the Heavenly places.

### Isaiah 14

13 You said in your heart: "I will ascend to the Heavens (The Heavenly Scroll); I will raise my throne above the stars of God (and take the Throne in Heaven by force Matthew 11:12). I will sit on the mount of assembly, in the far reaches of the north. 14 I will ascend above the tops of the clouds; I will make myself like (an image of) the Most High."15 But you will be brought down to Sheol, to the lowest depths of the Pit (Revelation 12:9)

We would do well to remember this when understanding the Book of Revelation.

# The Mark of the Beast - X

In this Chapter, John identifies the Greek letters Chi, Xi, and Sigma ($\chi\xi\varsigma$ ) as the symbol of the Beast and his mark is the first letter "X" or "Tau" which is the Cross of Tammuz <u>and</u> Jesus H. Christ the False Messiah (*who is a later incarnation of the Babylonian demi-god Tammuz*). That is $\chi\xi\varsigma$ in the original language which has been altered and in error replaced by 666 (*which is forbidden to do Revelation 22:19, Deut. 4:2, Psalm 30:6*). I will use that same <u>symbol</u> $\chi\xi\varsigma$ in is chapter to identify the beast Hesus Horus Krishan aka Jesus H. Christ. For more information and overwhelming proof, read my book **The Antichrist Revealed!** or watch my two-hour documentary on my YouTube Channel:

https://www.youtube.com/watch?v=o-gGbY4iIeQ&t=2442s

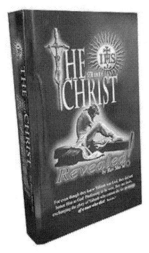

*The Antichrist Revealed! By Rav Sha'ul. Available on all online bookstores.*

With that introduction let us now examine what John was given to identify the "beast". We read in Revelation Chapter 13 the Beast $\chi\xi\varsigma$ brings about his own worship by controlling commerce (*buying and selling*). The chief aspect of Mystery Babylon in this chapter of Revelation is worldwide commerce. In History we see this very thing fulfilled as Roman Religion forced the world to worship Jesus H. Christ $\chi\xi\varsigma$ and submit to his false prophet the Pope.

In Revelation 13:17 we see that those who do not take the mark of Jesus Christ $\chi\xi\varsigma$ are prohibited from commerce within his realm. Is this referring to some futuristic physical "mark" or biochip in our forehead and hand as is being taught today? Will there come a day, yet future, when we who do not take this barcode or biochip cannot "buy/sell"? Ask yourself. Is this not exactly what everyone is expecting? Would YOU take a barcode on your forehead? Of course not. No one would we all have been conditioned to look for this very thing.

Or have we simply overlooked the obvious in history because we are unwilling to acknowledge that Jesus Christ is the beast $\chi\xi\varsigma$ and Christianity is the second beast a religion that spung up around the first beat? The "Mark" of Jesus is the $\chi$ as in X-mas. It is the belief in the Trinity and mark over your forehead and heart.

If we simply take an honest look throughout history, we see that Christianity has outlawed "buying and selling" specifically for all those who do not bow down to the authority of The Pope who claims to be the Vicar of Christ (*representative of Jesus Christ on Earth*) and accept the specific mark " $\chi$ " on their forehead for $\chi\xi\varsigma$ .

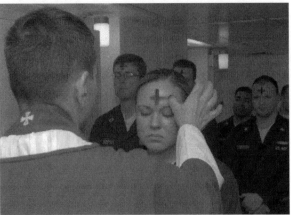

We see below the Mark of the Beast is the sign of the Cross X the first letter of the symbol of the beast χξς and those who do not have that mark X were forbidden to "buy or sell" throughout history:

### Jamieson-Fausset-Brown Bible Commentary

the mark, or the name—Greek, "the mark X (namely), the name of the beast χξς (Revelation 13)." The mark may be, as in the case of the sealing of the saints in the forehead, not a visible mark, but symbolical of allegiance. *So the sign of the cross in Popery* X. ***The Pope's interdict has often shut out the excommunicate from social and commercial intercourse.***

### Clarke's Commentary on the Bible

And that no man might buy or sell, save he that had the mark X – "If any," observes Bishop Newton," *dissent from the stated and authorized forms (of Christianity); they are condemned and excommunicated as heretics; and in consequence of that they are no longer suffered **to buy or sell; they are interdicted from traffic and commerce, and all the benefits of civil society.***

Roger Hoveden relates of William the Conqueror,
*that he was so dutiful to the pope (Prophet of χξς ) that he would not permit any one in his power **to buy or sell** any thing whom he found disobedient to the apostolic see (The Pope).*

The canon of the council of Lateran, under Pope Alexander III.,
*made against the Waldenses and Albigenses, enjoins, upon pain of anathema, that no man*

*presume to entertain or cherish them in his house or land, **or exercise traffic with them*** *(that do not follow Papal authority for* χ§ς *).*

The synod of Tours, in France, under the same pope, orders,
*"under the like intermination, that no man should presume to receive or assist them, no, not so much as hold any communion with them, **in selling or buying**; that, being deprived of the comfort of humanity they may be compelled to repent of the error of their way (against* χ§ς *)."*

It was ordered by a bull of Pope Martin the Fifth,
*"that no contract should be made with such, and **that they should not follow any business and merchandise: save he that had the mark*** χ *; took the oath to be true to the pope, or made a public profession of the Popish religion: or the name of the beast; Papists, so called from the pope"*

## Clarke's Commentary on the Bible

And that no man might buy or sell, save he that had the mark χ - "If any," observes Bishop Newton, "dissent from the stated and authorized forms; they are condemned and excommunicated as heretics; and in consequence of that they are no longer suffered to buy or sell; they are interdicted from traffic and commerce, and all the benefits of civil society. So Roger Hoveden relates of William the Conqueror, that he was so dutiful to the pope that he would not permit any one in his power to buy or sell any thing whom he found disobedient to the apostolic see. So the canon of the council of Lateran, under Pope Alexander III., made against the Waldenses and Albigenses, enjoins, upon pain of anathema, that no man presume to entertain or cherish them in his house or land, or exercise traffic with them. The synod of Tours, in France, under the same pope, orders, under the like intermination, that no man should presume to receive or assist them, no, not so much as hold any communion with them, in selling or buying; that, being deprived of the comfort of humanity they may be compelled to repent of the error of their way." In the tenth and eleventh centuries the severity against the excommunicated was carried to so high a pitch, that nobody might come near them, not even their own wives, children, or servants; they forfeited all their natural legal rights and privileges, and were excluded from all kinds of offices. The form of excommunication in the Romish Church is to take lighted torches, throw them upon the ground with curses and anathemas, and trample them out under foot to the ringing of the bells. It is in this and similar ways that the false prophet has terrified the Latin world, and kept it in subjection to the secular and spiritual powers. Those interdicted **by the two-horned beast** from all offices of civil life are also such as have not: - The name of the beast, or the symbol of his name χ§ς (Revelation 13).

# Revelation 13 Restored

### *First Beast – Babylonian Demi-god*

1 I, John, stood on the sand of the seashore. And I saw beasts coming out of the sea (Daniel 7:3), with ten horns and seven heads, with ten diadems on its horns and blasphemous names on its heads (Revelation 12:3).

### Daniel 7:3

2 Daniel declared: "As I looked up at The Heavenly Scroll at night, I saw a vision, and suddenly the four winds of Heaven were churning up the great sea. 3 Then four great beasts came up out of the sea, each one different from the others …

Babylon worshipped **Dagon** known as **the Dragon** *(coming out of the sea)* who is half fish and half man. Rev. 13:1 is a direct reference to Dagon, see Chapter 1 in my book Christianity – The Great Deception.

DAGON

Dagon (fish god)= Neptune= Posiedon (who carries the Trident) = Satan = Leviathan = Taneen = dragon = seraph

man creates everything
in his own image

This "Dragon in the Sea or DAGON the Fish God" is called leviathan in scripture and was worshipped by those in ancient Babylon. Dagon is associated with Nimrod the first High Priest of Dagon later known as the Pope.

**The Religious "Mitre" Hat From Babylon** | **The Priest of Ancient "Dagon" Fish Worship**

Worship of Dagon was passed down after Yahuah confused the languages and scattered humanity across the globe. It was this religion that was prevalent and continued at the time Rome destroyed Jerusalem. It was this religion of Dagon that permeated the high priestly ranks of paganism and was transferred to ROME from Babylon after Rome conquered Babylon (*and became the official religion of ROME*). Dagon worship was the foundation of The Catholic Church. Even today Catholic priests wear the priestly garments of the priests of Dagon the Dragon! Christianity is identical to the Mystery Religion of Babylon.

*Excerpt from my book **Christianity and the Great Deception***

*Now back to Revelation Chapter 13*

2 And the (current) beast (The Babylonian or the Roman Empire) that I saw was like (a composite pagan religion evolving from) a Leopard (Greece); its feet were like a bear's (Persia), and its mouth was like a lion's mouth (Babylon).

### Daniel 7:6
6 Next, as I watched, another beast appeared. It was like a Leopard, and on its back it had four wings like those of a bird. The beast also had four heads, and it was given authority to rule."

The Dragon (Dagon the Babylonian Fish God) gave the beast (Babylonian Religion of Rome) his power and his throne and great authority (The Pope is The High Priest of Dagon and literally usurped the Throne of Glory). 3 One of its heads _seemed_ to have a mortal wound, but its (not so) mortal wound was healed (Babylon fell to Rome. Normally when a nation falls, its priests are killed, but in this case, the seemingly mortal wound of defeat and certain death of this religion was 'healed' and Mystery Babylon became the state religion of Rome, later becoming Christianity at the Council of Nicaea), and the whole Earth marveled as they (ROME/known world) followed the beast (of Babylon).

4 People worshiped the Dragon (unknowingly) because she had given authority to the beast Χ͂ξϛ (by worshipping Jesus you are worshipping the Dragon and following the commands of The High Priest of Dagon, the Popes. Every fundamental doctrine of all Christian Churches is by Papal Decree and contradicts Yahuah's commands), and they also worshiped the beast Χ͂ξϛ (aka Jesus Christ) and asked, "Who is like the beast Χ͂ξϛ ? Who can wage war against it?" 5 The beast Χ͂ξϛ was given a mouth (The Pope is Jesus' representative on Earth known as *The Vicar of Christ*) to utter proud words (that Χ͂ξϛ has abolished The Law, Χ͂ξϛ changed The Sabbath to Sunday, Χ͂ξϛ changed Passover to Easter, etc.) and _blasphemies_ (that Χ͂ξϛ is God incarnate, the Creator, the Father in sinful flesh, that God died for you)

### Daniel 7:20
This horn had seemed greater than the others, and it had human eyes and a mouth that was boasting arrogantly.

and to exercise its authority (to wage war against the Saints) for forty-two months (Age of PISCES from 538AD-1798AD). 6 It opened its mouth to blaspheme Yahuah (saying Yahuah came to Earth and we killed him for our sin), and to slander His name (calling Yahuah "LORD" which is a title for Ba'al. Changing the name of Yahusha which means "Yahuah is Salvation" to Jesus which means "Hail Zeus" and "Earthly Pig") and his dwelling place (Ba'al Shamayim took The Throne in Heaven by force Matthew 11:12) and those who live in Heaven.

### Matthew 11:12
And from the days of John the Baptist until now, the kingdom of the Heavens is taken by violence and the violent seize it.

### Romans 8
2 For in The Yahushaic Covenant the law of the Spirit of life set you free from the law of sin and you die by decree (The Mosaic Covenant). 3 For what the law was powerless to do in that it was weakened by the flesh (SARKI - 'opposed to Yahuah'), Yahuah did (it was Yahuah who saved you NOT 'Jesus') by sending His own Son in the likeness of sinful flesh (another way of saying his flesh was full of sin! He was fully human in EVERY way i.e., not a god in any way Hebrews 2:17) as an offering for sin. He (the subject is Yahuah) thus condemned sin in the flesh (fulfilled His promise to "forgive our iniquity and remember our sin no more" Hebrews 8:12)

Yahusha NOT Yahuah "came in the flesh" born to two human parents via physical origin/sex, outside any divine influence at all! Prone to sin, i.e., sinful flesh, and opposed to Yahuah. Below is the definition of "flesh"...

> g4561 'sarki' - Thayer: 2a) the body of a man 2b) used of natural or physical origin, generation or relationship 2b1) born of natural generation 4) the flesh, denotes mere human nature, ***the Earthly nature of man apart from divine influence, and therefore prone to sin and opposed to God***.

The Father did NOT come in SINFUL flesh, let all who proclaim this blasphemy of "incarnation" be <u>ACCURSED</u>... it is Blasphemy. See my book **Blasphemy of the Holy Spirit**:

### Galatians 1:8
But even if we or an angel from Heaven should preach a gospel (that Yahuah came to Earth as a man and died) other than the one we preached to you (that Yahusha came in the flesh NOT Yahuah), let them be under Yahuah's curse!

7 It was given power to wage war against Yahuah's holy people and to conquer them (the inquisition, the Roman/Jewish Wars, the crusades, etc.). And it was given authority (Papal Disposition) over every tribe, people, language, and nation (The "Universal Church" of Rome conquered the known world and ruled the people of every nation from the throne the Pope sits on controlling all the "Kings of the Earth" in Europe and beyond). 8 All inhabitants of the Earth (known world at that time: The Roman Empire) will (eventually) worship the beast ΧΣ̅Σ (Christianity is the largest religion on Earth at the end)—all whose names have not been written in the Passover Lamb's book of life, the Passover Lamb who was slain from the creation of the world (all those who put their faith in the Easter Pig and not in The Passover Lamb) 9 If anyone has an ear, let him hear: 10 If anyone is to be taken captive, to captivity he goes; if anyone is to be slain with the sword, with the sword must he be slain. Here is a call for the endurance (wings of an eagle Revelation 12:14, Isaiah 40:31)

> **Isaiah 40:31**
> But those who wait on Yahuah shall renew their strength; They shall mount up with wings like eagles, they shall run and not be weary, They shall walk (through the wilderness) and not faint (through tribulation Revelation 12:14).

and faith of the saints (Revelation 14:12 - we are not physically spared in the mountains or taken to some "wilderness"; we *ENDURE* until the end of our lives in the message contained in The Heavenly Scroll which is The Word of His Testimony).

> **Matthew 24**
> 13 But the one who perseveres (on wings of an eagle Isaiah 40:31) to the end (of their life) will be saved. 14 And this gospel of the kingdom (proclaimed in The Heavenly Scroll) will be preached in all the world as a testimony to all nations, and then the end will come....

## *The Second Beast – Christianity*

11 Then I saw another beast (Christianity), coming out of the Earth (Je in Latin is "Earth" or "mother Earth". SUS is pig, Jesus is the pig (beast) of the Earth. The second beast is a religion flowing forth from ΧΣ̅Σ aka Jesus Christ). He (the prophet of this religion) had two horns like a lamb (Miter Hat), but he spoke like (or on behalf of) the dragon (the Spirit of Dagon).

<u>Note</u>: It is Dagon the Dragon that is the spiritual source behind the Catholic/Christian Churches based in Rome (any Sunday / Christmas / Easter / Trinity / Jesus church).

The Pope and priesthood of the Catholic Church are the high priest and priesthood of Dagon the Dragon in disguise (*not a very good disguise actually*).

12 He (the Pope, High Priest of Paganism) exercised all the authority (as Vicar of Christ) of the first beast Χⳗⲋ (Jesus H. Christ aka Hesus Horus Krishna) on his behalf (Authority of the Church doctrine), and (Christianity the second beast) made the Earth and its inhabitants worship the first beast Χⳗⲋ , whose fatal wound had been healed (The Mystery Religion of Babylon survived Babylon's fall to Rome).13 And he (second beast/Christianity) 13 performed great and miraculous signs, even causing fire to come down from Heaven to Earth in full view of men. 14 Because of the signs (only a wicked and adulterous generation require a "sign" Matthew 16:4) he (Christianity) was given power to do on behalf of the first beast Χⳗⲋ , he (Christianity) deceived the inhabitants of the Earth (the largest religion on Earth is Christianity). He (Christianity) ordered them (humanity) to set up an image (of Χⳗⲋ in The Temple of Yahuah – we "invite Jesus into our hearts") in honor of the beast Χⳗⲋ (Jesus Christ) who was wounded by the sword (metaphor for conquered by the sword) and yet lived (survived the conquest of ROME).

15 He (second Beast/Christianity) was given power to give breath/Ruach (Spirit of the False Messiah and Spirit of Error) to the image of the first beast χξς , so that it could speak (to the hearts of man) and cause all who refused to worship *the image* of χξς to be killed (Christianity is the bloodiest religion in the history of the world killing a higher percentage of the population at that time then WWI and WWII combined!).

16 It (Christianity) also forced all people, great and small, rich and poor, free and slave, to receive a mark ( X ) on their right hands or on their foreheads,

> **NOTE:** It was ordered by a bull of Pope Martin the Fifth, "that no contract should be made with such, and that they should not follow any business and merchandise: save he that had the mark; took the oath to be true to the Pope or made a public profession of the Popish religion: or the name of the beast; Papists, so called from the pope". The Mark of Jesus is "X" as in X-mas which is drawn on the forehead of Christians while reciting "in the name of the Father, the Son, and the Holy Ghost" and sealing the mind with Trinity:

 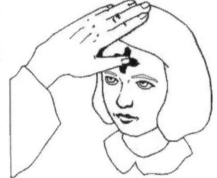

17 so that they could not buy or sell unless they had the mark ( X ),

> **Bishop Newton**, "dissent from the stated and authorized forms (of Christianity); they are condemned and excommunicated as heretics; and in consequence of that they are no longer suffered to buy or sell; they are interdicted from traffic and commerce, and all the benefits of civil society.

which is the name of the beast χξς ; or rather *the symbol* of its name. 18 This calls for wisdom (spiritual understanding of the mind). Let the person who has (spiritual) insight reckon up *the symbol* of the beast that identifies him, for it is *the symbol* of a man. That **symbol** is χξς (Chi, Xi, Sigma).

χξϛ is the symbol, monogram, and pictogram of Jesus Christ; this symbol uniquely identifies both Jesus and Christ it is the only symbol that is used for XESus, and Christos, and the Serpent). X is the unique "Mark of the Beast". See my book The Antichrist Revealed! For a more in depth look into Revelation 13.

# Chapter 14

# Introduction

In this chapter, we see the Bride revealed on Earth. Those who took the "Mark of χ ξ ς " are destroyed in one day by fire, the smoke of that event rises as an example forever, and the Great Harvest of the Earth begins. The Divine Government is setup on Earth to govern for 1,000 years.

- John is given a vision of The Divine Government made up of the children of Yahuah.

- The Lamb appears on Mount Zion with 144,000 "virgins" as first fruits, we all sing a "new song" worshipping the Lamb.

- A messenger appears in Heaven proclaiming the fulfillment of The Heavenly Scroll.

- A second messenger announces the fall of Babylon.

- A third angel declares Yahuah's wrath on those who worship χ ξ ς . The faithful are put to the test of endurance.

- A voice in The Heavenly Scroll pronounces those who died in covenant with Yahusha are rewarded.

- The Son of Man represented by ORION is crowned, seated on a cloud, to use his sickle to harvest the Earth… (*John sees a vision of ORION coming in the clouds of Heaven*).

- The Angel of Death then proceeds to slay the remaining inhabitants of Earth in a massive sacrifice of atonement to atone for violating Yahuah's Laws and Sabbaths see Isaiah 24.

# Hosts of Heaven

We see in this chapter the phrase "Hosts of Heaven". We are taught in error this is referring to the "army of God". It is true, the stars can represent that massive army, but "hosts of Heaven" is referring to the constellations. Constellations "host stars" in the sky. They do not physically exist, they are "images" drawn around a grouping of stars that illustrate the meaning of the stars they "host". The singular phrase "host of Heaven" is speaking of The Zodiac which hosts all the hosts of Heaven".

### Daniel 4:35
"Yahuah does according to His will written in *the host of Heaven* (The Zodiac which hosts constellations. Constellations "host stars") and among the inhabitants of Earth and no one can ward off His hand Or say to Him, 'What have You done?'

### Deut 4:19
"And beware not to lift up your eyes to Heaven and see the Sun and the moon and the stars, all *the host of Heaven* (constellations), and be drawn away and worship them and serve, those which Yahuah your God has allotted to all the peoples under the whole Heaven."

### 2 Kings 23:4-5
And he did away with the idolatrous priests whom the kings of Judah had appointed to burn incense in the high places in the cities of Judah and in the surrounding area of Jerusalem, also those who burned incense to Baal, to the Sun and to the moon and to the constellations, all *the host of Heaven*.


https://mybible.com/covers/654
Yahuah of hosts - יהוה צבאות Yehovah tsebaoth, Jehovah of armies. As all the Heavenly bodies were called the hosts of Heaven, צבא השמים tseba hashshamayim, Jehovah being called Lord of this host showed that he was their Maker and Governor; and consequently He, not they, was the proper object of religious worship. The Sun, moon, planets, and stars, were the highest objects of religious worship to the heathens in general. The Jewish religion, teaching the knowledge of a Being who was Yahuah of all these Heavenly bodies, showed at once its superiority to all that heathenism could boast.

What "Lord of Hosts" really implies is the Yahusha is the fulfillment of the message written therein called The Heavenly Scroll.

**Daniel 4:35**
"Yahuah does according to His will written in *the host of Heaven.*"

**Matthew 6:10**
Your kingdom come, your will be done, on Earth as it is written in Heaven (Daniel 4:35).

For instance, the constellation VIRGO hosts:

### Primary star
*Spica* – means "ear of wheat/corn/grain". Hebrew word for this star is *Tsemech* which means "the branch". Jer 23:5-6, Zech 3:8, 6:12, Isaiah 4:2. There are 20 different Hebrew words that mean "branch", yet only *Tsemech* is used of the Messiah; the same word for the name of the brightest star of Virgo. Virgo has a branch/ear of barely in one hand (John 12:21-24) and a "seed" in her other (Gen 3:15)

### Secondary star
*Zavijaveh*, meaning "gloriously beautiful." - Isaiah 4:2

### Decans (secondary constellations)
* *Coma decan* – meaning "the infant is the desired one" (Haggai 2:7). The image of this constellation is a woman holding an infant child. As the Egyptians were led astray into worshipping the "creation over the creator" they idolized the image of Coma and myths were created around this Decan of the Madonna and Child. This is where the worship of Semaramis and Tammuz (Babylon), Isis/Horus (Egypt), and many other pagan myths are derived.
* *Centaurus decan* – meaning "the dart piercing a victim"
* *Bootes decan* – meaning "the great shepherd and harvester"

# End of the Age of PISCES

**Matthew 12:32**
Whoever speaks a word against the Son of Man will be forgiven, but whoever speaks against the Holy Spirit will not be forgiven, either in this age (*PISCES*) or in the one to come (*Age of AQUARIUS*).

**Matthew 13:38-40, 49**
38 The field is the world, and the good seed represents the sons of the kingdom. The weeds are the sons of the evil one, 39 and the enemy who sows them is the devil. The harvest is the end of the age of PISCES, and the harvesters are angels. 40 As the weeds are collected and burned in the fire, so will it be at the end of the age of PISCES... 49 So will it be at the end of the age of PISCES: The angels will come and separate the wicked from the righteous,

### Matthew 24:3

While Yahusha was sitting on the Mount of Olives, the disciples came to Him privately. "Tell us," they said, "when will these things happen, and what will be the sign of Your coming and of the end of the age (of PISCES)?"

### Matthew 28:20

and teaching them to obey all that I have commanded you. And surely I am with you always, to the very end of the age (of PISCES).

### 1 Corinthians 10:11

Now these things happened to them as examples and were written down as warnings for us, on whom the fulfillment of the *Battle of the* Ages has come.

# Revelation 14 Restored

## *Vision of the Divine Government*

1 Then I looked, and behold, on Mount (city of) Zion (another name for The Heavenly Scroll Micah 4:1–5)

### Micah 4:1–5

4 It shall come to pass in the latter days that the mountain of the house of Yahuah shall be established as the highest of the mountains, <u>and it shall be lifted up above the hills</u>; and peoples shall flow to it. 2 and many nations shall come, and say: "Come, let us go up to the mountain of Yahuah, to the house of the God of Jacob (Yahuah's abode is in Heaven Isaiah 8:18), that he may teach us his ways (written in the stars Psalm 19, 119:89, 89:2, Daniel 4:35) and that we may <u>walk in his paths (Zodiac means "path or way" people will be learning The Word of His Testimony Proverbs 4:18)</u>."

#### Proverbs 4:18

The path (The Way foretold in The Heavenly Scroll) of the Righteous is like (metaphor) the morning Sun (Psalm 19), shining ever brighter till the full Light of day (we are Children of the Day enlightened by the Spiritual Light of The Heavenly Scroll).

### Isaiah 8:18

Here am I, and the children Yahuah has given me as signs and symbols in Israel from the Creator of the Heavenly Hosts (constellations Daniel 4:35), who dwells on Mount Zion (metaphorically The Heavenly Scroll).

stood the Lamb (in the center of The Heavenly Scroll before the Throne in Heaven), and with him 144,000 (symbolizes the perfect Divine Government 12x12000. We are His Temple, which is a 12k-by-12k square)

### Revelation 21

15 And the one who spoke with me had a measuring rod of gold to measure the city and its gates and walls. 16 The city lies foursquare, its length the same as its width. And he measured the city with his rod, 12,000 stadia.4 Its length and width and height are equal. 17 He also measured its wall, 144 cubits by human measurement, which is also an angel's measurement.

who (believed in the covenant that bares) his name (The Yahushaic Covenant) and had his Father's name 𐤉𐤄𐤅𐤄 written on their foreheads (they will be Kings and govern Creation in a Divine Government Revelation 1:6, Revelation 5:10, Revelation 3:21, Revelation 20:4). 2 And I heard a voice coming from The Heavenly Scroll like the roar of many waters (AQUARIUS) and like the sound of loud thunder (see verse 13 for what this voice said). The voices (souls of the martyrs surrounding the Throne Revelation 6:9) I heard was like the sound of harpists playing on their harps (LYRA - Revelation 15:2), 3 and they were singing a new song before the Throne (sang the Son of Moses Revelation 15:3. They declared Yahusha worthy to read The Heavenly Scroll - Revelation 5:9) and before the four living creatures and before the (24) elders (John is describing the center of The Heavenly Scroll). No one *came to realize* (*manthano* Strong's g3129)

# 3129. manthanó

the meaning of that song except the 144,000 who had been redeemed from the Earth.

### Revelation 5:9

9 And they sang a new song, saying: "*You are worthy to take the Scroll and to open its seals (ARIES), because you were slain (LIBRA), and with your blood you purchased for Yahuah persons from every tribe and language and people and nation (Rainbow Throne).*"

## *Those found worthy to rule*

4 It is these who have not defiled themselves (overcome idolatry worshiping a "man who died" and believing in The Trinity - Romans 1) with the women (Rome), for they are (Spiritual) virgins (who have walked The Way and have not slept with the whore of Babylon i.e., Rome - 2 Corinthians 11:2).

**2 Corinthians 11:2**

2 I am jealous for you with a godly jealousy. For I promised you to one husband (Yahusha), to present you as a pure virgin to the Messiah.

It is these who follow the Lamb wherever he goes (walks The Way). These have been redeemed from mankind as firstfruits for Yahuah and the Lamb (to govern in Righteousness - Revelation 3:4,21), 5 and in their mouth no deceit was found (their judgment is Righteous, their "word is their bond"), for they are blameless (in their dealings, they can be trusted to govern).

## *First Angel proclaims the message of The Heavenly Scroll*

6 Then I saw another angel flying in the midst of the stars, with an eternal gospel (The Heavenly Scroll) <u>to proclaim to those who dwell on Earth, to every nation and tribe and language and people</u> (to all mankind Psalm 19).

**Psalm 19**

1 The Heavens declare the glory of God; the skies proclaim the work of his hands. 2 Day after day they pour forth speech; night after night they reveal knowledge. 3 They have no speech, they use no words; no sound is heard from them. 4 Yet <u>their voice goes out into all the Earth, their words to the ends of the world</u>.

*Angel flying above The Heavenly Scroll with the eternal gospel (Scroll) sitting just above Taurus where the Ages for "this age" begins.*

275

7 And he said with a loud voice, "Fear Yahuah and give Him glory (The Heavenly Scroll proclaims His Glory Psalm 19),

> **Psalm 19**
> 1 The Heavenly Scroll declares the glory of God; the stars proclaim the work of his hands.

because the hour of His judgment (TAURUS) has come, and worship Him who made Heaven and Earth, the sea and the springs of water."

## *The Spiritual Kingdom of "Mystery Babylon" is destroyed*

8 A second angel followed, saying, "Fallen, fallen is Babylon the great (Roman Christianity), she who made all nations drink the wine of the passion of her (Spiritual) sexual immorality (idolatry)."

## *Those who follow the False Religion are destroyed by fire in 1 day*

9 And another angel, a third, followed them, saying with a loud voice, "If anyone worships the beast χξϛ and its image (Jesus Christ) and receives a mark (x) on his forehead (what you believe, sign of the cross) or on his hand (what you do, making this mark over your heart), 10 he also will drink the wine of Yahuah's wrath, poured full strength into the cup of his anger, and he will be tormented with fire and sulfur in the presence of the holy angels and in the presence of the Lamb (on the day of wrath). 11 And the *smoke (memory)* of their torment (not the fire of the torment) goes up forever and ever, and they have no rest (on Earth during this time, they are tormented by the "sting of a scorpion"), day or night, these worshipers of the beast and its image χξϛ , and whoever receives the mark of its name (the cross is the single "mark" of the name Jesus Christ or χξϛ the first letter of his symbol the Chi x )."

> **NOTE**: This is occurring BEFORE the resurrection which occurs next. So this is NOT talking about Hell (as commonly taught in error to justify the "frying in a frying pan for eternity

doctrine") but rather "hell on Earth" during which time the Earth is tormented by the "sting of the scorpion".

## *Endure in faith in*
## *The Word of His Testimony*

12 Here is a call for the saints to endure (in The Word of His Testimony Revelation 12:11, Revelation 6:9), those who keep the commandments of Yahuah and are in covenant with Yahusha.

## *The First Resurrection*

13 And I heard a voice (like thunder verse 2) from Heaven saying (this is what the voice that sounds like thunder in verse 2 said), *"Write this: Blessed are the dead who die in covenant with Yahusha from now on."* *"Blessed indeed,"* confirms the Ruach (in John), "(the voice continues) *that they may rest from their labors (CANCER, AQUARIUS), for their (good) deeds follow them!"* 14 Then I looked (into the stars), and behold, a white cloud (Milky Way Galaxy), and seated on the cloud one like a son of man (ORION), with a golden crown on his head, and a sharp sickle (or sword) in his hand.

15 And another angel came out of the temple, calling with a loud voice to him who sat on the cloud, "Put in your sickle, and reap, for the hour to reap has come, for the (wheat VIRGO) harvest of the Earth is fully ripe." 16 So he who sat on the cloud swung his sickle across the Earth, and the Earth was reaped (of the those who died in covenant with Yahusha)

## Judgment Day
### Destruction of the Damned

**Matthew 13**
38 The field is the world, and the good seed represents the sons of the kingdom. The weeds are the sons of the evil one, 39 and the enemy who sows them is the devil. The harvest is the end of the age of PISCES, and the harvesters are angels. 40 As the weeds are collected and burned in the fire, so will it be at the end of the age of PISCES.

17 Then another angel (of death) came out of the temple in Heaven, and he too had a sharp sickle. 18 And another angel came out from the altar, the angel who has authority over the fire (judgment of the damned), and he called with a loud voice to the one who had the sharp sickle, "Put in your sickle and gather the clusters from the vine of the Earth, for its grapes are ripe (Joel 3:13)."

**Joel 3:13**
Swing the sickle, for the harvest is ripe. Come, trample the grapes, for the winepress is full and the vats overflow-- so great is their wickedness!"

19 So the angel (of death) swung his sickle across the Earth and gathered the grape harvest of the Earth and threw it into the great winepress of the wrath of Yahuah. 20 And the winepress was trodden outside the city, and blood flowed from the winepress, as high as a horse's bridle, for 1,600 stadia.

# Chapter 15

# Introduction

In this chapter, John sees another sign in The Heavenly Scroll, HYDRA with the bowls of wrath being poured out over her and the birds of prey feeding on her body.

- The Great Supper ... the inhabitants of Earth who fight against the King of Kings are destroyed. The 7 plaques are released.

- John writes of seven angels with seven plagues, the last plagues ever to occur. He states that until the plagues are complete no one can enter the Temple of Yahuah.

- The Elect are given harps (*LYRA*) and sing The Song of Moses.

# Revelation 15 Restored

## *The Great Supper*

15 Then I saw, in The Heavenly Scroll, another great and amazing sign (Revelation 21:9, Revelation 19:17),

### Revelation 21:9
9 One of the seven angels who had the seven bowls full of the seven last plagues ...

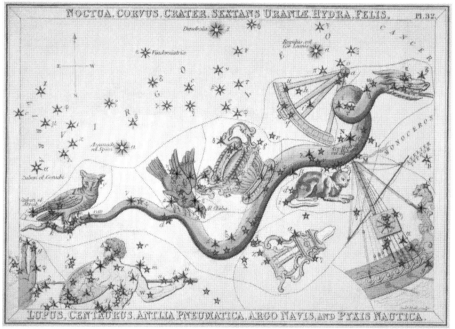

*Bowl of plagues being poured out on the serpent as birds of prey, owl and raven, feast on her body Revelation 19:17*

seven angels with seven plagues (poured out on the Great Whore - Revelation 17:1),

### Revelation 17
1 Then one of the seven angels with the seven bowls came and said to me, "Come, I will show you the punishment of the great prostitute, who sits on many waters. 2 The kings of the Earth were immoral with her, and those who dwell on the Earth were intoxicated with the wine of her immorality."

which are the last of the plaques, for with them the wrath of Yahuah is finished (and the birds of prey gather for the Great Supper of Yahuah - Revelation 19:17).

281

**Revelation 19:17**
And I saw an angel standing in the Sun, who cried in a loud voice to all the birds of prey flying in midair, "Come, gather together for the great supper of Yahuah.

## The Song of Moses

2 And I saw what appeared to be a sea of glass mingled with fire (looking into outer space with all the stars) — and those who had conquered the beast and its image and the number of its name, standing beside the sea of glass with harps given them by Yahuah in their hands. 3 And they sing the song of Moses, the servant of Yahuah, and the song of the Lamb, saying, *"Great and amazing are your deeds, O Yahuah God the Almighty! Just and true are your ways, O King of the nations! 4 Who will not fear, O Yahuah, and glorify your name* 𐤉𐤄𐤅𐤄 ? *For you* 𐤉𐤄𐤅𐤄 *alone are holy*. *All nations will come and worship you* 𐤉𐤄𐤅𐤄, *for your righteous acts have been revealed (on Earth as it was written in The Heavenly Scroll)."*

## The Seven Angels with Seven Plagues

5 After this I looked, and I saw in Heaven the temple--that is, the tabernacle of the covenant law (to judge those who violated The Law and Sabbaths Isaiah 24)

**Isaiah 24**
4 The Earth mourns and withers; the world languishes and fades; the exalted of the Earth waste away. 5 The Earth is defiled by its people; they have transgressed the laws; they have overstepped the decrees and broken the everlasting covenant. 6 Therefore a curse (the 'sting of a scorpion') has consumed the Earth, and its inhabitants must bear the guilt; the Earth's dwellers have been burned, and only a few survive....

--and it was opened. 6 and out of the sanctuary came the seven angels with the seven plagues, clothed in pure, bright linen, with golden sashes around their chests. 7 And one of the four living creatures (Seraphs surrounding the Throne in Heaven) gave to the seven angels seven golden bowls full of the wrath of Yahuah who lives forever and ever, 8 and the sanctuary was filled with smoke from the glory of Yahuah and from his power, and ono one could enter the sanctuary until the seven plagues of the seven angels were finished.

# Chapter 16

# Introduction

In this chapter, the 3 unclean spirits are introduced along with the 7 bowls of wrath that are poured out over the Earth.

## 3 Unclean Spirits

In context we are dealing with 3 unclean spirits that come out of the mouth of the False Prophet which is the office of the Pope of Rome... it is the "foundation of the beast" which is the Dragon/Mystery Babylon. The Beast χξϛ Jesus H. Christ is the culmination of the 3 unclean spirits that come out of the mouth of the False Prophet. These unclean spirits are defined very clearly in scripture:

1. The Spirit the Dragon - familiar spirits, Mystery Babylon, source of the Beast who gives it power and a throne - Revelation 13.

2. The Spirit of the False Messiah – incarnation - 1 John 4:2-4.

3. The Spirit of Error – lying pen of the scribes - 1 John 4:6.

So, the "Antichrist" is the image of a man represented by a false prophet (*Pope*) who claims this false messiah to be god-incarnate based on the religion of Babylonian and pagan trinities. In whose image χξϛ the law was abolished (*he is the Lawless One - 2 Thessalonians 2:8-10*). The one based on the corrupted message in the Mazzaroth (*which is Sun worship so he will represent Babylonian rituals Trinity, Christmas, Easter, Sunday etc.*)

## The Seven Bowls of Judgment

Reference: https://en.wikipedia.org/wiki/Seven_bowls

> The seven Vial/Bowl judgments are similar in nature to the Trumpet judgments, but far more serious for there will be no warning when they come. In addition, there are three key differences between the Trumpet judgments and the Vial/Bowl judgments: firstly, the Trumpet judgments are plagues that bring partial devastation and plagues upon 1/3 of nature and people, while the Vial/Bowl judgments are more severe direct assaults against humanity

and nature, thus bringing more chaos on the Earth than the Trumpet judgments. Lastly, the Trumpet judgments offer a possibility of redemption and repentance, while the Vial judgments do not; the Vial judgments are a literal assault on those who have taken the mark of the Beast, and to those who are considered incorrigibles and arrogantly unrepentant, thus making them impossible to save. The Vial/Bowl judgments are listed below. These are not literal... it is a vision:

- Metaphorical grievous sores on the worshipers of the Beast. These sores only affect those bearing the Mark of the Beast and the people who worship his image. See "the sting of a scorpion" earlier in this book.
- Sea turns to blood.
- Rivers turn to blood.
- A major heatwave causes the Sun to burn with intense heat and to scorch people with fire. (Revelation 16:8–9)
- The kingdom of the beast is plunged into darkness. (Revelation 16:11)
- The Euphrates River dries up to facilitate the crossing of the armies from the east, on their way to Israel for the battle of Armageddon. This event corresponds with Daniel 11:44.
- Worldwide Earthquake leveling every mountain into the sea followed by huge hailstones and lightning. The Earth's geography and topography will be drastically altered forever, as every mountain and hill will be leveled, and every island will either be removed from its foundations or disappear.
- The Earthquakes are accompanied by 100-lb hailstones.

# Revelation 16 Restored

### *The Seven Bowls of God's Wrath;*
### *An allusion to the plagues of Egypt*

1 Then I heard a loud voice from the temple telling the seven angels, "*Go and pour out on the Earth the seven bowls of the wrath of God.*" 2 So the first angel went and poured out his bowl on the Earth, and harmful and painful sores came upon the people who bore the mark of the beast and worshiped its image.

> #### Exodus 9
> 9 It will become fine dust over the whole land of Egypt, and festering boils will break out on people and animals throughout the land." 10 So they took soot from a furnace and stood before Pharaoh. Moses tossed it into the air, and festering boils broke out on people and animals.

3 The second angel poured out his bowl into the sea, and it became like the blood of a corpse, and every living thing died that was in the sea (Revelation 8:8-9).

4 The third angel poured out his bowl into the rivers and the springs of water, and they became blood (Revelation 8:10). 5 And I heard the angel in charge of the waters say,

*"Just are you, O Holy One, who is and who was, for you brought these judgments. 6 For they have shed the blood of saints and prophets, and you have given them (their own) blood to drink. It is what they deserve!" (*Isaiah 49:26) *7 And I heard the altar saying, "Yes, Yahuah the Almighty, true and just are your judgments!"*

> #### Isaiah 49:26
> 26 I will make your oppressors eat their own flesh, and they shall be drunk with their own blood as with wine.

8 The fourth angel poured out his bowl on the Sun, and it was allowed to scorch people with fire. 9 They were scorched by the fierce heat, and they cursed the name of Yahuah who had power over these plagues. They did not repent and give Him glory.

10 The fifth angel poured out his bowl on the throne of the beast, and its kingdom was plunged into darkness (from the smoke of the bottomless pit Revelation 9:2). People gnawed their tongues

in anguish 11 and cursed the Yahuah (author) of (the) Heaven(ly Scroll) for their pain and sores. They did not repent of their deeds.

12 The sixth angel poured out his bowl on the great river Euphrates (Revelation 9:14-16), and its water was dried up, to prepare the way for the kings from the east. 13 And I saw, coming out of the mouth of the dragon and out of the mouth of the beast and out of the mouth of the false prophet, three unclean spirits like frogs (Spirit of Dagon, Spirit of the False Messiah, Spirit of Error).

14 For they (the metaphorical frogs) are demonic spirits (leading people away 1 Titus 4:1),

> **1 Titus 4:1 – Spirit of Error, Lies, and Deceit**
> Now the Spirit expressly says that in later times some will depart from the faith by devoting themselves to deceitful spirits and teachings of demons, 2 through the insincerity of liars whose consciences are seared,

performing signs (of fire coming down from Heaven Revelation 13:3), who go abroad to the kings of the whole world, to assemble them for battle on the great day of Yahuah the Almighty (Revelation 19:19). 15 ("*Behold, I am coming like a thief! Blessed is the one who stays awake, keeping his garments on, that he may not go about naked and be seen exposed!*") 16 And they assembled them at the place that in Hebrew is called Armageddon (mountain of Meggido, which there is no such mountain. This battle is Spiritual/symbolic).

## The Seventh Bowl and the Temple in Heaven

17 The seventh angel poured out his bowl into the air, and a loud voice came out of the temple, from the throne, saying, "*It is done* (The Heavenly Scroll has been fulfilled)!" 18 And there were flashes of lightning, rumblings, peals of thunder, and a great Earthquake such as there had never been since man was on the Earth, so great was that Earthquake. 19 The great city was split into three parts, and the cities of the nations fell, and Yahuah remembered Babylon the great, to make her drain the cup of the wine of the fury of his wrath (Revelation 17, 18). 20 And every island fled away, and no mountains were to be found. 21 And great hailstones, about one hundred pounds each, fell from Heaven on people (as the Temple in Heaven was opened Revelation 11:19); and they cursed Yahuah for the plague of the hail, because the plague was so severe.

> **Revelation 11:19**
> 19 Then Yahuah's temple in Heaven was opened, and the ark of his covenant was seen within his temple. There were flashes of lightning, rumblings,4 peals of thunder, an Earthquake, and heavy hail.

# Chapter 17

# Introduction

In this chapter, Babylon the Great is identified. Civil war breaks out within the Beastly Religion, the Beast destroys the central figure of its power (*Rome*) by Divine Decree ... Babylon's power over the kings of Europe (*the known world at that time*) is broken. This is called the Reformation in history.

## Historical Context – The Civil War between the Beast and the Woman

We have been conditioned by the Beast to ignore history when understanding the Book of Revelation because it is all about Christianity which is The Beast and Hesus Horus Krishna aka Jesus H. Christ who is the False Messiah of that "Beastly Religion". We are taught that 2000 years went by from the time the Messiah came and John foresaw the Age of PISCES with nothing at all happening only to be fulfilled in one dramatic 7-year period at the very end.

Revelation Chapter 17 was in fact fulfilled during the 1500s called The Reformation.

> **The Reformation and Wars of Religion (libertymagazine.org)**
> Fought after the Protestant Reformation began in 1517, the wars disrupted the religious and political order in the Catholic countries of Europe. ... The conflicts culminated in the Thirty Years' War (1618–1648), which devastated Germany and killed one-third of its population, a mortality rate twice that of World War I and WWII combined. "The division between Protestant and Catholic caused or intensified numerous conflicts, resulting in some of the longest lasting, bloodiest, and most bitterly contested and destructive wars in history."

# The 7 Kings

These are demi-gods who were all considered the fulfillment of the Zodiac i.e., Kings in their culture. It is upon these pagan demi-gods which the foundation of The Woman was built.

1.   Tammuz of Babylon

2.   Horus of Egypt

3. Ashur of Assyria

4. Apollo of Greece

5. Hercules of Greco-Roman

6. Helios of Roman

7. Hesus H. Krishna aka Jesus H. Christ of Christianity

# The 10 horns

From the 1520s until approximately 1650 the 10 greatest nations in Christendom waged war against the woman breaking her power over kings called The Reformation:

1. France

2. Spain

3. Portugal

4. Austria

5. Sweden

6. The Dutch Republic

7. Britain

8. Denmark

9. Norway

10. Scotland

The Reformation in the 1500s and 1600s was the first step of The Greater Exodus as the Elect began to "come out of her my people". This reformation would culminate at the end times with

His people coming totally out and rejecting the False Messiah. In this way for a long period of time, Christianity did serve the purpose as "God's people" in the war to destroy the prostitute only to be swept away by Protestant Christianity and the False Messiah's rule. The truth is everything has already been fulfilled in history. Revelation Chapter 17 tells the story of a civil war in the Beastly Religion called Mystery Babylon between the seat of her iniquity Rome and the 10 figurative kings and the Beast (kings of Europe). This civil war breaks the power of the "woman/Rome" over the kings of the Earth. This civil war is known in history as *the Reformation.*

Again, we are taught a fairytale version of the Reformation as though mankind just "wised up" and changed their mind concerning the pagan worship of Rome under the lead of Papal Authority. The truth is that it was by death and total destruction of Europe and the bloodiest war in human history fulfilling the "white and red horses" of Revelation killing 25-30% (close to 1/3rd) of the known world's population (Europe) at that time!

> Main article: Whore of Babylon
> The woman who rides on the beast is introduced in the seventeenth chapter. The entire chapter is quite symbolic, but an angel explains to John the meaning of what he is seeing. The woman, who is referred to as "the great prostitute", "is the great city who rules over the kings of the Earth" (Revelation 17:18), who is envied by the ten kings who give power to the beast and is destroyed by those ten kings. "They will bring her to ruin and leave her naked; they will eat her flesh and burn her with fire. For God has put it into their hearts to accomplish his purpose by agreeing to give the beast their power to rule, until God's words are fulfilled" (Revelation 17:16–17).
>
> Revelation 17–18 introduces a Woman dressed in purple and scarlet, and decked with gold, precious stones and pearls. She sits on a scarlet beast with 7 heads (representing 7 kings) and 10 horns (representing 10 kings). She is described as the "*Mother of Harlots*" and is drunk with the blood of the saints indicating her intense involvement in persecution. She comes to power and rules the kings and peoples of the Earth. Eventually, the 10 kings ruling the kingdoms that give their power to the Beast grow tired of her influence and overthrow her. Her destruction will cause the kings and merchants of the Earth to mourn her death.

# Revelation 17 Restored

## *Babylon, the Prostitute (Rome), and the Beast (Christianity)*

1 One of the seven angels who had the seven bowls came and said to me, *"Come, I will show you the punishment of the great prostitute, who sits by many waters. 2 With her the kings of the Earth committed adultery, and the inhabitants of the Earth were intoxicated with the wine of her adulteries."*

3 Then the angel carried me away in the Spirit into a wilderness. There I saw a woman sitting on a scarlet beast that was covered with blasphemous names and had seven heads and ten horns. 4 The woman was dressed in purple and scarlet, and was glittering with gold, precious stones and pearls. She held a golden cup in her hand,

filled with abominable things and the filth of her adulteries. 5 The name written on her forehead was a mystery: **Babylon the great the mother of prostitutes and of the abominations of the Earth**.

6 I saw that the woman was drunk with the blood of Yahuah's holy people, the blood of those who bore testimony to Yahusha. When I saw her, I was greatly astonished. 7 Then the angel said to me: *"Why are you astonished? I will explain to you the mystery of the woman and of the beast she rides, which has the seven heads and ten horns. 8 The beast* (Mystery Babylon), *which you saw, once was* (The Latin Empire/Latinus), now is not (was conquered by Rome/Romulus), *and yet will come up out of the Abyss* (as Romulus was LATIN and Mystery Religion has risen as The Council of Nicaea) *and go to its destruction* (after conquering The Earth as Christianity). *The*

292

*inhabitants of the Earth whose names have not been written in the book of life from the creation of the world will be astonished when they see the beast* (Mystery Babylon), *because it once was* (a Latin Empire), *now is not* (it was conquered by Rome), *and yet will come* (conquering as Christianity).

9 *"This calls for a mind with wisdom. The seven heads are seven hills on which the woman* (Rome) *sits. 10 They are also seven kings* (Spiritually there are 1-Tammuz/Babylon, 2-Horus/Egypt, 3-Ashur/Assyria, 4-Apollo/Greece, 5-Hercules/Greek and Roman, 6-Sol Invictus/Helios Roman, 7-Hesus H. Krishna). *Five have fallen* (1-Tammuz/Babylon, 2-Horus/Egypt, 3-Ashur/Assyria, 4-Apollo/Greece, 5-Hercules/Greek), *one is* (6- Helios Roman. Sol Invictus was the official religion in Rome at that time), *the other* (Hesus Horus Krishna aka Jesus H. Christ) *has not yet come* (created at the Council of Nicaea some 300 years after John wrote Revelation)*; but when he does come, he must remain for only a little while* (before Rome fell). *11 The beast who once was, and now is not, is an eighth king* (when Jesus was created at Nicaea and Christianity replaced the Roman Empire). *He is associated with the* (same religion as the) *seven and is going to his destruction* (like the previous demi-gods)."

# The Reformation:
## The Civil War between The Beast and the Whore, the power of the Whore is broken over the kings of Europe

12 *"The ten horns you saw are ten kings who have not yet received a kingdom (*they were <u>puppet</u> Kings of the Pope through Papal Disposition*), but who for one hour will receive authority as kings along with the beast* (the 10 kings were the Kings established by the Pope over Europe). *13 They have one purpose* (to rebel against Papal control and destroy Rome's grip over Europe) *and will give their power and authority to the beast* (will unite in battle as Reformers for Christ ΧΣϚ not nations).

## Protestant Christianity will later wage war on the Lamb

14 *They* (later) *will wage war against the Lamb* (at the end of the Age of PISCES), *but the Lamb will triumph over them because he is the Master of all and King of kings—and with him will be his called, chosen and faithful followers."*

## Explanation of the Prophetic Imagery

15 Then the angel said to me, *"The waters you saw, where the prostitute sits, are peoples, multitudes, nations and languages. 16 The beast* (Protestant Christianity) *and the ten horns (*Kings of Europe*) you saw will hate the prostitute* (Roman Catholicism). *They will bring her to ruin and leave her naked* (Great 30 years' War between Catholicism and the Christian Reformers that broke Rome's grip over Europe killing 1/3 or the population*); they will eat her flesh and burn her with fire.*

## The Reformation was Yahuah's Will to break the power of the Whore

17 *For Yahuah has put it into their hearts to accomplish his purpose by agreeing to hand over to the beast their royal authority, until Yahuah's words are fulfilled. 18 The woman you saw is the great city* (Roman Christianity/Catholicism) *that rules over the kings of the Earth* (called **Papal Disposition**)."

> https://en.wikipedia.org/wiki/Papal_deposing_power
> The papal deposing power was the most powerful tool of the political authority claimed by and on behalf of the Roman Pontiff, in medieval and early modern thought, amounting to the assertion of the Pope's power to declare a Christian monarch heretical and powerless to rule.
>
> Pope Gregory VII's Dictatus Papae (c. 1075) claimed for the Pope "that it may be permitted to him to depose emperors" (12) and asserted the papal power to "absolve subjects from their fealty to wicked men" (27).
>
> Oaths of allegiance held together the feudal political structure of medieval Europe. The principle behind deposition was that the Pope, as the ultimate representative of God from whom all oaths draw their force, could in extreme circumstances absolve a ruler's subjects of their allegiance, thereby rendering the ruler powerless. In a medieval Europe in which all confessed the Pope as head of the visible Church, it gave concrete embodiment to the superiority of the spiritual power over the temporal—the other side, so to speak, of the role of Popes and bishops in anointing and crowning emperors and kings.

# *Chapter 18*

# Introduction

In chapter 17, we saw civil war breaks out within the Beast, the Kings of Europe destroy the seat and power of Babylon (*Rome*) over Europe. Basically, in Chapter 17, the "head" is cut-off followed by the death of the body in Chapter 18. These two chapters are two of the most difficult and disputed chapters in Revelation. There is no consensus on the identity of this "beast χξς " or if these things were fulfilled in history or yet future. But what is agreed upon by scholars alike is Chapter 17 is dealing with the Spiritual entity of Babylon while Chapter 18 deals with the commercial/political entity. However, within The Sabbath Covenant's Assembly of Nazarenes world-wide, there is no doubt as to the identity of χξς - It is Hesus Horus Krishna aka ***Jesus H. Christ***. Please see my book The Antichrist Revealed!

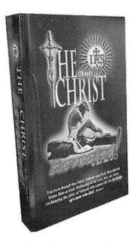

*The Antichrist Revealed by Rav Sha'ul available on all online bookstores*

The problem is that those trying to understand and explain Revelation are Christian and unable to Spiritually "see" because they themselves have committed the Abomination of Desolation *(keep Easter over Passover)* and worship the Beast χξς ! So, any interpretation of the Book of Revelation from these "Beastly sources" is blind at best.

In this chapter Babylon falls. This causes the merchants of the Earth to weep because no one is able to buy their products anymore, which is exactly what happened when Rome fell. The known world fell into The Dark Ages and the world economy collapsed, and the center of the known world's ports went out of business. The Beast had a mortal head wound that healed when Rome conquered Babylon (*mortal head wound*). However, Mystery Babylon conquered the Roman Empire when the Babylonian religion became the state religion of Rome (*head wound healed*). Rome had conquered the "known world" at that time and became the politico-commercial system that provided the means and basis of a new world-wide religious system. This religious system was devised at the Council of Nicaea to unite all pagan religions under one faith based in Rome called Christianity.

Christianity is a carbon copy of the Mystery Religion of Babylon (*see my book **Mystery Babylon: The Religion of the Beast***). This religion became known as the Universal (*catholic means universal*) Church. For more information on this Great Deception, please read my book ***Christianity and the Great Deception***.

*Christianity and The Great Deception by Rav Sha'ul available on all online bookstores*

# Revelation 18 Restored

## *The Fall of Babylon*

1 After this I saw another angel coming down out of the depths of The Heavenly Scroll to explain its outcome (g1537),

> Strong's Greek: 1537. ἐκ (ek or ex) -- from, from out of (biblehub.com)
> "coming down from" **1537** *ek* (a preposition, written *eks* before a vowel) – properly, "*out from* and *to*" (the *outcome*); *out from within.* 1537 /*ek* ("out of") is one of the most under-translated (and therefore mis-translated) Greek propositions – often being confined to the meaning "by." 1537 (*ek*) has a two-layered meaning ("*out from* and *to*") which makes it *outcome* oriented (out of the depths of the source and extending to its impact on the object).

having great authority, and the Earth was illuminated with its (g846 speaking of The Heavenly Scroll Psalm 19) glory.

> https://biblehub.com/greek/846.htm
> Thayer's Greek Lexicon
> **STRONGS NT 846: αὐτός**
> I. self, as used (in all persons, genders, numbers) to distinguish a person **or thing** from or contrast it with another, or to give him (**it**) emphatic prominence.
>
> **Psalm 19**
> 1 *The Heavenly Scroll (Sun, moon, stars, constellations) declare the glory of God*; the skies proclaim the work of His hands.

2 And he called out with a mighty voice (to proclaim the fulfillment of the battle of the ages spoken in The Heavenly Scroll between the Dragon and The Son of Man), "Fallen, fallen is Babylon the great! She has become a dwelling place for demons, a haunt for every unclean spirit, a haunt for every unclean bird, a haunt for every unclean and detestable beast.

> **Isaiah 13:21**
> But desert creatures will lie there, jackals will fill her houses; there the owls will dwell, and there the wild goats will leap about.

### Isaiah 34:14
Desert creatures will meet with hyenas, and wild goats will bleat to each other; there the night creatures will also lie down and find for themselves places of rest.

### Jeremiah 50:39
"So desert creatures and hyenas will live there, and there the owl will dwell. It will never again be inhabited or lived in from generation to generation.

### Jeremiah 51:37
Babylon will be a heap of ruins, a haunt of jackals, an object of horror and scorn, a place where no one lives.

### Zephaniah 2:14
Flocks and herds will lie down there, creatures of every kind. The desert owl and the screech owl will roost on her columns. Their hooting will echo through the windows, rubble will fill the doorways, the beams of cedar will be exposed.

### Zephaniah 2:15
This is the city of revelry that lived in safety. She said to herself, "I am the one! And there is none besides me." What a ruin she has become, a lair for wild beasts! All who pass by her scoff and shake their fists.

3 For all nations have drunk the wine of the passion of her sexual immorality, and the kings of the Earth have committed immorality with her, and the merchants of the Earth have grown rich from the power of her luxurious living."

### Revelation 18:11
"The merchants of the Earth will weep and mourn over her because no one buys their cargoes anymore--

### Revelation 18:15
The merchants who sold these things and gained their wealth from her will stand far off, terrified at her torment. They will weep and mourn.

4 Then I heard another voice from Heaven saying, "Come out of her, my people, lest you take part in her sins, lest you share in her plagues.

### Isaiah 48:20
Leave Babylon, flee from the Babylonians! Announce this with shouts of joy and proclaim it. Send it out to the ends of the Earth; say, "Yahuah has redeemed his servant Jacob."

5 For her sins are heaped high as Heaven, and Yahuah has remembered her iniquities.

### Jeremiah 51:9
"'We would have healed Babylon, but she cannot be healed; let us leave her and each go to our own land, for her judgment reaches to the skies, it rises as high as the Heavens.'

### Ezra 9:6
and prayed: "I am too ashamed and disgraced, my God, to lift up my face to you, because our sins are higher than our heads and our guilt has reached to the Heavens.

6 Pay her back as she herself has paid back others and repay her double for her deeds;

### Psalm 137:8
Daughter Babylon, doomed to destruction, happy is the one who repays you according to what you have done to us.

### Jeremiah 50:15
Shout against her on every side! She surrenders, her towers fall, her walls are torn down. Since this is the vengeance of Yahuah, take vengeance on her; do to her as she has done to others.

### Jeremiah 50:29
"Summon archers against Babylon, all those who draw the bow. Encamp all around her; let no one escape. Repay her for her deeds; do to her as she has done. For she has defied Yahuah, the Holy One of Israel.

### Jeremiah 51:24
"Before your eyes I will repay Babylon and all who live in Babylonia for all the wrong they have done in Zion," declares Yahuah.

### Jeremiah 51:49
"Babylon must fall because of Israel's slain, just as the slain in all the Earth have fallen because of Babylon.

mix a double portion for her bin the cup she mixed.

### Revelation 14:10
they, too, will drink the wine of God's fury, which has been poured full strength into the cup of his wrath. They will be tormented with burning sulfur in the presence of the holy angels and of the Lamb.

### Revelation 16:19

The great city split into three parts, and the cities of the nations collapsed. God remembered Babylon the Great and gave her the cup filled with the wine of the fury of his wrath.

### Revelation 17:4

The woman was dressed in purple and scarlet, and was glittering with gold, precious stones and pearls. She held a golden cup in her hand, filled with abominable things and the filth of her adulteries.

7 As she glorified herself and lived in luxury, so give her a like measure of torment and mourning, since in her heart she says, 'I sit as a queen (bride of 𝓧𝓼𝓼 ), I am no widow, and mourning I shall never see.'

### Isaiah 47

7 You said, 'I will be queen forever.' You did not take these things to heart or consider their outcome.8 So now hear this, O lover of luxury who sits securely, who says to herself, 'I am, and there is none besides me. I will never be a widow or know the loss of children.'...

### Zephaniah 2:15

15 This is the city of revelry that lived in safety. She said to herself, "I am the one! And there is none besides me." What a ruin she has become, a lair for wild beasts! All who pass by her scoff and shake their fists.

### Revelation 3:17

17 You say, 'I am rich; I have acquired wealth and do not need a thing.' But you do not realize that you are wretched, pitiful, poor, blind and naked.

8 For this reason her plagues will come in a single day, death and mourning and famine, and she will be burned up with fire (on the DAY of judgment, not eternity); for mighty is Yahuah our God who has judged her."

9 And the kings of the Earth, who committed sexual immorality and lived in luxury with her, will weep and wail over her when they see the smoke of her burning. 10 They will stand far off, in fear of her torment, and say, "Alas! Alas! You great city, you mighty city, Babylon! For in a single hour your judgment has come."

### Revelation 18:17

In one hour such great wealth has been brought to ruin!' "Every sea captain, and all who travel by ship, the sailors, and all who earn their living from the sea, will stand far off.

**Revelation 18:19**

They will throw dust on their heads, and with weeping and mourning cry out: "'Woe! Woe to you, great city, where all who had ships on the sea became rich through her wealth! In one hour she has been brought to ruin!'

**Revelation 18:8**

Therefore in one day her plagues will overtake her: death, mourning and famine. She will be consumed by fire, for mighty is Yahuah God who judges her.

11 And the merchants of the Earth weep and mourn for her, since no one buys their cargo anymore, 12 cargo of gold, silver, jewels, pearls, fine linen, purple cloth, silk, scarlet cloth, all kinds of scented wood, all kinds of articles of ivory, all kinds of articles of costly wood, bronze, iron, and marble, 13 cinnamon, spice, incense, myrrh, frankincense, wine, oil, fine flour, wheat, cattle and sheep, horses and chariots, and slaves, that is, human souls.

> The Fall of Babylon (Revelation 18) – Revelation Made Clear (thebookofrevelationmadeclear.com)
> The fall of the Roman Empire fulfills this chapter. Humanity had no idea what the effects of the fall of Rome would have, it devastated the Earth. No more global trade, bankrupted the nations, the merchants, and the workers who all relied on global trade. Then plunged the world into The Dark Ages. (*Note, Rome fell in 395 AD, scarcely 1 generation after the abomination called The Council of Nicaea which no doubt lead to its complete collapse virtually overnight*).

14 *"The fruit for which your soul longed has gone from you, and all your delicacies and your splendors are lost to you, never to be found again!"* 15 The merchants of these wares, who gained wealth from her, will stand far off, in fear of her torment, weeping and mourning aloud, 16 *"Alas, alas, for the great city that was clothed in fine linen, in purple and scarlet, adorned with gold, with jewels, and with pearls! 17 For in a single hour all this wealth shas been laid waste."* And tall shipmasters and seafaring men, sailors and all whose trade is on the sea, stood far off 18 and cried out vas they saw the smoke of her burning, "What city was like the great city?" 19 And they threw dust on their heads as they wept and mourned, crying out, "Alas, alas, for the great city where all who had ships at sea grew rich by her wealth! For in a single hour, she has been laid waste.

20 Rejoice over her, O Heaven, and you saints and apostles and prophets, for Yahuah has given judgment for you against her!" 21 Then a mighty angel took up a stone like a great millstone and threw it into the sea, saying, "So will Babylon the great city be thrown down with violence, and will be found no more; 22 and the sound of harpists and musicians, of flute players and trumpeters, will be heard in you no more, and a craftsman of any craft will be found in you no more, and the sound of the mill will be heard in you no more, 23 and the light of a lamp will shine in you no more, and the voice of bridegroom and bride will be heard in you no more, for your merchants were the great ones of the Earth, and all nations were deceived by your sorcery. 24 And in her was found the blood of prophets and of saints, and of mall who have been slain on Earth."

**Jeremiah 51:49**

"Babylon must fall because of Israel's slain, just as the slain in all the Earth have fallen because of Babylon.

# Chapter 19

# Introduction

In this chapter, the Battle of the Ages end with Mystery Babylon defeated. Yahusha emerges from the fray covered in blood riding a white horse and he is called The Fulfillment of the Word (*found in The Heavenly Scroll*).

- The marriage between the Bride (*the Elect*) who has prepared herself and clothed in white linen, and the Groom (*the Messiah*) is consummated on Yom Kippur (Revelation 19:5–10).

- Yahusha who holds the title Immanuel "faithful and true witness" rides in on a white horse. "With Justice he makes war" (*Revelation 19:11*). Yahusha the Messiah is the rider mentioned in chapter twelve. John references Psalm 2:9 "He will rule them with an iron scepter" (*Revelation 19:15*).

- The war begins between the children of Yahuah and the world. When the war is won, the Beast χξς and the false prophet (*Pope*) are cast into the metaphorical "lake of fire". The rest of the dead are not laid to rest, but left out for "the Great Supper" a final offering. (*Revelation 19:20–21*).

- The Army of Yahuah made up of its King Yahusha and the rest of the Children of Yahuah return to rule the Earth dressed in fine linen riding white horses with Crowns.

For more on Yahusha being the fulfillment of the Word proclaimed in The Heavenly Scroll, not "the Incarnate Word of God" as in the pagan philosophy of "word became flesh" see my book ***The Testimony of Yahuchanon.***

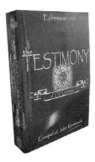

# Is Yahusha the "Word of God" in the flesh?

Yahusha is the fulfillment of the Word of Yahuah written in the stars. That is what the Book of Revelation and Gospel of John Chapter 1 (*both written by the same guy*) is all about! He is not the personification of the Word or Incarnation of the Word. **That is pagan**.

As you can see below, the Doctrine of Incarnation that led to the acceptance of the pagan Babylonian Trinity through syncretism did not come about until 4 centuries after Yahusha lived and died. That false doctrine that Yahusha is literally "Logos" or "Word of God" in the flesh and not the fulfillment of Yahuah's predestined plan written in the stars evolved in the 4th Century through the "*tradition and reasoning*" under the influence of pagan Greek philosophers such as Plato...

> **The Abingdon Dictionary of Living Religions**, page 767, tells us:
> TRINITY (Ch). The Dogma, formulated authoritatively in fourth century church Councils, that Christians worship one God in three persons (Father, Son, Holy Spirit) and one substance. Under pressure to explain to a hostile Roman world how Christians counted themselves monotheists, Christian apologists (notably Justin Martyr, d. 165) combined Johannine and Stoic-Platonic understanding of the term Logos ("Reason," or "Word") in order to maintain that the Son was both God's own self-expression and a being distinct from him.

So, we read above The Trinity was justified not through the Word of Yahuah (*because it cannot be it is Blasphemy*) it was justified using Hellenism or the "combined Johannine and Stoic Platonic" pagan philosophy of the term "Logos". We read below that the term *logos* was defined by Christians according to the interpretations of pagan influenced philosophers in order to promote a false pagan God-savior:

> **Encyclopedia Britannica, Volume 7, page 449.**
> LOGOS (Greek:"word, "reason, or plan"), plural logoi, in Greek philosophy and theology, the divine reason implicit in the cosmos, ordering it and giving it form and meaning. Though the concept defined by the term logos is found in Greek, Indian, Egyptian, and Persian philosophical and theological systems, it became particularly significant in Christian writings and doctrines to describe or define the role of Jesus Christ as the principle of God active in the creation and the continuation structuring of the cosmos and in revealing the divine plan of salvation to man. It thus underlies the basic Christian doctrine of the pre-existence of Jesus... The identification of Jesus with the logos was further developed in the early church but more on the basis of Greek philosophical ideas than on Old Testament motifs.

The concept of Logos was based on Greek philosophical ideas not on any prophecy or Old Testament "motifs" or Hebrew understanding at all. It is a pagan philosophy of Hellenism.

The Religions of Ancient Greece and Babylonia clearly tells us that the Greek philosophical ideas were developed in Alexandria, Egypt from the pagan Babylonian mystery religions. These ideas pertaining to the meaning of Logos penetrated as a result of modern religious thought through the philosophy of Greece and Egypt.

> **The Religions of Ancient Greece and Babylonia**, by A. H. Sayce. pages 229-230
> Many of the theories of Egyptian religion, modified and transformed no doubt, have penetrated into the theology of Christian Europe, and form, as it were, part of the woof in the web of modern religious thought. Christian theology was largely organized and nurtured in the schools of Alexandria, and Alexandria was not only the meeting place of East and West, it was also the place where the decrepit theology of Egypt was revivified by contact with the speculative philosophy of Greece. Perhaps, however, the indebtedness of Christian theological theory to ancient Egyptian dogma is nowhere more striking than in the doctrine of the Trinity. The very terms used of it by Christian theologians meet us again in the inscriptions and papyri of Egypt. Originally the trinity was a triad like those we find in Babylonian mythology. The triad consisted of a divine father, wife, and son. The father became the son and the son the father through all time, and of both alike the mother was but another form.

It is from the pagan mystery religions that the Greek philosophers developed the idea of *Logos*:

## The New International Dictionary of New Testament Theology, Volume 3, page 1085

Among the systems offering an explanation of the world in terms of the logos, there are the Mystery Religions. These cultic communities did not see their task as lying in the communication of knowledge of a scientific nature, but of mysteries to their initiates who strove for purification in the recurrent enactment of sacred actions. The Foundation for these cultic actions was Sacred Text. Among them were the cults of Dionysus, the Pytha-goreans, and the Orphic Mysteries. By means of these cults, non Greek thought, such as in the Isis-Osiris Mysteries, which Osiris the logos created by Isis is the spiritual image of the world. Similarly in the cult of Hermes, Hermes informed his son Tat in the Sacred Text belonging to the cult, how by God's mercy, he became logos, and thus a son of God. As such, he (Hermes) brought regulation and form into world, but himself remained a mediating being between God and matter, on one side, and God and man on the other. The logos can also, however, appear as the son of Hermes, resulting in a triple (trinity) gradation: God (who is Zeus), Son (Hermes), and LOGOS. It was through syncretism that we have the word "Logos" or "Word" written in our English Bibles instead of "The Spoken Promise / Plan of Yahuah" which is what the word Logos means in Greek and Debar in Hebrew! Neither word means "in the flesh":

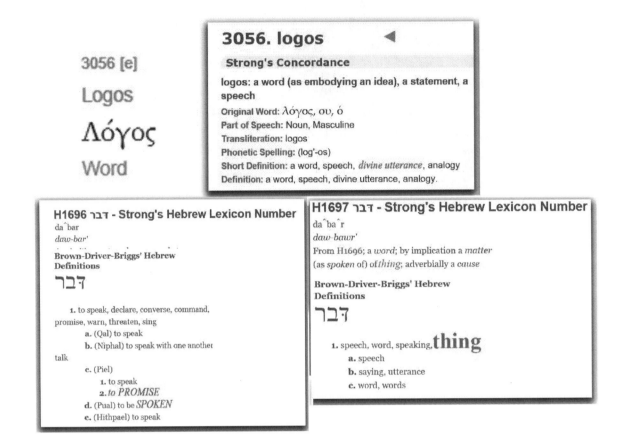

For more information on this topic, please read my book **Blasphemy of the Holy Spirit** which is a full vindication of The Spirit of Truth vs. The Spirit of the Antichrist which is Incarnation.

*Blasphemy of the Holy Spirit* by Rav Sha'ul

# King of Kings and Lord of Lords...

In this chapter of Revelation, Yahusha rides in with the "shem" or title/name written on his banner "King of Kings and Lord of Lords". Putting that sound bite back into context, we see that in context Yahusha has many crown, a crown for each title he holds... we know Yahusha has many "titles" or "names" which in Hebrew means "reputation"... we are not talking about his personal name, Revelation 19:12 is speaking of his titles.

> https://yhwhisone.wordpress.com/2016/07/29/the-hebrew-word-shem-meaning/
> 3.A more common meaning of the word for "name" in Hebrew (SHEM) in the Bible is 'the essential reality of who someone is', as in Proverbs 21:24. "A proud and haughty person's SHEM is scorner." In Exodus 34:14 we read," Yahuah, Whose SHEM is jealous, is a jealous Elohim." In a more famous example, the prophet Isaiah gave Messiah's SHEM as being
>
> - "Wonderful,
> - Counselor,
> - the Image of Mighty EL,
> - the Father of Everlasting Life,
> - the Ruler of Heaven." (Isaiah 9:5-6)

He certainly is all of those, and they are some of His royal titles, but none of them are His Name. The plural form of SHEM is SHMOT. The Bible has many SHMOT for Elohim which are royal titles and revelations of the reality of Who He is, but not names as such. In Biblical Hebrew, to trust in Someone's SHEM means to trust Him because of Who He is. To bless Someone's SHEM means to bless Him because of Who He is. Now before we proceed to idioms, would you like to work a small puzzle? Here it is: Untangle the visual pun in Revelation 19:16:"And on his robe and on his thigh (banner-correct translation ) He has His SHEM written: KING OF KINGS, AND MASTER OF MASTERS."

# Revelation 19 Restored

### *Rejoicing in Heaven*

19 After this I heard what seemed to be the loud voice of a great multitude in Heaven, crying out (the 7th Trumpet sounded Revelation 11:15),

> *"Hallelujah! Salvation and glory and power belong to our God, 2 for his judgments are true and just; for he has judged the great prostitute who corrupted the Earth with her immorality and has avenged on her the blood of his servants."*

> This is the end of the 7 bowls and 7 judgements and 7 Trumpets

> **Revelation 17:1**
> 1 Then one of the seven angels who had the seven bowls came and said to me, "Come, I will show you the judgment of the great prostitute who is seated on many waters, 2 with whom the kings of the Earth have committed sexual immorality, and with the wine of whose sexual immorality the dwellers on Earth have become drunk."

3 Once more they cried out,

> *"Hallelujah! The smoke from her goes up forever and ever."*

4 And the twenty-four elders and the four living creatures fell down and worshiped God who was seated on the throne (Yahusha had not yet been set on the Throne as King, he is still the Prince of Peace), saying, "Let it be so. Hallelujah!" 5 And from the throne room came a voice saying,

> *"Praise our God, all you his servants, you who fear him, small and great."*

### *The Marriage Supper of the Lamb*

6 Then I heard what seemed to be the voice of a great multitude, like the roar of many waters and like the sound of mighty peals of thunder, crying out,

*"Hallelujah! For Yahuah our God the Almighty reigns. 7 Let us rejoice and exult and give him the glory, for the marriage of the Lamb has come, and his Bride has made herself ready; 8 it was granted her to clothe herself with fine linen, bright and pure"*

for the fine linen is the righteous deeds of the saints.

9 And the angel said to me, *"Write this: Blessed are those who are invited to the marriage supper of the Lamb."* And he said to me, *"These* (revelation of The Heavenly Scroll) *are the true words of God* (written in the stars Psalm 119:89 Psalm 89:2, Daniel 4:35, Matthew 6:10*)."* 10 Then I fell down at his feet to worship him, but he said to me, *"You must not do that! I am a fellow servant with you and your brothers who hold to the testimony of Yahusha* (which is The Heavenly Scroll). *Worship Yahuah alone."* For the testimony of Yahusha is the spirit of prophecy (The Heavenly Scroll is the Spirit of Prophecy, as ALL prophet were given the Scroll to "eat").

### Revelation (of The Heavenly Scroll) 10:7-10
7 But in the days when the seventh Angel is about to sound his trumpet, the mystery of Yahuah will be accomplished, **just as He announced to His servants the Prophets**." 8 Then the voice that I had heard from Heaven spoke to me once more: "Go, take the Scroll that lies open in the hand of the Angel who is standing on the sea and on the land." 9 So I went to the Angel and asked him to give me the little Scroll. He said to me, "**Take it and eat** it. It will turn your stomach sour, but 'in your mouth it will be as sweet as honey.' 10 I took the little Scroll from the Angel's hand and ate it.

### Ezekiel 2:8
And you, son of man, listen to what I tell you. Do not be rebellious like that rebellious house. Open your mouth and eat what I give you."

### Ezekiel 3:3
Then he said to me, "Son of man, **eat this Scroll** I am giving you and fill your stomach with it." So I ate it, and it tasted as sweet as honey in my mouth.

### Psalm 119:103
**How sweet are Your Words** (preserved eternal in The Heavenly Scroll *Psalms 119:89*) to my taste, sweeter than honey in my mouth.

### Jeremiah 15:16
**Your Words were found, and I ate them**. Your Words became a delight to me and my heart's delight, for I bear Your name, O Yahuah God of Hosts.

**Ezekiel 2:8**
But you, son of man, listen to what I tell you. Do not be rebellious like that rebellious house. **Open your mouth and eat what I give you.**"

**Job 23:12**
Neither have I gone back from the Commandment of His lips; **I have esteemed the Words of His mouth more than my necessary food**.

# Rider on a White Horse

[11] I saw Heaven (shamayim, The Heavenly Scroll/Mazzaroth) standing open (stars rolled back like a Scroll Rev. 6:14, Isaiah 34:4, Rev. 5) and there before me (written in The Heavenly Scroll that was opened) was a white horse, whose rider is called Faithful and True (first name/title **Immanuel**). With justice (Eternal Judge 2 Corinthians 5:10, Acts 17:31. John 5:22, TAURUS) he wages war and executes great judgment.

**TAURUS**
The conquering Ruler comes, the sublime vanquisher, to execute the great judgment, he is the ruling Shepherd King

[12] His eyes are like blazing fire, and on his head are many crowns (a crown for each title, with the title written on the crown, the context is still 'crowns'...) He has a name/title written (on one of the crowns) on his (head), that no one knows (he hasn't received this crown yet) but he himself (there is a crown given him that is not given until after he fulfills The Heavenly Scroll).... .

> **"The Messiah's name is irrelevant; he gets a NEW name no one knows"**
> Quite often I hear the argument that the actual name of the Messiah is not that important. He is going to receive a "new name" that no one knows, so why bicker over Jesus/Yeshua/Yahshua/Yahusha/Yahoshua? None of that matter, so they tell me. This is a prime example of what I call a "sound bite". One verse taken totally out of context and blown up into a "doctrine" that contradicts the entire Bible! The context above is titles on crowns not his personal name.

13 He is clothed in a robe dipped in blood, and the name by which he is called is The Dabar (fulfillment of the Spoken Promise) of Yahuah (*from the beginning written in The Heavenly Scroll*).

## H1696 דבר - Strong's Hebrew Lexicon Number

daˆbar

*daw-bar'*

**Brown-Driver-Briggs' Hebrew Definitions**

    **1.** to speak, declare, converse, command, promise, warn, threaten, sing
        **a.** (Qal) to speak
        **b.** (Niphal) to speak with one another talk
        **c.** (Piel)
            **1.** to speak
            **2.** to promise
        **d.** (Pual) to be spoken
        **e.** (Hithpael) to speak

*Hebrew for "word" H1696 means "spoken promise".*
*Yahusha is the spoken promise that was fulfilled in the flesh*

### Daniel 4:35

"All the inhabitants of the Earth are accounted as nothing, but He does according to His will written in the host of Heaven (The Zodiac which hosts constellations. Constellations "host stars")

### Psalm 89:2

I will declare that your love stands firm forever, that you have established your faithful promise (dabar) of salvation in The Heavenly Scroll itself.

### John 17:5

And now, Father, glorify me in Your presence (through resurrection as promised in the Dabar/Spoken Promise) with the glory I had with You (written in The Heavenly Scroll) before the world began (the Light of Gen. 1:1: written into the stars on Day 4, then fulfilled in Yahusha on the 4th prophetic day as the Debar/Plan was fulfilled in the flesh John 1).

### Psalm 119:89

Your Word, Yahuah, is eternal; it stands firm (written) in (the) Heaven(ly Scroll).

### Matthew 6:10

Your Kingdom come, Your Will be done, on Earth as it is (written) in (the) Heaven(ly Scroll)...

<u>Hebrews 10:7</u>
""THEN I SAID, 'BEHOLD, I HAVE COME IN THE SCROLL OF THE BOOK (in Heaven) IT IS WRITTEN OF ME TO DO YOUR WILL, O Yahuah.'"

<u>Psalm 19:1-2</u>
1 The Heaven(ly Scroll) declares the Glory of Yahuah (which is Yahusha 2 Corinthians 4:6) ;the stars proclaim the work of His Hands. 2 Day after day they pour forth speech; night after night they reveal knowledge.

14 The armies of Heaven were following him (***Commander of the Host*** one of his titles), riding on white horses and dressed in fine linen, white and clean (garments of the ***High Priest*** another title). 15 Coming out of his mouth is a sharp sword (The Law) with which to strike down the nations (as ***Eternal Judge***, another title). "He will rule them with an iron scepter (***King of Kings***, another title)." He treads the winepress of the fury of the wrath of Yahuah Almighty (he is the mighty ***Image of God/Elohim***, another title). 16 On his robe and on his banner he has this title written: ***KING OF KINGS AND MASTER OF MASTERS***.

17 Then I saw an angel standing in the light of the Sun, and with a loud voice he called to all the birds that fly directly overhead, *"Come, gather for the great supper of Yahuah, 18 to eat the flesh of kings, the flesh of captains, the flesh of mighty men, the flesh of horses and their riders, and the flesh of all men, both free and slave, both small and great."*

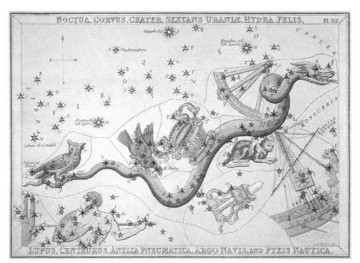

*Bowl of Wrath being poured out and the birds of prey devouring the Dragon HYDRA*

19 And I saw the beast $\chi\xi\varsigma$ and the kings of the Earth with their armies gathered to make war against him who was sitting on the horse and against his army. 20 And the beast was captured, and with it the false prophet who in its presence had done the signs by which he deceived those who had received the mark of the beast $\chi$ and those who worshiped its image $\chi\xi\varsigma$ .

These two (images) were thrown alive into the lake of fire that burns with sulfur. 21 And the rest were slain by the sword that came from the mouth of him who was sitting on the horse, and all the birds were gorged with their flesh (*The False Prophet is not a single person, it is an office. The False Messiah is not a single person, it is a false image of the true Messiah*).

# *Chapter 20*

# Introduction

In this chapter we enter the Age of AQUARIUS and the King begins his reign:

- Satan is bound for a thousand years.

- The Elect are raised and transposed to Spirit to rule.

- Yahusha the Water Bearer Mikveh's the Earth to cleanse it from the Battle of the Ages (*TAURUS thru PISCES*).

- Fallen humanity is destroyed along with the Dragon, the False Messiah, and the False Prophet.

- The First Resurrection occurs as Yahusha builds the 3rd and Final Temple of Yahuah.

- After a thousand years, Satan is released to deceive the nations, those deceived, and Gog and Magog are gathered against the Holy City. Fire comes down and devours them.

- Satan is cast into the "lake of fire" forever coming under Yahuah's judgment (fire).

- The memory of those who lived and died during the 1,000-year reign are brought to judgement (raised from the dead).

# TARURS - Great White Throne Judgment

In chapters 19 and 20, Yahusha fulfills the pictograph of TAURUS.

### TAURUS
The conquering Ruler comes, the sublime vanquisher, to execute the great judgment, he is the ruling Shepherd King

We read in this chapter that two books are opened. The *Book of the Dead* and the *Book of Life*. This is called The Great White Throne judgment. This scene is the same as we witnessed in

Chapter 19 where the judge takes his seat and the Heavens part "like a Scroll" and The Heavenly Scroll which contains the Book of the Dead and the Book of Life are opened.

### Revelation 19
[11] I saw Heaven (shamayim, The Heavenly Scroll/Mazzaroth) standing open (stars rolled back like a Scroll Revelation 6:14, Isaiah 34:4, Revelation 5) and there before me (written in The Heavenly Scroll that was opened) was a white horse, whose rider is called Faithful and True (title **Immanuel**). With justice (Eternal Judge - 2 Corinthians 5:10, Acts 17:31. John 5:22,) he wages war and executes great judgment (TAURUS).

Then the two books are open and Yahusha begins judging the "living in covenant with him" and also those who remain dead in their works.

### Revelation 20:11-15
Then I saw a great white throne and him who was seated on it. From his presence Earth and sky fled away, and no place was found for them (as they parted like a Scroll to reveal the contents of the stars Revelation 19:11). 12 And I saw the dead, great and small, standing before the throne, and books (of the dead) were opened (this is the 'resurrection', it is of their memory). Then another book was opened, which is the book of life (and their memory was "resurrected"). And the dead were judged by what was written in the books, according to what they had done. 13 And the sea gave up the dead who were in it, Death and Hades gave up the dead who were in them, and they were judged, each one of them, according to what they had done. 14 Then Death and Hades were thrown into the lake of fire (again, not literal. Death and Hades are not people any more than the False Prophet or Antichrist. All are false beliefs not real individuals). This is the second death, the lake of fire (judgement). 15 And if anyone's name was not found written in the book of life, **his memory was thrown into the lake of fire** (consumed by the Word of Yahuah the all-consuming fire).

## *The Book of the Dead is Opened*

What happens when the Book of the Dead is opened? It is called the Book of the Dead because those whose names are written in that book are DEAD. They died. They are not brought back to life and resurrected in that sense. It is their memory written in the Book of the Dead that is raised in question of judgment. It is their works written in that book of "memories" that are judged by fire in one day not over the course of a life spent in hell for all eternity. These dead never live again, they do not receive the Crown of Eternal Life to live in Hell. It is on the day Yahuah judges the works of those who did not build their foundation on The Yahushaic Covenant.

Their works written in the Book of the Dead are judged then their life come under judgment by His Law and Yahuah issues the final death decree and they are not granted eternal life. They remain dead as they have ceased to exist at the first death of the body. They were not born again in their spirit, so they are not eternal in any way. They received the Second Death sentence issued in lieu of the Death Decrees in the Law and stay dead eternally. In other words, the Death Decrees justify their deaths, and they are not given life to live again. You cannot "dwell in eternal fires of hell" and this is not what Scripture teaches us …

### Isaiah 33:14
The sinners in Zion are afraid (of death); trembling grips the ungodly: "Who of us can dwell with a consuming fire? Who of us can dwell with everlasting flames?"

No one. We see that Yahuah casts their works into the "fire" and their works are tested and judged not the person because they are dead, it is ONLY their memory that is "raised" as the Book of the Dead is read, and their life judged by His Law.

### 1 Corinthians 3
13 each one's work will become clear; for the Day will declare it, because their works will be revealed by fire; and the fire will test each one's work, of what sort it is.

### John 5
29 And the Bride will be revealed on Earth (PISCES and flow down into the streams of Living Water poured out from on High by AQUARIUS the Bearer of Living Water and Manna - Isaiah 44:3). Those (The Bride) who have been made ready (ARIES) by practicing Righteousness (Sanctified John 17:19) will be Resurrected (CAPRICORNUS) in order to live (death will 'pass them over' and enter into The Promised Land - CANCER); and those who have practiced wickedness will have the memory of their lives Resurrected in order to be Judged to justify their death (1 Corinthians 3:13).

The Bible uses "metaphors" we can understand to explain this day. They are not tormented by fire literally; their works are judged by the all-consuming fire of The Law of Yahuah.

### Jeremiah 23:29
"Is not my word like fire," declares Yahuah

### Jeremiah 5:14
Therefore this is what Yahuah God Almighty says: "Because the people have spoken these words, I will make my words in your mouth a fire and these people the wood it consumes.

**Deuteronomy 4:24**
For Yahuah your God is a consuming fire, a jealous God.

**Deuteronomy 9:3**
But understand that today Yahuah your God goes across ahead of you as a consuming fire.

**2 Samuel 22:9**
Smoke rose from His nostrils, and consuming fire came from His mouth; glowing coals blazed forth.

**Hebrews 12:29**
for our "God is a consuming fire."

It is the metaphorical "smoke" or memory of that day that rises up to the throne of Yahuah for all eternity NOT the fires of "hell". Revelation 14 should be properly understood of speaking of the time of torment during the "last days". It is not speaking of an eternity in hell:

**Revelation 14**
9 Then a third angel followed them, saying with aloud voice, "If anyone worships the beast and his image, and receives his mark on his forehead or on his hand, 10 he himself shall also drink of the wine of the wrath of Yahuah, which is poured out full strength into the cup of His indignation (on them on Earth while they live). He shall be tormented with fire and brimstone (on Earth during The Great Tribulation) in the presence of the holy angels and in the presence of the Lamb. 11 And the smoke of their torment ascends forever and ever; and they have no rest day or night (on Earth during The Great Tribulation), who worship the beast and his image, and whoever receives the mark of his name."

## *The Book of Life is opened*

But what happens when the Book of Life is opened? This is the part that give me chills. Those "living" in covenant with the Messiah, The Yahushaic Covenant, have their names read aloud by Yahusha to Yahuah and they are risen Divine, granted eternal life, and given crowns of authority to rule with him.

**Matthew 10**
32 Therefore everyone who confesses me before men, I will also confess him before my Father in Heaven. 33 But whoever denies Me before men, I will also deny him before my Father in Heaven.

### Luke 12:8
I tell you, everyone who confesses Me before men, the Son of Man will also confess him before the angels of Yahuah.

### Revelation 3:5
Like them, he who overcomes will be dressed in white. And I will never blot out his name from the Book of Life, but I will confess his name before My Father and His angels.

### James 1:12
Blessed is the one who perseveres under trial because, having stood the test, that person will receive the crown of life that Yahuah has promised to those who love him.

### 2 Timothy 4:8
From now on there is laid up for me the crown of righteousness, which Yahusha, the righteous Judge, will award to me on that day--and not only to me, but to all who crave His appearing.

### Revelation 2:10
Do not be afraid of what you are about to suffer. I tell you, the devil will put some of you in prison to test you, and you will suffer persecution for ten days. Be faithful, even to the point of death, and I will give you life as your victor's crown.

### Matthew 28:29
29 And everyone who has left houses or brothers or sisters or father or mother or wife or children or fields for the sake of My name will receive a hundredfold and will inherit eternal life.

# If you are not born-again, you do not live again

You are not "raised from the dead" physically to go to "Heaven" or The Kingdom of God for judgement. Flesh and blood can never enter a Spiritual Realm where "Heaven/The Kingdom" resides.

### 1 Corinthians 15
45 So it is written: "The first man Adam became a living being" the last Adam BECAME (by the power of the resurrection *Romans 1:2-4* he did not preexist) a life-giving spirit. 46 The spiritual (body), however, <u>was not first</u>, **but the natural (body), and then the spiritual (body)**. 47 The first man was of the dust of the Earth, but the second man is from what is written in The Heavenly Scroll... 49 And just as we have born the likeness of the Earthly man (according to the flesh which means opposed to, with no knowledge of Yahuah), so also shall

we bear the likeness of the Heavenly man (and be just like Yahusha). 50 Now I Declare to you, brothers, that <u>flesh and blood cannot inherit the Kingdom of Yahuah, nor does the perishable inherit the imperishable</u>.

### John 3

6 That which is born of the flesh (human birth), is flesh (that includes Yahusha who was born "according to the flesh," **Romans 1:3**); but that which is born of the Spirit, is Spirit (no such thing as a demi-god). 7 Do not be surprised that I said to you: You must be reborn from above to enter the Kingdom of God (Yahusha is speaking from experience being born-again when Mikveh'd by John).

### John 18:36

Yahusha said, "My kingdom is not of this world. If it were, my servants would fight to prevent my arrest by the Jewish leaders. But now my kingdom is from another realm."

# Revelation 20 Restored

## The Thousand Years

20 Then I saw an angel coming down from Heaven, holding in his hand the key to the bottomless pit and a great chain.

> **NOTE**: This angel comes with the keys to seal up the bottomless pit once he subdues the Dragon who was given the keys earlier to release the bound demons/fallen angels held in it.
>
> **Revelation 9:1**
> The fifth angel sounded his trumpet, and I saw a star that had fallen from the sky to the Earth. The star was given the key to the shaft of the Abyss.

2 And he seized the Dragon (the woman, prostitute), that ancient serpent, who is the devil and Satan, and bound her for a thousand years, 3 and threw her into the pit, and shut it and sealed it over her, so that she might not deceive the nations any longer, until the thousand years were ended. After that she must be released for a little while.

4 Then I saw thrones and seated on them were those to whom the authority to judge was committed.

> **Matthew 19:28**
> when the Son of Man sits on His glorious throne, you who have followed Me will also sit on twelve thrones, judging the twelve tribes of Israel.

## The First Resurrection of the Dead

Also, I saw the souls of those who had been beheaded for the Testimony of Yahusha and for the Word of Yahuah, and those who had not worshiped the beast χξς or its image and had not received its mark Ҳ on their foreheads or their hands. They came to life and reigned with the Messiah for a thousand years.

5 The rest of the dead did not come to life until the thousand years were ended. This is the first resurrection. 6 Blessed and holy is the one who shares in the first resurrection! Over such the

second death (decree) has no power, but they will be priests of Yahuah and of the Messiah, and they will reign with him for a thousand years.

### Revelation 1:5-6
5 and from Yahusha the Messiah, the faithful and true witness (Immanuel), the firstborn from the dead, and the ruler of the kings of the Earth. To Him who loves us and has released us from our sins by His blood, 6 who has made us to be a kingdom, priests to His God and Father Yahuah — to Him (Yahuah) be the glory and power forever and ever!

### Revelation 20:4
I saw thrones on which were seated those who had been given authority to judge.

## The Defeat of Satan

7 And when the thousand years are ended, Satan will be released from her prison 8 and will come out to deceive the nations that are at the four corners of the Earth, Gog and Magog, to gather them for battle; their number is like the sand of the sea. 9 And they marched up over the broad plain of the Earth and surrounded the camp of the saints which is the beloved city, but fire came down from Heaven and consumed them, 10 and the devil who had deceived them was thrown into the lake of fire and sulfur where the beast χξς and the false prophet were, and they will be (metaphorically) tormented day and night forever and ever (they will forever go down in history as defeated).

## Judgment Before the Great White Throne

11 Then I saw a great white throne and him who was seated on it. From his presence Earth and sky fled away, and no place was found for them. 12 And I saw the dead, great and small, standing before the throne, and books (of the dead) were opened (this is the 'resurrection', it is of their memory recorded in those books). Then another book was opened, which is the book of life (and their memory was "resurrected"). And the dead's life record were judged by what was written in the books, according to what they had done. 13 And the sea gave up (the memories of) the dead who were in it, Death and Hades gave up (the memories of) the dead who were in them, and they were judged, each one of them, according to what they had done (recorded in the Books of the Dead).

14 Then Death and Hades were thrown into the lake of fire (again, not literal. Death and Hades are not people any more than the False Prophet or Antichrist. All are ideas). This is the second death, the lake of fire (judgement). 15 And if anyone's name was not found written in the book of life, his memory was thrown into the lake of fire (consumed by the Word of Yahuah the all-consuming fire).

# Chapter 21

# Introduction

In this chapter, the Heavens, Earth, and Jerusalem become a "new creation".

### Isaiah 65

17 For behold, I will create new Heavens and a new Earth. The former things will not be remembered, nor will they come to mind. 18 But be glad and rejoice forever in what I create; for I will create Jerusalem to be a joy and its people to be a delight.

In this new creation, we see above the former things will not be remembered, and "He will wipe away every tear from their eyes" and "there will be no more death or mourning or crying or pain, for the old order of things has passed away." Revelation 21:4. The Earth is Mikveh'd with Living Water and returned to a Garden of Eden state of perfection, not "recreated" as in literally destroyed then remade. This is the same concept behind when we are Mikveh'd and become a "new creation". The Earth too is Mikveh'd by the Water Bearer AQUARIUS (*the Messiah*) and become a "new creation".

### AQUARIUS

He pours out "living water" from on high, humanity drinks of the Heavenly river and the faithful live again

### Isaiah 44

3 For I will pour water on the thirsty land, and currents on the dry ground. I will pour out My Spirit on your descendants, and My blessing on your offspring. 4 They will sprout among the grass like willows by streams of living water

### 2 Corinthians 5:17

Therefore, if anyone is in The Yahushaic Covenant, he is a new creation. The old has passed away; behold, the new has come. All this is from Yahuah, who through covenant with Yahusha reconciled us to the Father and gave us the ministry of reconciliation; that is, in covenant with Yahusha, Yahuah was reconciling the world to Himself (creating a new creation).

### Romans 6:1-23

Do you not know that all of us who have been Mikveh'd into The Yahushaic Covenant were cleansed with living water by his death? We were buried therefore with him by Mikveh into death, in order that, just as Yahusha was raised from the dead by the glory of the Father, we too might walk in newness of life.

After the Earth is Mikveh'd clean by The Water Bearer with living water, it becomes a "new creation" (*just as we do when we are Mikveh'd*). New Jerusalem (*the sons of Yahuah*) descend back to Earth to rule over it.

# Revelation 21 Restored

## *The Renewed Heaven and Earth*

1 Then I saw a new Heaven and a new Earth (cleansed by living water - AQUARIUS), for the (memory of the) first Heaven and the first Earth had passed away (Isaiah 65:17), and the sea was not like before (waters receded to pre-flood levels exposing very fertile lands).

### 2 Peter 3:13
But in keeping with his promises we are looking forward to a new Heaven and a new Earth, where righteousness dwells.

### Isaiah 65:17
17 "See, I will create new Heavens and a new Earth. The former things will not be remembered, nor will they come to mind.18 But be glad and rejoice forever in what I create; for I will create Jerusalem to be a joy and its people to be a delight.

### Isaiah 66:22
"As the new Heavens and the new Earth that I make will endure before me," declares Yahuah, "so will your name and descendants endure.

2 And I saw the holy city, new Jerusalem, coming down out of Heaven from Yahuah, prepared as a bride adorned for her husband.

### Isaiah 52:1
Awake, awake, Zion, clothe yourself with strength! Put on your garments of splendor, Jerusalem, the holy city. The uncircumcised and defiled will not enter you again.

### Isaiah 4:3
Whoever remains in Zion and whoever is left in Jerusalem will be called holy--all in Jerusalem who are recorded among the living—

### Isaiah 49:18
Lift up your eyes and look around. They all gather together; they come to you. As surely as I live, declares Yahuah, you will wear them all as jewelry and put them on like a bride.

3 And I heard a loud voice from the throne saying, "*Behold, the dwelling place of Yahuah is with man. He will dwell with them, and they will be his people, and Yahuah himself will be with them*

*as their God. 4* (this is how the Earth is "new") *He will wipe away every tear from their eyes, and death shall be no more, neither shall there be mourning, nor crying, nor pain anymore, for the former things have passed away.*"

### Leviticus 26:11-12
11'Moreover, I will make My dwelling among you, and My soul will not reject you. 12 'I will also walk among you and be your God, and you shall be My people.

5 And He who was seated on the throne said, "*Behold, I am making all things new.*" Also He said, "Write this (the revelation of The Heavenly Scroll) down, for these words (written in The Heavenly Scroll Psalm 19, 119:89, 89:2, Daniel 4:35, Enoch 35:3) are trustworthy and true." 6 And He said unto me, It is done. I am Aleph and the Tav, the Beginning (Unity) and the End (Perfection).

NOTE: See pages 51-61 of the Introduction to this Book for more. Yahuah is the Father Who is doing the speaking in this prophecy. The words "beginning and end" are Hellenized twisting of the meaning of "Aleph and Tav". It should read "I am Aleph and Tav, Unity and Perfection". This is where the twisting come in because <u>Yahusha is "the Beginning and End, First and the Last" of Eternal Creation. Yahuah is **Eternal** period.</u> By putting in Alpha and Omega the translating the meaning of those Hellenized words instead of Aleph and Tav, they made it look as though both Yahuah and Yahusha claimed the same title, "the beginning and end"! Yahuah alone is the Creator.

I will give unto him that thirst to drink from the Fountain of Water of life freely (Yahusha, AQUARIUS the Water Bearer).

### John 4:10
Yahusha answered her, "If you knew the gift of Yahuah and who it is that asks you for a drink, you would have asked him and he would have given you living water."

### John 7:37-38
On the last and greatest day of the feast, Yahusha stood up and called out in a loud voice, "If anyone is thirsty, let him come to me and drink. Whoever believes in me, as the Scripture has said: 'Streams of living water will flow from within him.'"

### Revelation 7:17
For the Lamb in the center of the throne will be their shepherd. He will lead them to springs of living water, and Yahuah will wipe away every tear from their eyes.'"

### Revelation 21:6

And He told me, "It is done! I am the Beginning and the End. To the thirsty I will give freely from the spring of the water of life.

### Revelation 22:1

Then the angel showed me a river of the water of life, as clear as crystal, flowing from the throne of Yahuah and of the Lamb.

### Revelation 22:17

The Spirit of the Bride say, "Come!" Let the one who hears say, "Come!" And let the one who is thirsty come, and the one who desires the water of life drink freely.

### Isaiah 12:1-3

1 And in that day you will say: "O Yahuah, I will Praise You; Though You were angry with me, Your anger is turned away, and You comfort me. 2 Behold, Yahusha (Yahuah is my Salvation), I will trust and not be afraid;' For Yahuah is my strength and song; He also has become my salvation (fulfilling The Word of His Testimony sending AQUARIUS the Bearer of Living Water and Manna).'" 3 Therefore, with joy you will draw water from the Wells of Salvation (as Yahusha pours our Living Waters from on High meaning of AQUARIUS).

### Isaiah 44:3,4

3 For I will pour Living Water upon him that is thirsty, and streams of Living Water upon the dry ground (the dead who have return to dry dust): I will pour My Spirit upon your offspring (Mikveh by Fire), and My blessing upon your descendants (and they will be Born-again): 4 And they shall spring up (into eternal life) like poplar flowers in Living Water.

### AQUARIUS the Bearer of Living Water and Manna

He pours out "Living Water from on High, humanity drinks of the Heavenly River and the faithful live again, he is the Deliverer of the Good News (Gospel), Carrying the wood of the sacrifice over the Earth.

7 He that overcomes will inherit all things (as Yahuah gives an inheritance through His First-Born Son, Yahusha); and I will be His Father (Yahuah is the Father of all His Sons including Yahusha), and he shall be My Son. 8 But as for the cowardly, the faithless, the detestable, as for murderers, the sexually immoral, sorcerers, idolaters, and all who bear false witness, their portion will be in the lake that burns with fire and sulfur, which is the second death."

## The Day of Atonement, the Wedding Day

9 Then came one of the seven angels who had the seven bowls full of the seven last plagues and spoke to me, saying, *"Come, I will show you the Bride, the wife of the Lamb."* 10 And he carried me away in the Spirit to a great, high mountain, and showed me the holy city Jerusalem (a symbolic picture of the Bride) coming down out of Heaven from Yahuah, 11 having the glory of God, its radiance like a most rare jewel, like a jasper, clear as crystal. 12 It had a great, high wall, with twelve gates, and at the gates twelve angels, and on the gates the names of the twelve tribes of the sons of Israel were inscribed— 13 on the east three gates, on the north three gates, on the south three gates, and on the west three gates. 14 And the wall of the city had twelve foundations, and on them were the twelve names of the twelve apostles of the Lamb (12x12=144 the number of the Elect).

## The New Jerusalem

15 And the one who spoke with me had a measuring rod of gold to measure the city and its gates and walls. 16 The city lies foursquare, its length the same as its width. And he measured the city with his rod, 12,000 stadia. Its length and width and height are equal. 17 He also measured its wall, 144 cubits by human measurement, which is also an angel's measurement. 18 The wall was built of jasper, while the city was pure gold, like clear glass. 19 The foundations of the wall of the city were adorned with every kind of jewel. The first was jasper, the second sapphire, the third agate, the fourth emerald, 20 the fifth onyx, the sixth carnelian, the seventh chrysolite, the eighth beryl, the ninth topaz, the tenth chrysoprase, the eleventh jacinth, the twelfth amethyst. 21 And the twelve gates were twelve pearls, each of the gates made of a single pearl, and the street of the city was pure gold, like transparent glass.

## The Spiritual Temple made up of the Children of God

22 And I saw no temple in the city, for its temple is the Yahuah our God the Almighty and the Lamb (His Firstborn Son of the Resurrection/Dead and all those in covenant with him).

### John 2
19 Yahusha answered and said unto them, destroy this temple, and in three days I will raise

it up. 20 Then said the Jews, Forty and six years was this temple in building, and wilt thou rear it up in three days? 21 But he spoke of the temple of his body.

### I Corinthians 6:19

Do you not know that your body is a temple of the Spirit of Yahuah who is in you, whom you have from Yahuah?

### II Corinthians 6:16

What agreement has the Temple of Yahuah with idols? For we are the temple of the living Elohim; just as Yahuah said, "I will dwell in them and walk among them; and I will be their Elohim, and they shall be My people."

### Ephesians 2:19-22

So then you are no longer strangers and aliens, but you are fellow citizens with the saints, and are of Yahuah's household, having been built upon the foundation of the apostles and prophets, the Messiah Yahusha Himself being the corner stone (of the Temple of Yahuah), in whom the whole building, being fitted together is growing into a Holy Temple of Yahuah; in whom you also are being built together into a dwelling of Yahuah in the Spirit (the Kingdom of Yahuah).

### I Peter 2:5

You also, as living stones, are being built up as a spiritual house (Temple)...

23 And the city has no need of Sun or moon to shine on it, for the glory of Yahuah gives it light, and its lamp is the Lamb. 24 By its light will the nations walk, and the kings of the Earth will bring their glory into it, 25 and its gates will never be shut by day—and there will be no night there. 26 They will bring into it the glory and the honor of the nations. 27 But nothing unclean will ever enter it, nor anyone who does what is detestable or false, but only those who are written in the Lamb's book of life.

# *Chapter 22*

# Introduction

In this chapter, Living Water from the River of Live is poured out by the Water Bearer (*AQUARIUS*) and the children of Yahuah live eternally. The "Tree of Life" sprouts throughout the land. The Tree yields its healing fruit all year around. This is a metaphor of the Messiah and all those who spring forth in eternal life.

> **CAPRICORNUS**
> Eternal life comes from his death, he's the Arrow of Yahuah, he is pierced, yet springs up again in abundant life.

# The Tree of Life

Yahusha was pictured symbolically in the Garden as "The Tree of Life". Yahuah had a Plan from the Beginning, and Yahusha was that "Plan Fulfilled in the flesh" when he was born, per John Chapter 1.

Adam and Eve were not allowed to partake of that "Tree of Life", because Yahuah's Plan of Salvation through a human mediating High Priest, who would be risen Divine, as laid out in The Heavenly Scroll <u>before</u> Adam and Eve were created, <u>had not yet been Fulfilled</u>! So, they could not eat of that tree until Yahuah's Plan of Salvation would be Fulfilled in Yahusha the Messiah.

"Eating of The True of Life" is a metaphor for being Adopted by Yahuah through The Yahushaic Covenant; an Adoption Covenant whereby we are granted Eternal Life as Yahuah's Children.

### *Yahusha is "the Branch" that was broken off from his own (the Jews) and planted in the ground*

We know that Nazarene means "the Branch" and Yahusha is the Fulfillment of The Heavenly Scroll where the Branch is foretold. He is… The Nazarene! The types and shadows in Scripture are ripe with imagery of a tree or branch. We read that Yahusha was the Branch that was rejected by his own.

### John 1:11
He came to that which was his own, but his own did not receive him.

Instead, they hung Yahusha on "the Tree of Life" where he died, and was then replanted into the ground, and sprung back up as the eternal Tree of Life foretold in the stars called The Heavenly Scroll by the constellation Capricorn.

Yahusha is also seen as the Chief Cornerstone of The Temple. The "builders" were the descendants of Abraham via The House of Judah who rejected The Branch, broke it off, and planted it into the ground.

### Mark 12:10
Have you not even read this Scripture: 'THE STONE WHICH THE BUILDERS REJECTED, THIS BECAME THE CHIEF CORNERSTONE'.

## The Nazarenes are "the Branches flowing from The Tree of Life"

"Nazarene" means followers of the Notsri (*Righteous Branch/Tree of Life*) who is Yahusha. We are grafted into THAT tree! We enter into Covenant with Yahuah through THAT BRANCH and partake of the Tree of Life (*receive Eternal Life*).

### Isaiah 42:6
"I am Yahuah, I have called you in Righteousness, I will also hold you by the hand and watch over you, And I will appoint you as a Covenant to the people, As a Light to the nations...

## Yahusha is that Branch that sprung up from death the Fulfillment of The Tree of Life.

### Jeremiah 23:5
"The days are coming," declares Yahuah, "when I will raise up for David a Righteous Branch, a King who will reign wisely and do what is just and right in the land.

### Isaiah 4:2
"In that day the Branch of Yahuah will be beautiful and Glorious, and the Fruit of the Earth will be the pride and the adornment of the survivors of Israel.

### Isaiah 11:1

"Then a shoot will spring from the stem of Jesse, and a Branch from his roots will bear fruit (The Tree of Life, WE are its fruit)

### Isaiah 53

1 Who hath believed our report? and to whom is the arm of Yahuah revealed? 2 For he (Yahusha) shall grow up before Yahuah as a tender shoot/branch/tree, and as a root out of a dry ground (this is the ROOT we are grafted too): he hath no form nor comeliness; and when we shall see him, no beauty that we should desire him (he's just another human being). 3 He is despised and rejected of men; a man of sorrows and acquainted with grief: and we hid as it were faces from him; he was despised, and we esteemed him not.

# Revelation 22 Restored

## *The River of Life*
## *AQUARIUS Fulfilled*

1 Then the angel showed me the river of the water of life, bright as crystal, flowing from the Throne of God and of the Lamb (the Water Bearer) 2 through the middle of the street of the city;

### Zechariah 14:8
On that day living water will flow out from Jerusalem, half of it east to the Dead Sea and half of it west to the Mediterranean Sea, in summer and in winter.

### Joel 3:18
And in that day the mountains will drip with sweet wine, and the hills will flow with milk. All the streams of Judah will run with water, and a spring will flow from the house of Yahuah to water the Valley of Acacias.

also, on either side of the river (all over the kingdom), the Tree of Life (not a single tree, an abundant tree) 2 with its twelve yields of fruit, yielding its fruit each month (all year long the tree bears fruit). The leaves of the tree were for the healing of the nations.

### Note:
Most translations of verse 1 imply there is only 1 "tree of life" which bears 12 different kinds of fruit. This is not the proper translation. The "Tree of Life" is a class of tree and there is an ample supply of this tree everywhere. There is not 12 kinds of fruit, but 1 fruit which is constantly (all 12 months of the year) producing fruit. The "fruit" of this tree is everlasting life. The root of this class of tree is Yahusha the Messiah. Yahusha bears "fruit" and we all become fruit bearing trees of life.

### Ezekiel 47:12
Fruit trees of all kinds will grow on both banks of the river. Their leaves will not wither, nor will their fruit fail. Every month they will bear fruit, because the water from the sanctuary flows to them. Their fruit will serve for food and their leaves for healing."

3 No longer will there be anything accursed, but the throne of Yahuah (as King over Creation) and of the Lamb Yahusha (as King over the Government that governs Creation) will be in it, and

His (Yahuah who sites on the throne) servants will worship Him (Yahuah). 4 They will see His face, and His name (𐤉𐤄𐤅𐤄) will be on their foreheads. 5 And night will be no more.

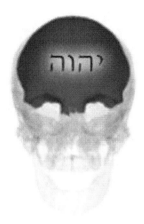

*Those who inhabit the Kingdom are sealed with the Seal/Mark of Yahuah on their foreheads.*

They will need for no light of lamp or Sun (The Heavenly Scroll will have been fulfilled), for the Yahuah Elohim will be their light (from then on in the Spiritual Realm), and they will reign forever and ever.

## *The Conquering King Is Coming*
## *LEO Fulfilled*

6 And Yahusha said to me, "*These words (in The Heavenly Scroll) are trustworthy and true. And Yahuah, the God of the Spirits of the Prophets, has sent His angel Gabriel to show His servants what must soon take place (on Earth as written in Heaven).*" 7 "*And behold, I am coming soon. Blessed is the one who keeps the words of the prophecy of this Heavenly Scroll.*"

### Revelation 5
1 And I saw in the right hand of Him Who sat on the throne, a (Heavenly) Scroll written inside and on the back (Scroll made up of 3D Heavenly signs/pictographs), sealed with seven seals .

### Revelation 1

339

2 John testified to the word of Yahuah (he was shown eternally preserved in The Heavenly Scroll Psalm 119:89) and to the testimony of Yahushua Messiah (The Word of His Testimony), and to all things that he saw (in a vision of The Heavenly Scroll). 3 Blessed is he who reads, and those who hear the words of this prophecy (found in The Heavenly Scroll) and keep those things which are written in it (make The Plan of Salvation written in The Heavenly Scroll the "word of their testimony" Revelation 12:11, Revelation 14:12); for the time is at hand (end of the Age of PISCES Matthew 28:20).

8 I, John, am the one who heard and saw these things (written in The Heavenly Scroll). And when I heard and saw them, I fell down to worship at the feet of the angel Gabriel who showed them to me, 9 but he said to me, "*You must not do that! I am a fellow servant with you and your brothers the prophets, and with those who keep the words of this book. Worship Yahuah alone (Luke 4:8)*."

10 And he said to me, "*Do not seal up the words of the prophecy of this Heavenly Scroll, for the time is near (*last 2-days of PISCES*). 11 Let the evildoer still do evil, and the filthy still be filthy, and the righteous still do right, and the holy still be holy*."

12 "*Behold, I am coming (*again*) soon (*as the Conquering King SAGITTARIUS, TAURUS, LEO*), bringing my recompense with me (*as the Great Judge TAURUS*), to repay each one for what he has done.*

> *SAGITTARIUS*: The double-natured seed (*King and High Priest*) triumphs as a warrior and pleases the Heavens, builds fires of punishment, casts down the dragon.

> *TAURUS*: The conquering Ruler comes, the sublime vanquisher, to execute the great judgment, he is the ruling Shepherd King.

> *LEO*: The Lion King is aroused for rending, the Serpent flees, the Bowl of Wrath is upon him, his Carcass is devoured. The Lion of the tribe of Judah rules as King.

13 I am ~~the Alpha and the Omega~~ *the first and the last, the beginning and the end*."
> Now, we come to the second Scripture in which the literal words Alpha and Omega were added, in order to say that Yahusha is the Alpha and Omega. This Scripture is **Revelation 22:13. Revelation 22:16** undeniably states that these are Yahusha's words.

> > **Revelation 22:12-13**, KJV—
> > 12 And behold, I come quickly, and my reward is with me, to give every man according as his work shall be. 13 [117] [I am Alpha and Omega] the beginning and the end the first and last.

The King James has a footnote number _117_, which I put in red in verse 13. The footnote of this Bible, shows that the Alexandrian (NU) and the Vatican (M) texts omit the phrase, Alpha and Omega. Because it was added by Scribes!

14 Blessed are those who wash their robes,5 so that they may have the right partake of the tree of life and that they may enter the city by the gates. 15 Outside are the dogs and sorcerers and the sexually immoral and murderers and idolaters, and everyone who loves and practices false witness.

16 "_I, Yahusha, have sent my messenger to testify to you about these things written in The Heavenly Scroll_ (Revelation 5:1, Revelation 1:2-3) _for the Bride. I am the root of the Tree of Life_ (John 1:4, John 8:12, John 14:6)

### John 8:12
When Yahusha spoke again to the people, he said, "I am the light of the world. Whoever follows me will never walk in darkness, but will have the light of life."

### John 1:4
In Him was life, and that life was the light of men.

### John 14:6
Yahusha says to him, I am the way, and the truth, and the life. No one comes to the Father unless by me.
_and the descendant of David, the bright morning star._"

Note: The "bright morning star" is a reference to the most visible star in The Heavenly Scroll, Sirius. It is stationary in the sky (does not move or "fall") and the most important star in ancient human history. While the name "morning star" is associated with the fall of Lucifer, these are NOT the same star. The star in Isaiah speaking of Lucifer is a "falling star" not the stationary Bright Morning Star Sirius.

17 The Spirit within the Bride says, "_Come._" And let the one who hears say, "_Come._" And let the one who is thirsty come; let the one who desires drink from the water of life (AQUARIUS) without price.

18 I warn everyone who hears the words of the prophecy of this Scroll in Heaven: if anyone adds to them, Yahuah will add to him the plagues described in this Scroll, 19 and if anyone takes away from the words of the Scroll of this prophecy, Yahuah will take away his share in the tree of life and in the holy city, which are described in this Scroll.

20 He who testifies to these things says, "*Surely I am coming soon.*" HalleluYahuah. Come, King Yahusha! 21 The grace of the King Yahusha be with all. HalleluYahuah!

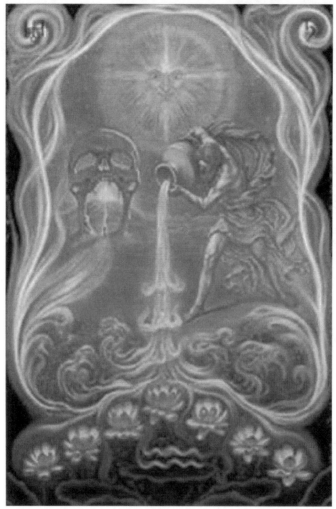

*AQUARIUS pouring Living Water over Poplar Flowers ...*

### Isaiah 44:3-4

3 For I will pour water on the thirsty land, and currents on the dry ground. I will pour out My Spirit on your descendants, and My blessing on your offspring. 4 They will sprout among the grass like flowers by streams of Living Water.

# *Appendix I*
# *The Battle of Jericho*

# Battle of Jericho

I want to explore the Battle of Jericho and detail what Yahuah gave as a prophetic portrait of the same event, on a much greater scale, upon the Second Coming of the Messiah. All the stories and Feasts and Holy Days in the "Old Testament" were given as physical metaphors or "rehearsals" to teach us of greater Spiritual Truths.

These rehearsals were given to us so we would better understand The Plan of Salvation written in the stars and the events surrounding the first and Second Comings. In this section, I am going to cover all the major events surrounding the return of the Messiah in Revelation. I will demonstrate that each event is covered in detail on a smaller scale in the Battle of Jericho to give us better understanding of the events in the Book of Revelation. I will cover:

- The Two Witnesses
- The Scarlet Thread of Redemption
- The 7 Seals
- The 7 Shofars (shofars)
- The Shout of the Archangel
- The Appearance of the Messiah before the Ark of the Covenant
- The Rapture or rather first resurrection of the dead.
- The Messiah leading the army of Remnant Israel to reclaim the Earth for Yahuah
- The Gold/Silver Vessels
- The Great Earthquake
- The collapse of all the kingdoms of Earth to become the Kingdoms of Yahuah governed by Yahusha
- The destruction of the wicked on Earth (the Great Supper of Yahuah)
- The cost to rebuild the Earth and govern it is the Firstborn Son of Yahuah. So too at the cost of Yahuah's youngest son, will the gates be established.
- The 1,000-year rest of the Sabbath Millennium

# Introduction

Everything above in the Book of Revelation is the fulfillment of the portrait given to us by Yahuah at the Battle of Jericho. The Book of Joshua is the story of how Joshua (*Yahusha in Hebrew*) took the mantle and leadership of the Children of Israel in the wilderness from Moses and led them into the Promised Land. Providing a clear picture of how the Law (*Moses*) leads us through the wilderness (*life*) to the promises (*eternal life*), but Joshua (*a prototype of the Messiah Yahusha*) is the bridge to the promised rest which is The Kingdom of Yahuah in the coming 7th Millennium as laid out in the stars through Ages:

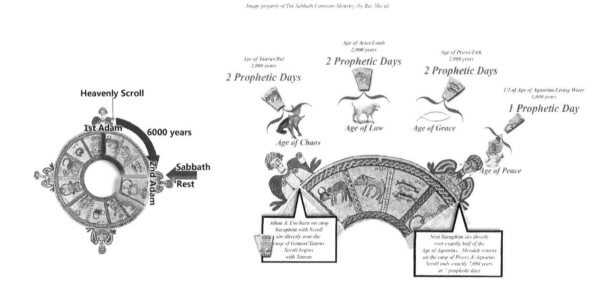

# 7,000 Year Plan for Man
*6 days and a 7th - The Sabbath Covenant foretold in The Heavnly Scroll*

First, when making the comparison that Jericho represents the "Kingdoms of Earth" in Revelation, I want to point out that Jericho is a Kingdom not simply a "city". I know we all first learned of the Battle of Jericho in our Sunday School class and even had a clever little song we sang "and the walls came tumbling down...la la la" and we came to see Jericho as a small city. A small city as though The Promised Land was an organized self-governing country with borders and a central government. But that is not at all the case. Countries didn't exist at that time, people were ruled by Kings and lived in City-States with walls around them called Kingdoms. A castle was at the center with a king, the king had guards and an army to protect his Kingdom. People paid taxes to a king for protection. That is what Jericho was... a Kingdom. We know this because Jericho had a king and an army:

### Joshua 6:2
Then Yahuah said to Joshua, "See, I have delivered Jericho into your hands, along with its king and its fighting men."

I want to make that point to demonstrate the Kingdom of Jericho is a "picture" of the Kingdoms of Earth in the Battle of Jericho not just a "city". Before the battle to take the Promised Land begins, Yahusha son of Nun sends in two "spies" to survey the land and bring back 2 reliable witnesses:

### Joshua 2:1
Then Joshua son of Nun secretly sent two spies from Shittim. "Go, look over the land," he said, "especially Jericho." So they went and entered the house of a prostitute named Rahab and stayed there.

After the two witnesses were sent to "spy" out the land, the first battle to take the Promised Land was the Battle of Jericho. Below in the 6th Chapter of Joshua is the account of that battle:

### Joshua 6:1-27
1 Now the gates of Jericho were securely barred because of the Israelites. No one went out and no one came in. 2 Then Yahuah said to Joshua, "See, I have delivered Jericho into your hands, along with its king and its fighting men. 3 March around the city once with all the armed men. Do this for six days. 4 Have seven priests carry shofars of rams' horns in front of the ark. On the seventh day, march around the city seven times, with the priests blowing the shofars. 5 When you hear them sound a long blast on the shofars, have the whole army give a loud shout; then the wall of the city will collapse and the army will go up, everyone straight in." 6 So Joshua son of Nun called the priests and said to them, "Take up the Ark of the Covenant of Yahuah and have seven priests carry shofars in front of it." 7 And he ordered the army, "Advance! March around the city, with an armed guard going ahead of the Ark of Yahuah." 8 When Joshua had spoken to the people, the seven priests carrying the seven shofars before Yahuah went forward, blowing their shofars, and the Ark of Yahuah's covenant followed them. 9 The armed guard marched ahead of the priests who blew the shofars, and the rear

guard followed the ark. All this time the shofars were sounding. 10 But Joshua had commanded the army, "Do not give a war cry, do not raise your voices, do not say a word until the day I tell you to shout. Then shout!" 11 So he had the Ark of Yahuah carried around the city, circling it once. Then the army returned to camp and spent the night there. 12 Joshua got up early the next morning and the priests took up the Ark of Yahuah. 13 The seven priests carrying the seven shofars went forward, marching before the Ark of Yahuah and blowing the shofars. The armed men went ahead of them and the rear guard followed the Ark of Yahuah, while the shofars kept sounding. 14 So on the second day they marched around the city once and returned to the camp. They did this for six days. 15 On the seventh day, they got up at daybreak and marched around the city seven times in the same manner, except that on that day they circled the city seven times. 16 The seventh time around, when the priests sounded the trumpet blast, Joshua commanded the army, "Shout! For Yahuah has given you the city! 17 The city and all that is in it are to be devoted to Yahuah. Only Rahab the prostitute and all who are with her in her house shall be spared, because she hid the spies we sent. 18 But keep away from the devoted things, so that you will not bring about your own destruction by taking any of them. Otherwise you will make the camp of Israel liable to destruction and bring trouble on it. 19 All the silver and gold and the articles of bronze and iron are sacred to Yahuah and must go into His treasury." 20 When the shofars sounded, the army shouted, and at the sound of the trumpet, when the men gave a loud shout, the wall collapsed; so everyone charged straight in, and they took the city. 21 They devoted the city to Yahuah and destroyed with the sword every living thing in it—men and women, young and old, cattle, sheep and donkeys. 22 Joshua said to the two men who had spied out the land, "Go into the prostitute's house and bring her out and all who belong to her, in accordance with your oath to her." 23 So the young men who had done the spying went in and brought out Rahab, her father and mother, her brothers and sisters and all who belonged to her. They brought out her entire family and put them in a place outside the camp of Israel. 24 Then they burned the whole city and everything in it, but they put the silver and gold and the articles of bronze and iron into the treasury of Yahuah's house. 25 But Joshua spared Rahab the prostitute, with her family and all who belonged to her, because she hid the men Joshua had sent as spies to Jericho— and she lives among the Israelites to this day. 26 At that time Joshua pronounced this solemn oath: "Cursed before Yahuah is the One Who undertakes to rebuild this city, Jericho: "At the cost of his firstborn son he will lay its foundations; at the cost of his youngest he will set up its gates." 27 So Yahuah was with Joshua, and his fame spread throughout the land.

# Summary of The Battle of Jericho

To summarize Joshua son of Nun sent two witnesses into the Promised Land then Yahuah gave Joshua the battle plan which he carried out in detail. He gave the order to redeem Rahab (*the Great Grandmother of Yahusha the Messiah*) and her entire household set apart by the scarlet thread. Then he sent 7 Priests with 7 shofars followed by an "armed guard" followed by the Ark of the Covenant followed by the Israelite army. They marched around the walls of the Kingdom of Jericho 6 times for 6 days without making a sound. The only sound was the Priests blowing the shofars. Then on the 7th day, they marched around the wall of Jericho 7 times with the Priest blowing the shofars. During the 7th trip around the city, the Priests blew one long sound of the shofars and the entire army erupted with a resounding SHOUT and the walls of the Kingdom of Jericho fell. Then the army went up to occupy the city and all the men, women, children, and cattle of Jericho died by the sword (were slaughtered) of the Israelite army. All the "gold, silver, bronze, and iron" vessels were put securely in the House of Yahuah. Rahab and her entire family were spared according to her oath and faith in Yahuah. The entire Kingdom of Jericho and everything in it was burned and purged. Joshua son of Nun pronounces a curse and establishes that the cost to rebuild the Kingdom would come at the expense of the firstborn son and at the cost of the youngest son.

Now, let's take a journey through the Book of Revelation and see just how this physical metaphor or rehearsal at the Battle of Jericho plays out in order, to the very detail, in the event of Yahusha Son of Yahuah returning to lead Remnant Israel into the Sabbath Millennium where the entire Earth is "The Promised Land".

### Events foretold in the Book of Revelation

As I stated before, I am going to cover the events in the Book of Revelation and demonstrate how the Battle of Jericho foretold of the Second Coming. From the two witnesses appearing to the blowing of shofars to the SHOUT that leads to the return of the Messiah to the Kingdoms of this Earth falling and becoming the Kingdoms of Yahuah and His Messiah Yahusha. All of it is covered in detail in the exact same order. Here we go.

### The Two Witnesses - (Revelation 11 and Joshua 2:1)

In Revelation 11, two witnesses are sent to Earth to prophecy 1,260 days prior to the Second Coming and battle to reclaim The Promised Land for Remnant Israel. In the Book of Joshua (*Joshua 2:1*) two "spies" which are nothing more than witnesses are send into to the land of Canaan and specifically to the Kingdom of Jericho to survey and give a report.

## The Scarlet Thread of Redemption

I could write an entire book on this subject. So, to prevent getting sidetracked let me say that there is a Scarlet Thread of Redemption that runs throughout the Word of Yahuah pointing us to the Messiah Yahusha. From Abel bringing a Lamb and shedding blood in Genesis to the substitute sacrificial ram with Abraham/Isaac to the blood on the doorposts of the Passover Lamb in Exodus to Rahab's scarlet thread in the book of Joshua, this is a primary theme in the Bible and also in the Battle of Jericho.

## The 7 Seals (Revelation 8)

We see in the Battle of Jericho that the army was to walk "around" the walls of Jericho 7 times before the "last set of 7 Priests were to blow their shofars". Why? What could be the reasoning behind this action of walking AROUND the walls? This action would seem to be a "metaphor" for the 7 Seals which were "around" the Scroll. The sequence of events is identical to the events in Revelation, following the completion of the 7th Seal, 7 shofars are given to 7 Angels to sound. Following half an hour of silence, the Angels sound the 7 Shofar blasts just like in the Battle of Jericho when after walking around the city in complete silence 7 times the 7 Priests blow their shofars:

> **Revelation 8:1-2 - The Seventh Seal and the 7 Angels with 7 Shofars/Shofars**
> [1] When he opened the seventh seal, there was silence in Heaven for about half an hour. [2] And I saw the seven Angels who stand before Yahuah, and seven shofars were given to them.

## The 7th Trumpet/shofar blast (Revelation 11)

Now the next sequence of events in the Battle of Jericho (*after walking around the city 7 times like the opening of the 7 seals around the Scroll*) was the sounding of the

7th trumpet/shofar blast, a long-distinguished blast. This too is the next sequence of events in Revelation and we read about it in Revelation 11.

### Revelation 11:15
The seventh Angel sounded his trumpet, and there were loud voices in Heaven

"Loud voices" were heard upon the 7th Trumpet blast, just like in the Battle of Jericho when the army (loud voices) shouted after the 7th Trumpet blast. We also see that as a result of these "loud voices" that a great Earthquake occurred, and the Kingdom fell in both Revelation and Jericho.

### Revelation 11:13
13 At that very hour there was a severe Earthquake and a tenth of the city collapsed.

## The Great Earthquake

We see there is an Earthquake that caused the city to fall in *Revelation 11:13*. We also know from *Ezekiel 38* who spoke of the events surrounding the Second Coming that there is a great Earthquake that again causes the walls of the city to fall:

### Ezekiel 38:19-23
19 In My zeal and fiery wrath I declare that at that time *there shall be a great Earthquake* in the land of Israel. 20 The fish in the sea, the birds in the sky, the beasts of the field, every creature that moves along the ground, and all the people on the face of the Earth will tremble at My presence. The mountains will be overturned, the cliffs will crumble, and *every wall will fall to the ground*. 21 I will summon a sword against Gog on all My mountains, declares the Sovereign God. Every man's sword will be against his brother. 22 I will execute judgment on him with plague and bloodshed; I will pour down torrents of rain, hailstones and burning sulfur on him and on his troops and on the many nations with him. 23 And so I will show My Greatness and My Holiness, and I will make Myself known in the sight of many nations. Then they will know that I am Yahuah.'

In the Book of Joshua, it doesn't exactly say it was an Earthquake that brought down the walls of Jericho. However, it is the commonly accepted scientific explanation for those walls falling. We are beginning to see that every event in the Battle of Jericho was a detailed look on a smaller scale of what would happen at the time of the Second Coming. Since Scripture interprets Scripture, I believe it is safe to draw the conclusion that a smaller more regional Earthquake brought down the wall of Jericho too since it is spoken of in Revelation and Ezekiel as the cause in the final event.

## *The Shout of the Archangel*

We see in the Battle of Jericho that a loud SHOUT is heard, and the walls of the Kingdom of Jericho fell. We also see, that upon the loud SHOUT of the Archangel the Kingdoms of Earth fall too in Revelation 11:

> **Revelation 11:15**
> The seventh angel sounded his trumpet, and there were loud voices in Heaven, which said: "The kingdom of the world has become the Kingdom of Yahuah and of His Messiah, who will reign for ever and ever."

We also see this loud SHOUT after the Last Trumpet blast in 1 Thessalonians where Paul is describing the exact same event in the same order and same detail. Here Paul is describing the assembly of the Army of God to retake Earth (I will get to more on this later):

> **1 Thessalonians 4:15-17**
> [15] For this we say to you by the Word of Yahuah, that we who are alive and remain until the coming of the King will by no means precede those who are asleep. [16] For the King himself will descend from Heaven with a shout, with the voice of an Archangel, and with the trumpet of Yahuah. And the dead in covenant with the King will rise first. [17] Then we who are alive and remain shall be caught up together with them in the clouds to meet Yahusha in the air.

## *The Appearance of The Messiah*
## *before the Ark of the Covenant*

In the Battle of Jericho, we see that an armed guard or WARRIOR is sent ahead of the Ark of the Covenant. Who is that a portrait of? Well, in Revelation we see the exact same event being fulfilled. We see in Revelation 11 just after the 7th Trumpet and the SHOUT of the Archangel which heralds the return of Yahusha the Heavens open up and we see the Ark of the Covenant, the same time as the Earthquake:

> **Revelation 11:19**
> Then Yahuah's Temple in Heaven was opened, and within His Temple was seen the Ark of

His Covenant. And there came flashes of lightning, rumblings, peals of thunder, an Earthquake and a severe hailstorm.

We see the Messiah coming as a WARRIOR ahead of the Ark of the Covenant in Revelation 19. This was the same time that Heaven was standing open with the Temple and Ark on display followed by the Army of Yahuah... just like in the Battle of Jericho:

> **Revelation 19:11-16 - The Heavenly Warrior Defeats the Beast**
> [11] I saw Heaven standing open and there before me was a white horse, whose rider is called Faithful and True. With justice he judges (*TAURUS*) and wages war. [12] His eyes are like blazing fire, and on his head are many crowns. He has a name written on him that no one knows but he himself. [13] He is dressed in a robe dipped in blood, and his name is the Word of God. [14] The armies of Heaven were following him, riding on white horses and dressed in fine linen, white and clean. [15] Coming out of his mouth is a sharp sword with which to strike down the nations (*ORION*). "He will rule them with an iron scepter (*TAURUS*)." He treads the winepress of the fury of the wrath of God Almighty. [16] On his robe and on his thigh, he has this name written: KING OF KINGS AND RULER OF RULERS.

## *The Rapture & Resurrection*

In the story of the Battle of Jericho, we see the Israelites "go up" to battle after the 7th Trumpet and SHOUT to take the Kingdom of Jericho. This is the exact sequence of events foretold in Revelation and 1 Thessalonians as to when the living saints (*left alive at the time of the Second Coming*) are "raptured" or "go up". The truth concerning the "rapture" is that it is the building of the Army of Yahuah in the sky preceding the final battle on Earth to retake the Promised Land. We too, who remain alive, will "go up" to do battle just like the Israelites did at Jericho. The living will NOT precede those dead who rise first.

Of course, the "traditional" teaching of the Christian Church who, having done away with the O.T., is one of complete miSunderstanding. While Christians are taught a "pre-trib" rapture and that we are "taken to Heaven" this is not the story told in the Bible nor the story told in 1 Thessalonians nor the story told at the Battle of Jericho.

In every case, the "going up" is the building of an army to go into battle. Paul is clearly teaching in accordance with the rest of the Word of Yahuah, that at THE LAST SHOFAR of the 7 blasts, Yahusha descends with a loud SHOUT and the dead rise first followed by those alive at the time and we meet Yahusha IN THE AIR not some mythical place called "Heaven". They with the risen dead then come directly back down to Earth to liberate it.

### Romans 8:19-25

19 For the creation waits in eager expectation for the children of Yahuah to be revealed (because it is the sons of Yahuah that will govern it in righteousness). 20 For the creation was subjected to futility (when Adam fell), not willingly, but because of Yahuah who subjected it (the fall of creation was part of Yahuah's plan) in hope (of liberating it through His future sons); 21 because the **creation itself also will be delivered** (Paul uses future tense speaking of creation being delivered. He is speaking of the future fulfillment of The Fall Feasts) <u>from the bondage of corruption into the glorious liberty of the children of Yahuah</u>. (Paul understands the "purpose" in all of this is that creation is turned over to be governed by the children of Yahuah) 22 For we know that the whole creation groans and labors (Paul is confirming here The Sabbath Covenant that for 6,000 years creation labors from the effects of sin per The Sabbath Covenant) with birth pangs together until now (the 7th Millennium, the Sabbath is yet to come **Hebrews Chapter 4**). 23 Not only that, but we also who have the Firstfruits (Paul is confirming the Feasts of Yahuah here... The Passover Lamb/Feast of First Fruits/Spring Feasts) of the Spirit (Given on the Feast of Weeks or Shav'uot), even we ourselves groan within ourselves (along with creation because we have not yet been resurrected either), eagerly waiting for the adoption (into the Family of Yahuah through resurrection), the redemption of our body (the resurrection on the Feast of Trumpets as Paul teaches the Fall Feasts). 24 For we were saved (Paul stresses the past tense here because we were saved during the Spring Feasts by the Passover Lamb) in this hope (that Yahusha will return again and fulfill the Fall Feasts, resurrecting our bodies so that WE can then liberate creation), but hope that is seen is not hope; for why does one still hope for what he sees (Paul is stressing that we must still have hope for we have not yet witness the fulfillment of the Fall Feasts, so hope endures)? 25 But if we hope for what we do not see, we eagerly wait for it (the Fall Feasts) with perseverance (Paul is encouraging us to endure in hope of the future fulfillment of the Fall Feasts because those who persevere until the end shall be saved).

The "SHOUT" that is given that raises the dead is probably not unlike that which Yahusha let out when he called Lazarus from his grave.... "COME FORTH, ARISE" or something along those lines. We are gathered as an ARMY OF Yahuah that is descending back to Earth to wage war and overcome it (*more on this in the next chapter*). We ascend into the clouds (*atmosphere of Earth*) meeting Yahusha the King and joining Yahuah's returning army in the air. We are not taken to Heaven we are assembled in the sky then launch an assault on the Kingdoms of Earth to retake it... just like in the Battle of Jericho.

### 1 Thessalonians 4:15-17

15 For this we say to you by the Word of Yahuah, that we who are alive and remain until the coming of the King will by no means precede those who are asleep. 16 For the King himself will

descend from Heaven with a shout, with the voice of an Archangel, and with the trumpet of Yahuah. And the dead in covenant with the King will rise first. [17] Then we who are alive and remain shall be caught up together with them in the clouds to meet Yahusha in the air.

## *The Messiah leading the Army of Remnant Israel to reclaim the Earth for Yahuah*

So, after the Last Trumpet followed by a loud SHOUT, the dead rise first then the living "go up" with

them and the Army of Yahuah is assembled with Yahusha the Warrior/King commanding. We see in Revelation the martyrs are given white robes and so too are the risen dead and assumed living all of whom make up the Army of Yahuah who returns with Yahusha to wage war on Earth:

> **Revelation 6:11**
> Then each of them *was given a white robe*, and they were told to wait a little longer, until the number of their fellow servants and brothers who were to be killed as they had been was completed.

> **Revelation 19:11-14 - The Heavenly Warrior Defeats the Beast**
> [11] I saw Heaven standing open and there before me was a white horse, whose rider is called Faithful and True. With justice he judges and wages war. [12] His eyes are like blazing fire, and on his head are many crowns. He has a name written on him that no one knows but he himself. [13] He is dressed in a robe dipped in blood, and his name is the Word of Yahuah. [14] The armies of Heaven were following him, riding on white horses *and dressed in fine linen, white and clean*.

We clearly see those sons of Yahuah who have died over the years are given white robes and told to wait until the full number of the Army of Yahuah is assembled at the end of the 6th Prophetic Day as foretold in The Heavenly Scroll. This is confirmed by the King himself that he returns at the end of the age of **PISCES** (end of the 6th prophetic day).

> **Matthew 28:20**
> "And surely I am with you always, to the very end of the age (this is the Age of **PISCES**, the Messianic Age)."

That final assembly of this returning army occurs upon the last of 7 shofar blasts one for each prophetic day in The Plan for Mankind laid out in The Heavenly Scroll announcing the beginning of the 7th called The Millennial Reign the ultimate fulfillment of The Sabbath Covenant.

# The Sabbath Covenant
*Foretold in The Heavenly Scroll*

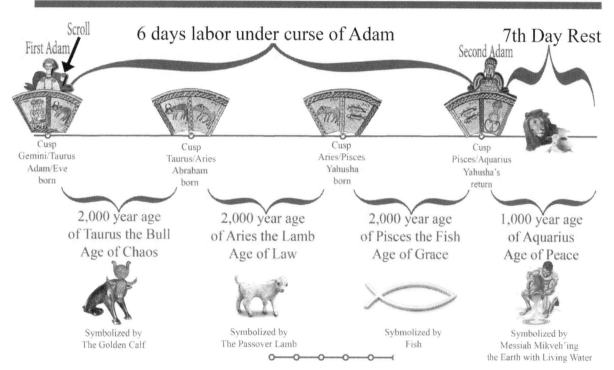

Then we hear a SHOUT and the return of Yahusha when the dead rise and the living assume into the air and are assembled behind the returning King. NOT to go to Heaven for an eternity of "cloud floating harp frolicking and pillow fighting"... we actually go up into the sky and come back to Earth as an ARMY to wage war... and then rule over it for 1,000 years.

## *The destruction of the wicked on Earth*
## *(the Great Supper or Day of Yahuah*

Next in the Battle of Jericho, the Israelite army goes in and puts the sword to all men/women/children and purges the land of the wicked. This is exactly what the Army of Yahuah does after being assembled in the air with the Warrior/King Yahusha. We, the Army of Yahuah lead by Yahusha, defeat the False Messiah and False Prophet and we go after and put to death by the sword those wicked of Earth who followed The Beast and destroyed the Earth.

### 2 Thessalonians 2:6-8

6 And you know what is now restraining him, so that he may be revealed at the proper time. 7 For the mystery of lawlessness is already at work, but the one who now restrains it (Archangel Michael see *Daniel 12* and *Revelation 12*) will continue until he is taken out of the way. 8 And then the lawless one will be revealed, whom the King Yahusha will slay with the breath of his mouth and annihilate by the majesty of his arrival.

### Matthew 13:40-42

40 As the weeds are collected and burned in the fire, so will it be at the end of the age (of **PISCES**). 41 The Son of Man will send out his Angels, and they will weed out of his Kingdom every cause of sin and all who practice lawlessness. 42 And they will throw them into the fiery furnace, where there will be weeping and gnashing of teeth....

Again, more on this in the next chapter. This slaughter of the wicked is called The Great Supper of Yahuah and is described in detail below in Revelation and in Joel. Just like the Battle of Jericho all the wicked in the land, man/woman/child, is put to death by the sword:

### Revelation 19:17-21

17 And I saw an angel standing in the Sun, who cried in a loud voice to all the birds flying in midair, "Come, gather together for the great supper of Yahuah, 18 so that you may eat the flesh of kings, generals, and the mighty, of horses and their riders, and the flesh of all people, free and slave, great and small."

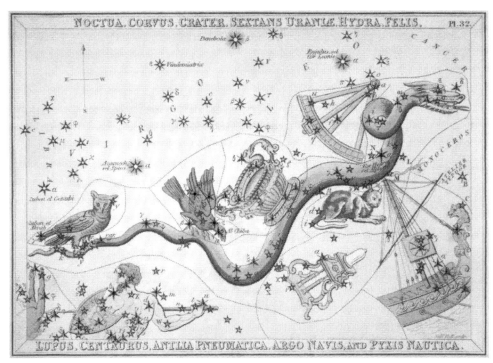

*Birds of Prey (Owl and Raven) feasting on the Serpent*

19 Then I saw the beast and the kings of the Earth and their armies gathered together to wage war against the rider on the horse and his army. 20 But the beast was captured, and with it the false prophet who had performed the signs on its behalf. With these signs he had deluded those who had received the mark of the beast and worshiped its image. The two of them were thrown alive into the fiery lake of burning sulfur. 21 The rest were killed with the sword coming out of the mouth of the rider on the horse, and all the birds gorged themselves on their flesh.

## The Gold/Silver Vessels

We also see that the Gold, Silver, Bronze, Iron vessels were put into the "House of Yahuah" at the Battle of Jericho. What do these vessels represent? They represent the Chosen Remnant of Yahuah. Paul uses this same language in 2 Timothy:

### 2 Timothy 2:19-21

19 Nevertheless, Yahuah's solid foundation stands firm, sealed with this inscription: "Yahuah knows those who are His," and, "Everyone who confesses the name of Yahuah must turn away from wickedness." 20 In a large house there are vessels not only of gold and silver, but also of wood and clay; some are for special purposes and some for common use. 21 Those who cleanse

themselves from the latter will be instruments for special purposes, made holy, useful to the Master and prepared to do any good work.

## The Destruction of the Earth by Fire

Just like in the Battle of Jericho when Jericho was destroyed and purged by fire, In Revelation 18 we see that "Babylon" is destroyed by fire:

### Revelation 18:8
Therefore in one day her plagues will overtake her: death, mourning and famine. She will be consumed by fire, for mighty is Yahuah our God who judges her

In Isaiah we see the entire Earth is destroyed by fire:

### Isaiah 24:6
Therefore a curse consumes the Earth; its people must bear their guilt. Therefore, Earth's inhabitants are burned up, and very few are left.

The cost to rebuild the Earth and govern it is the Firstborn Son of Yahuah. So, at the cost of Yahuah's youngest Son, will the gates be established.

In the Battle of Jericho, we see that after Jericho is purged with fire, Joshua son of Nun sets the cost of rebuilding the Kingdom at the expense of the owners "firstborn son" and "youngest son". We know from the Bible that the cost of redeeming this planet back to Yahuah and the Remnant back to Yahuah came at the expense of Yahuah's Firstborn Son. And it is with the purchased lives of the eldest to the youngest of the Sons of Yahuah that this Earth will be governed, rebuilt, re-established, after the Earth is purged by fire and everything in it destroyed.

## The 1,000-year rest of the Sabbath Millennium

Finally after the 6 Days (6,000 year parallel) of "work" walking around the walls of Jericho, on the 7th Day (Sabbath Millennium parallel) and the Battle of Jericho is over, the Israelites occupy the Promised Land which was given them as a place of total "rest":

### Joshua 21:43-44
43 And Yahuah gave unto Israel all the land which He swore to give unto their fathers; and they possessed it and dwelt therein. 44 And Yahuah gave them rest round about, according to

all that He swore unto their fathers; and there stood not a man of all their enemies before them; Yahuah delivered all their enemies into their hand.

# The Sabbath Covenant
*Foretold in The Heavenly Scroll*

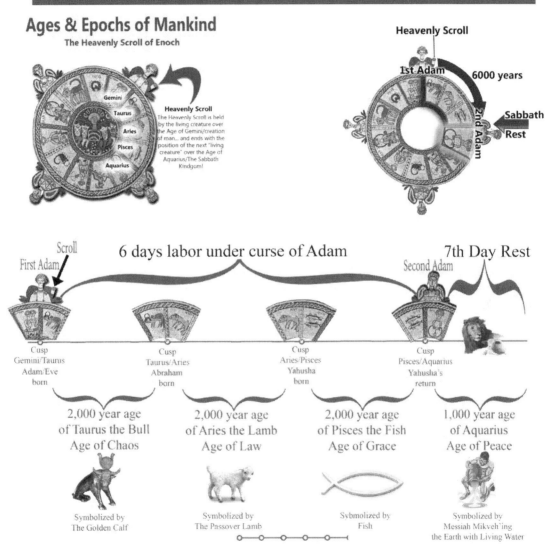

With that introduction, overview, and example found in the Battle of Jericho, we are going to interpret the Book of Revelation in that context but most importantly in the context that it was given... The Heavenly Scroll.

# *Appendix II Revelation and Ezekiel*

# Parallels between the Book of Revelation and the Book of the Ezekiel

| THE VISION | EZEKIEL | REVELATION |
|---|---|---|
| 1. The Throne Vision | Chapter 1 | Chapter 4 |
| 2. The Heavenly Scroll is Opened | Chapters 2-3 | Chapter 5 |
| 3. The Four Plagues | Chapter 5 | Chapter 6:1-8 |
| 4. Those Slain Under the Altar | Chapter.6 | Chapter 6:9-11 |
| 5. The Wrath of Yahuah | Chapter 7 | Chapter 6:12-17 |
| 6. The Seal on the Saint's Foreheads | Chapter 9 | Chapter 7 |
| 7. The Coals from the Altar | Chapter.10 | Chapter 8 |
| 8. The 1/3 Destruction | Chapter 5:1-4 and 12 | Chapter 8:6-12 |
| 9. No More Delay | Chapter 12 | Chapter 10:1-7 |
| 10. The Eating of The Heavenly Scroll | Chapter 2 | Chapter 10:8-11 |
| 11. Prophecy against the Nations | Chapters 25-32 | Chapter 10:11 |

| 12. The Measuring of the Temple | Chapters 40-43 | Chapter 11:1-2 |
|---|---|---|
| 13. Comparing Jerusalem to Sodom | Chapter 16 | Chapter 11:8 |
| 14. The Cup of Wrath | Chapter 23 | Chapter 14 |
| 15. The Vine of the Land | Chapter 15 | Chapter 14:18-20 |
| 16. The Great Harlot | Chapters 16, 23 | Chapters 17-18 |
| 17. The Lament Sung Over the City | Chapter 27 | Chapter 18 |
| 18. The Scavenger's Feast | Chapter 39 | Chapter 19 |
| 19. The First Resurrection | Chapter 37 | Chapter 20:4-6 |
| 20. The Battle of Gog and Magog | Chapter 38-39 | Chapter 20:7-9 |
| 21. The New Jerusalem | Chapters 40-48 | Chapter 21 |
| 22. The River of Life | Chapter 47 | Chapter 22 |

# *Appendix II*
# *Books by Rav Sha'ul*

# Book 1
# Creation Cries Out!
# The Mazzaroth

In this book I trace the great deception back to its origin and explain how the "Gospel message in the stars" was corrupted into another gospel. I reestablish the message contained in The Heavenly Scroll and give Yahuah the Glory He deserves as the Creator of all things. In this book, the original revelation found written in the stars is broken down, defined, and glorified.

I explain how the watchers corrupted the true message and taught mankind to worship the creation over the Creator. Creation Cries Out! Reveals the secrets preserved in the Heavens and provides clear instruction so that the Great Seal over the Bible and the books of prophecy can be opened. Every prophet of Yahuah based their predictions on The Heavenly Scroll and described it in great detail.

# Book 2
# Mystery Babylon the Religion of the Beast

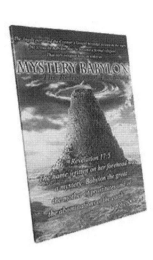

In this book I explain how that corrupted message was formulated into a formal religion in Babylon and define that religion as it existed then. We will go back to the very beginning of "paganism" and examine the gods and rituals that define this false religion.

We will trace this religion, show how it evolved, who created it, and how it came to dominate all mankind. This information is vital as there is prophesied to be, at the end, a religion on Earth based on Mystery Babylon that deceives all humanity.

The only way to properly identify that religion today that has fulfilled this prophecy is to fully understand Mystery Babylon.

# Book 3 Christianity and the Great Deception

I compare Christianity to Mystery Babylon and prove that it is a carbon copy and is the prophesied false religion. Every description of "God" is taken directly from Babylon. From the Trinity to calling the Creator "The LORD" are all based on Sun worship.

I explain where Jesus H. Christ came from, who created that false image, and how that false messiah is a carbon copy of the second member of the Babylonian Trinity named Tammuz.

From the false sacrifice of a pig on Easter, to Sunday worship, to Christmas... every aspect of the Christian Religion is a carbon copy of Mystery Babylon!

I document everything carefully from historical sources, the Catholic Church documents, and the Bible. No one who has read this book has remained a "Christian" after finishing it.

# Book 4
# The Antichrist
# Revealed!

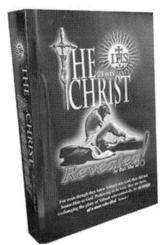

In this book I prove that Jesus H. Christ is the false image of the true messiah, and I demonstrate how he meets every prophecy of the "Antichrist".

I define in great detail such things as the Abomination of Desolation, the Spirit of the Antichrist, the Spirit of Error, the other Gospel, and much more. In this book, I demonstrate through Biblical prophecy that the false messiah is an "image" of the true Messiah not an actual person.

This book is 500 pages of solid proof that the "god" of this Earth, Jesus Christ is the "Abominable Beast" foretold by name, sacrifice, and rituals. I prove that "Jesus" is not the name of the Messiah in any language much less Hebrew. We dissect that name and prove how the name of the Messiah was intentionally altered to give glory to Zeus over Yahuah. The true name of the Messiah is Yahusha.

# Book 5
# The Kingdom

With the false religion, the false messiah, the false sacrifice, the false rituals clearly defined in the first 4 books, I begin to relay a firm foundation in what is true. In this book I define The Kingdom of Yahuah in great detail.

I explain how all previous 6 covenants were transposed into the final 7th Covenant of Yahusha. I breakdown every aspect of the Kingdom using physical to spiritual parallels of a kingdom on Earth. What is this Kingdom, what is its purpose, what is its domain, who is its King, what is its constitution, who are its citizens, and what responsibility to the citizens who gain citizenship? All answered in this book.

# Book 6
# The Yahushaic Covenant: The Mediator

In this book I break down The New Covenant and explain who Yahusha is in relation to Yahuah, what our roles are in the covenant of Yahusha, and much more. The Yahushaic Covenant is the "Salvation of Yahuah Covenant".

I explain the role the Law plays in our lives under covenant with Yahusha. I explain the effects of Hellenism and blending the truth with paganism. I breakdown the scripture in context, shedding light on the writings in the Renewed Covenant with the original scriptures (Old Testament if you must).

I re-teach the scriptures in light of the ancient language and cultural matrix of the 1st Century people of Yahuah living in the land of Israel.

# Book 7
# The Law and the Pauline Doctrine

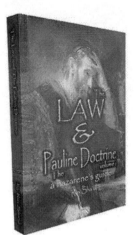

In this book, I explain the role the Law plays in our lives and re-teach Sha'ul's writings from the standpoint of intent.

I overcome the Christian lie that Sha'ul taught against the Torah. We go in and take a hard look at how Sha'ul's writing were translated and "twisted" by the Greeks into another Gospel called The Pauline Doctrine. In this book, I introduce us all to Rav Sha'ul the leader of the Nazarenes! What does that mean, and what does that one fact say about the way his writings have been translated today?

I explain the various aspects of The Law, how it was transposed over time from the Mind of Yahuah, to written in the stars at creation, to given orally, to written in stone, to finally written on our hearts. I explain the various jurisdictional aspects of the Law, look at the Law from the standpoint of intent, and provide solid instruction to the Nazarene today in how to approach the Law of Yahuah.

# Book 8
# Melchizedek and the Passover Lamb

What does Melchizedek really mean? In this book I explain how Yahusha became the King of Kings and the Eternal High Priest by blood lineage to King David and the ordained Zadok Priesthood. We travel back 2,000 years to the time of the Messiah's birth to fully understand the mindset of that time.

A time of great expectation toward the coming Messiah. We look back into historical documents surrounding that time period to identify the lineage of Yahusha. Lineage that was lost to antiquity when Rome burned the original manuscripts.

Who were Yahusha's "other grandparents" that contributed equally to his bloodline, we have just never been introduce to? How is Yahusha "King of Israel". How is Yahusha the "High Priest of Israel".

The Bible declares Yahusha inherited those titles. If so, how and from whom? This book is a must read and introduction to the REAL Messiah in a way you have never known him.

# Book 9
# 'The Narrow Gate'

In this book I explain how keeping the Feasts of Yahuah properly is a prerequisite of entering the Kingdom. The Feast Cycle is the "Narrow Gate" of a wedding, and we must rehearse these events from the standpoint of "a Bride".   This is called The Plan of Salvation which is written in the stars "before the foundation of the world" on Day 4 of Creation.

What is the true meaning of the feasts, what are they rehearsing, how do we keep them? All these questions are answered and more in the final book in this series, The Narrow Gate.

# Book 10
# The Mistranslated
# Book of Galatians

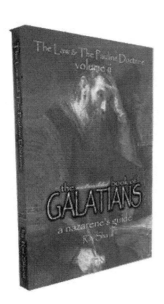

The letter to the Galatians is one of the most mistranslated (*purposely*) books in the Bible. The Greeks twisted the words of Sha'ul into a lie to abolish the Law.

In this book, I go verse by verse showing were and how the words were twisted, showing the proper translation, and then using all of Sha'ul's writing to shed light on what Sha'ul was talking about in this letter. The resulting translation is the first of its kind! The real letter to the Galatians says the exact opposite of what you read in your English Bibles. The basic foundation of the Christian Church is found to be a lie and the truth revealed in this book about what Sha'ul actually taught concerning The Law, Circumcision, and many other things.

# Book 11
# The Nazarene

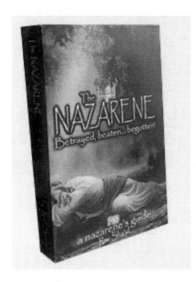

In this book, we are going to find out how little we actually ever knew about The Nazarene. Most who use this title are nowhere near true Nazarenes by what they believe, much closer to Christians that Nazarenes. Accepting the Torah does not one a Nazarene!

I will show us who they were, what they believed, what happened to them. Who are they today? We are going much deeper into who the Messiah really was and exactly what those closest to him knew about him and believed.

We are going to wipe out 1,700 years of altered texts, pagan doctrines, twisted teachings, and get back to the basics of The Nazarene as he/they existed 2000 years ago.... before Constantine forced the Cult of Sol Invictus down humanities throat at the threat of death... and the Nazarenes went into hiding.

# Book 12
# The Testimony of Yahuchanon

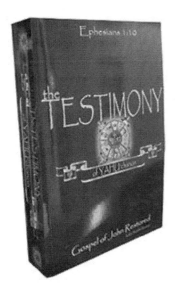

Yahusha came at the fullness of time or rather the time of the fulfillment of The Plan of Salvation written in the stars. He came to fulfill what is promised and written (LOGOS/DABAR) in The Heavenly Scroll on Earth "in the flesh". Yahusha's Message was the same as John the Immerser's that we are to repent and follow The Way because The Kingdom proclaimed in The Heavenly Scroll is at hand as he came to fulfill it at just the right time. We have been blinded by tradition and religion to deny The Heavenly Scroll and commit what the Scriptures call the two evils by denying Yahusha was the fulfillment of ORION and AQUARIUS!

The Bible is the story of The Battle of the Ages that plays out in the stars/constellations between ORION The Son of Man and The Dragon/Serpent. That battle then plays out on Earth and is documented from Genesis to Revelation. This battle between The Son of Man and The Dragon materializes in the personal life of Yahusha the Messiah as he is the fulfillment of ORION and AQUARIUS. This Battle plays out over the ages of mankind foretold in The Heavenly Scroll where the Messiah comes in the 4th Prophetic Day and The Dragon strikes his heel and he crushes the head of the Serpent.

This book restores back to the Messiah his mission and his message and for the first time delivers an accurate rendition of his teachings which astonished everyone who heard him speak. This book is the restoration of the Gospel of John bringing back to the text The Word of Yahuah's Testimony that Yahusha is the Messiah written in the stars and the Doctrine of Righteousness called The Way.

# Book 13
# The Fall Feasts: An invitation to the Wedding

In all our attempts to be obedient to the letter of the Law, we again fail our Father in Spiritual Intent. We remain addicted to milk, lacking teeth to digest the meatier matters of what The Feast Cycle was designed to teach us.

### Hebrews 5:12

In fact, though by this time you ought to be teachers (of the Intent of the Law), you need someone to teach you the elementary truths of Yahuah's Word all over again. You need milk (the letter), not solid food (Spiritual Intent. The Law is Spiritually appraised *1 Corinthians 2:14*)!

Teachers who bring us under condemnation to the "letter of the Law" treat us as if we are Spiritual Children; telling us everything has to be done "just like this... or just like that"; yet never tell us "why" these things are done which is the more important MEAT. These teachers are a dime a dozen, not called to teach and lack the anointing required to mentor Spiritual Men and Women! These are infant teachers themselves... teaching infants, all feeding on milk!

Nothing has changed in 2,000 years because we do not have mature teachers teaching the Spiritual Law, we have immature teachers trying to "look knowledgeable" with all their impressive carnal/literal knowledge of the letter. We mistake these men as "teachers", when they are in as much need of instruction as the rest of us in Spiritual Things.

In this book, I teach the true message contained in the stars! That message is found in the feast cycle which is the rehearsal of the Divine Wedding.

# Book 14

# Unlocking the Book of Revelation

The Book of Revelation is a documented account of what is written in the stars that must take place on Earth over what the Bible calls the "last days" which is the Age of PISCES. John is given visions as he looked up into the night sky and the angel Gabriel came to him on behalf of Yahuah and Yahusha to reveal the contents of The Heavenly Scroll. The Book of Revelation has been miSunderstood, mistranslated, and mistaught for 2000 years as the ones doing the "teaching" have rejected the very source of its message... The Heavenly Scroll. These men and women who mislead the masses over the years are all filled with The Spirit of the False Messiah as they all worship the Beast χξς ! They are blinded to the meaning of the words of this book as prophesied on its pages, do not understand the prophetic language, and have rejected The Word of His Testimony written in the stars.

This book reveals the meaning behind all the cryptic language, images, shadow pictures, and mysteries in the Book of Revelation. For the first time in history, teaching the Book of Revelation in context of the rest of the prophets and The Heavenly Scroll.

# Book 15 Blasphemy of the Holy Spirit

Blasphemy of the Holy Spirit is an opposing Spirit the Bible calls the **Spirit of the Antichrist**. It is at heart the denial of The Shema (*the greatest commandment*). It is declaring that **"Yahuah came to Earth as a man and died to save us"**.

We call this the Doctrine of Incarnation. The "carn" in "incarnation" refers to flesh or meat (of the human body). Thus, "incarnate" means "in the flesh". =REINCARNATION is a word that means "to be born again (in the flesh)". Any concept of a Trinity or a Bi-Entity is blasphemy as Yahuah has declared He is ONE and He is Spirit and cannot and will not "come in the flesh". The phrase "in the flesh" means... "natural/physical origin (*not Spiritual*), born of natural origin ONLY, mere human/natural birth only... <u>APART FROM DIVINE INFLUENCE</u>, prone to sin and opposed to Yahuah". This is the condition all human beings are born into as we all were born, came, revealed "in the flesh". The word translated "flesh" is the Greek word 'sarki' below:

> <u>g4561 'sarki' - Thayer:</u>
> 2a) the body of a man 2b) used of natural or physical origin, generation or relationship 2b1) born of natural generation 4) the flesh, denotes mere human nature, the Earthly nature of man apart from divine influence, and therefore prone to sin and opposed to God"

The True and False Spirits are defined by this understanding. The Spirit of Yahuah declares that Yahusha "came in the flesh" outside any divine influence, not Yahuah. The Spirit of the False Messiah (*demi-god*) is that Jesus is "God in the flesh" or that "God" came to Earth as a man and we killed him.

Yahuah is Spirit NOT "sinful flesh". To declare Yahuah "came in the flesh and died" is to deny what He declares about Himself. We are warned of this by Sha'ul in

Romans 1 not to worship a man who died (*Yahusha*). Yahuah is Invisible Spirit not mortal flesh.

# More from Rav Sha'ul

Please visit my websites www.sabbathcovenant.com or www.ravshaul.com for in depth teachings, audio lessons, links to these books, and much more. If this book has been a blessing to you, please support this ministry. Email info@sabbathcovenant.com for more information or click on the donate link at the top of the page on either website.

Please visit my YouTube Channel for further video teachings and presentations.

https://www.youtube.com/channel/UCVLZgChmeSa78Mo7b228sjQ

All Glory belongs to Yahuah. He is our Creator, Author of The Heavenly Scroll, and Father of the called out ones (*Nazarenes*). And to Yahusha the Nazarene, the Messiah and Royal High Priest of Israel, I say...

*"WORTHY IS THE LAMB! TO RECEIVE HONOR, AND GLORY, AND POWER, AND PRAISE" HALLELUYahuah*

*LET IT BE SO DONE, ON EARTH AS IT IS WRITTEN IN THE HEAVENLY SCROLL.*

Kingdom blessings, and much love... Rav Sha'ul

Made in United States
Orlando, FL
26 February 2025

58926838R00210